Doing English Grammar

Grammar is integral to teaching English as a second language, and yet there is often a disconnect between theory and practice. This book bridges that gap by introducing key theories of English grammar and showing how they can be applied in teaching. By drawing on an eclectic range of sources, and using a multidisciplinary approach, Berry links advances in our knowledge of grammar, from theoretical and descriptive viewpoints, with developments in pedagogical practices, to provide a comprehensive overview of the whole process of grammar. The second part of the book contains four case studies of key areas of English grammar in which the insights of the earlier chapters are applied, illustrating how grammar theory is used in practice. Offering new insights into the way English grammar works, this book is invaluable for all professionals who 'do' English grammar: teachers, grammarians, textbook writers and syllabus designers, testers and researchers.

Roger Berry has been involved in English Grammar as teacher, teacher-trainer, author, lecturer, examiner and researcher. He has published six books on the subject, the most recent being *English Grammar: A Resource Book for Students*, 2nd edition (2018).

THE CAMBRIDGE APPLIED LINGUISTICS SERIES

The authority on cutting-edge Applied Linguistics research

Series Editors   2007–present: Carol A. Chapelle and Susan Hunston
                        1988–2007: Michael H. Long and Jack C. Richards

For a complete list of titles please visit: www.cambridge.org

Recent titles in this series:

Learner Corpus Research Meets Second Language Acquisition
Bert Le Bruyn and Magali Paquot

Second Language Speech Fluency
From Research to Practice Parvaneh Tavakoli and Clare Wright

Ontologies of English
Conceptualising the Language for Learning, Teaching, and Assessment
Edited by Christopher J. Hall and Rachel Wicaksono

Task-Based Language Teaching
Theory and Practice Rod Ellis, Peter Skehan, Shaofeng Li, Natsuko Shintani and Craig Lambert

Feedback in Second Language Writing
Contexts and Issues
Edited by Ken Hyland and Fiona Hyland

Language and Television Series
A Linguistic Approach to TV Dialogue
Monika Bednarek

Intelligibility, Oral Communication, and the Teaching of Pronunciation
John M. Levis

Multilingual Education
Between Language Learning and Translanguaging
Edited by Jasone Cenoz and Durk Gorter

Learning Vocabulary in Another Language
2nd Edition I. S. P. Nation

Narrative Research in Applied Linguistics
Edited by Gary Barkhuizen

Teacher Research in Language Teaching
A Critical Analysis Simon Borg

Figurative Language, Genre and Register
Alice Deignan, Jeannette Littlemore and Elena Semino

Exploring ELF
Academic English Shaped by Non-native Speakers Anna Mauranen

Genres across the Disciplines
Student Writing in Higher Education Hilary Nesi and Sheena Gardner

Disciplinary Identities
Individuality and Community in Academic Discourse Ken Hyland

Replication Research in Applied Linguistics
Edited by Graeme Porte

The Language of Business Meetings
Michael Handford

Reading in a Second Language
Moving from Theory to Practice William Grabe

Modelling and Assessing Vocabulary Knowledge
Edited by Helmut Daller, James Milton and Jeanine Treffers-Daller

Practice in a Second Language
Perspectives from Applied Linguistics and Cognitive Psychology
Edited by Robert M. DeKeyser

Task-Based Language Education
From Theory to Practice
Edited by Kris van den Branden

Second Language Needs Analysis
Edited by Michael H. Long

Insights into Second Language Reading
A Cross-Linguistic Approach Keiko Koda

Research Genres
Exploration and Applications John M. Swales

Critical Pedagogies and Language Learning
Edited by Bonny Norton and Kelleen Toohey

Exploring the Dynamics of Second Language Writing
Edited by Barbara Kroll

Understanding Expertise in Teaching
Case Studies of Second Language Teachers
Amy B. M. Tsui

Criterion-Referenced Language Testing
James Dean Brown and Thom Hudson

Corpora in Applied Linguistics
Susan Hunston

Pragmatics in Language Teaching
Edited by Kenneth R. Rose and Gabriele Kasper

Cognition and Second Language Instruction
Edited by Peter Robinson

Research Perspectives on English for Academic Purposes
Edited by John Flowerdew and Matthew Peacock

Computer Applications in Second Language Acquisition
Foundations for Teaching, Testing and Research Carol A. Chapelle

Doing English Grammar
Roger Berry

Doing English Grammar
Theory, Description and Practice

Roger Berry

CAMBRIDGE
UNIVERSITY PRESS

University Printing House, Cambridge CB2 8BS, United Kingdom

One Liberty Plaza, 20th Floor, New York, NY 10006, USA

477 Williamstown Road, Port Melbourne, VIC 3207, Australia

314–321, 3rd Floor, Plot 3, Splendor Forum, Jasola District Centre, New Delhi – 110025, India

79 Anson Road, #06–04/06, Singapore 079906

Cambridge University Press is part of the University of Cambridge.

It furthers the University's mission by disseminating knowledge in the pursuit of education, learning, and research at the highest international levels of excellence.

www.cambridge.org
Information on this title: www.cambridge.org/9781108419994
DOI: 10.1017/9781108325745

© Roger Berry 2021

This publication is in copyright. Subject to statutory exception and to the provisions of relevant collective licensing agreements, no reproduction of any part may take place without the written permission of Cambridge University Press.

First published 2021

A catalogue record for this publication is available from the British Library.

ISBN 978-1-108-41999-4 Hardback
ISBN 978-1-108-41281-0 Paperback

Cambridge University Press has no responsibility for the persistence or accuracy of URLs for external or third-party internet websites referred to in this publication and does not guarantee that any content on such websites is, or will remain, accurate or appropriate.

Contents

	List of Figures	xi
	List of Tables	xii
	Editors' Preface	xiii
	Introduction	1
I.1	Who Is This Book For?	1
I.2	Why Another Book on Grammar?	1
I.3	Aims	2
	References	2
1	***The Place of Grammar***	**3**
1.1	Introduction	3
1.2	Attitudes to Grammar	3
1.3	Grammar in Methods and Approaches	6
1.4	Second Language Acquisition (SLA) Studies and the Role of Formal Instruction	10
1.5	Problems with SLA Research into Formal Instruction	11
1.6	Teacher Language Awareness	13
1.7	Conclusion	14
	Note	15
	References	15
2	***What Is Grammar?***	**17**
2.1	Introduction	17
2.2	The Scope of Grammar	17
2.3	Defining Grammar	18
2.4	Grammar and Meaning: Convention and Creativity	20
2.5	How Languages 'Do' Grammar	23
2.5.1	Strategy 1: Vary the Word Order	23
2.5.2	Strategy 2: Change the Shape of Words	24
2.5.3	Strategy 3: Add Little 'Function' Words	24
2.5.4	Strategy 4: Use Suprasegmental Features	24
2.5.5	Combining Strategies	25
2.6	Three Distinctions	26

2.6.1	Distinction 1: Primary vs Secondary Grammar	26
2.6.2	Distinction 2: Descriptive vs Prescriptive Grammar	27
2.6.3	Distinction 3: Scientific vs Pedagogic Grammar	30
2.7	Pedagogic Grammar as Process	31
2.8	Theoretical Approaches to Grammar	33
2.8.1	Modern Traditional Grammar	34
2.9	Descriptive Inputs to Pedagogical Grammar as Process	36
2.9.1	Historical Accounts	37
2.9.2	Contrastive Accounts	38
2.9.3	Other Descriptive Areas	39
2.10	Conclusion	40
	Activity	41
	Comment	41
	Notes	41
	References	42
3	***The Need for New Descriptions***	**43**
3.1	Introduction	43
3.2	Reason 1: The Language Changes	43
3.2.1	Reasons for Change	45
3.3	Reason 2: Our Current Accounts Are Wrong	48
3.3.1	Reasons for Misconceptions	53
3.4	Reason 3: New Grammatical Phenomena Are 'Discovered'	54
3.5	Reason 4: The Scope of Grammar – and Therefore the Phenomena Which Need Describing – Is Extended	56
3.6	Reason 5: There Are Alternative Ways of Looking at Old Problems	59
3.7	Two Major Problems	61
3.7.1	Metalinguistic Relativity	61
3.7.2	Poor Transmission	62
3.8	Conclusion	63
	Activity: Conditional Sentences	63
	Comment	64
	Notes	66
	References	66
4	***Working with Terminology***	**68**
4.1	Introduction	68
4.2	Attitudes to Terminology	68
4.3	Understanding Terminology	69
4.4	The Pros and Cons of Terminology	73
4.5	What Goes Wrong with Terminology?	75

4.6	Researching Terminology	79
4.7	Evaluating Terminology	82
4.8	Changing Terms	84
4.9	Using Terminology Effectively in the Classroom	86
4.10	Conclusion: Towards the Appropriate Use of Terminology	86
	Activity	87
	Comments	88
	References	89
5	*Issues in Grammatical Description*	92
5.1	Introduction	92
5.2	Basic Issues in Describing Grammar	93
5.2.1	Depth and Refinement	93
5.2.2	Distinguishing Uses	94
5.2.3	An Example: The Present Simple	96
5.2.4	Formality	98
5.2.5	Acceptability	99
5.3	Modality	101
5.4	Personality	107
5.5	Sub-technical Vocabulary	111
5.6	Exemplification	112
5.6.1	Advantages of Authentic Examples	113
5.6.2	Disadvantages of Authentic Examples	114
5.6.3	Adapting Examples	115
5.6.4	The Purpose of Exemplification	116
5.6.5	Authenticity Revisited	117
5.6.6	A Third Approach	118
5.6.7	Contrived vs Authentic: A Summary	118
5.7	Comparing Texts	119
5.7.1	Analysis	120
5.8	Conclusion	122
	Activity	122
	Comment	122
	Notes	123
	References	123
6	*Grammar in Operation*	125
6.1	Introduction	125
6.2	Syllabuses	125
6.3	Rules of Thumb	129
6.4	Exercises and Activities	132
6.4.1	Gap-Filling Exercises	133

6.4.2	Other Types of Exercise	134
6.5	Error Correction	135
6.6	Tests	137
6.6.1	Tests of L1 Speakers	137
6.6.2	Tests of L2 Learners	138
6.6.3	Tests of Teachers	140
6.7	Attitudes to Grammar: Innovative Activities	142
6.8	Conclusion	144
	Activity	144
	Comment	145
	Notes	145
	References	146
7	*Case Study 1: The Articles*	147
7.1	Introduction	147
7.2	Understanding Articles	147
7.2.1	The Indefinite Article	148
7.2.2	The Definite Article	150
7.2.3	Further Information about the Articles	153
7.3	The Contrastive Background	154
7.4	The Historical Background	155
7.5	Learners and Articles	155
7.6	The Current Situation	156
7.7	What to Do	160
7.7.1	Overall Strategy	160
7.7.2	Introducing the Definite Article	160
7.7.3	Rules	161
7.7.4	Terms	162
7.7.5	Exercises	162
7.8	Conclusion	165
	Activity	166
	Notes	167
	References	167
8	*Case Study 2: The Comparison of Adjectives*	168
8.1	Introduction	168
8.2	The Background	169
8.3	The Meanings of Comparison	171
8.4	Other Comparative Structures	171
8.5	The Comparative and Historical Background	171
8.6	Learners and Comparison	172
8.7	Researching Comparison	173
8.8	In the Classroom	176
8.8.1	Rules	176

8.8.2	Exercises	178
8.8.3	Terminology	179
8.9	Conclusion	180
	Activity	181
	Comment	181
	Notes	182
	References	183
9	*Case Study 3: The Personal Pronouns*	184
9.1	Introduction	184
9.2	The Background (1)	184
9.3	The Personal Pronoun Paradigm	185
9.3.1	Person	186
9.3.2	Number	187
9.3.3	Gender	188
9.3.4	Case	189
9.3.5	Related Forms	189
9.3.6	Summary	190
9.4	*They* as Singular Pronoun	190
9.4.1	A New Reflexive Pronoun?	192
9.5	Generic *You*	194
9.6	The Background (2)	196
9.6.1	Contrastive Evidence	196
9.6.2	Historical Evidence	197
9.7	Learners and Personal Pronouns	198
9.8	The Current Pedagogic Situation	199
9.8.1	Coverage in Materials	199
9.8.2	Coverage of Generic 'You'	199
9.9	What to Do?	200
9.9.1	Strategy	200
9.9.2	Activities	201
9.9.3	Terminology	202
9.10	Conclusion	202
	A Postscript	204
	Activity	204
	Comment	205
	Notes	206
	References	206
10	*Case Study 4: Reported Speech*	209
10.1	Introduction	209
10.2	Backshift	209
10.3	The Status of Reported Speech (1)	210
10.4	The Background	212

10.4.1	Origin	212
10.4.2	Deixis	212
10.5	The Status of Reported Speech (2)	213
10.5.1	The Relationship between Direct and Reported Speech	214
10.6	An Explanation: Distancing	215
10.6.1	Backshift from Past Tense to Past Perfect	216
10.7	Reporting in the Classroom	216
10.7.1	The Current Situation	216
10.7.2	A Revised Strategy	217
10.7.3	Rules and Terms	218
10.7.4	Alternative Areas of Reporting to Focus On	218
10.7.5	Suggestions for Activities	220
10.8	Conclusion	222
	Activity	223
	Comment	224
	Note	224
	References	225
	Conclusion	226
C.1	Summing Up	226
C.2	Problems and Solutions	228
	Appendices	230
	Appendix 1 (from Chapter 3): Results from Berry (2014)	230
	Appendix 2 (from Chapter 5): Texts Used in METALANG 1	232
	Appendix 3 (from Chapter 5): Results from Berry (2009a)	233
	Index	234

Figure

2.1 The process of pedagogic grammar (from Berry
    1999: 32)   32

Tables

5.1	Incidence of can and main adverbs with use(d) and say	106
5.2	Incidence of pronouns with CAN and USE in SWAN and COBUILD	109
5.3	Adverbs correlated with pronouns and can in MURPHY	111
7.1	The difference between the and a with singular count nouns.	161
8.1	Results from Hilpert	181
9.1	The traditional personal pronoun paradigm, with axes for person and number.	185
9.2	Frequency of themself over twenty-five years	193
9.3	A revised version of the personal pronoun paradigm	203
A.1	The frequency of the seven items in METALANG I compared to Cobuild Direct (All frequencies are per one million words)	233

Editors' Preface

Grammar can be problematic for teachers of English. Academic publications on grammar sometimes confuse rather than enlighten teachers by presenting a variety of theoretical models, each with its own array of terminology. The advice given to teachers on the role of grammar in teaching can be inconsistent and often does not take into account research into teaching and learning grammar.

This book situates itself firmly on the side of the teacher to tackle the need for constructive dialogue between the theoretician and the practitioner. Roger Berry uses his extensive experience as a researcher and teacher educator as he demystifies terminology, explains concepts, engages with the research, and argues for the interconnectedness of theory and practice.

A number of themes run through this book. One is a challenge to teachers to consider critically statements about correctness in grammar, in the light of both old and new sources of evidence. Numerous examples are used to show that 'rules of thumb' can be useful sometimes, but misleading in other cases. Another theme is an invitation to applied linguists to regard books about grammar, and the people who write them, as valid objects of study. Chapter 5 reports research into the language of grammar books themselves; unusually, it does so in terms of the writing process and the complex decisions that writers about grammar are faced with. A third theme throughout the book is the need for teachers to consider the purpose and context of each pedagogical encounter when deciding what grammatical points to teach and how to teach them. The emphasis on flexibility and a response to individual situations is a key aspect of this book. Berry also notes the ongoing need for revisions to descriptions of grammar, either because the language changes or because the methods used to investigate it do.

The book is enhanced by a series of insightful case studies based on commonly taught areas of English grammar: the article system, comparative adjectives, the personal pronoun system, and reported speech. Each of these chapters contains new, often surprising, observations and demonstrates in practical terms how the arguments made throughout the book translate into how and when specific items are taught. Berry also deals comprehensively with the role of grammar in different aspects of the pedagogic process, including syllabus design, testing and assessment. Most of the chapters in the book are accompanied by activities that encourage thoughtful engagement with the chapter topics.

Teaching grammar can be difficult. This book demystifies the topic and demonstrates how interaction among theory, research and practice can benefit all three perspectives on grammar. It is a valuable addition to the series.

Introduction

I.1 Who Is This Book For?

The book is aimed at any professionals who are involved in the teaching of English grammar to learners, whether they be

- writers of descriptions of grammar for learners or teachers;
- syllabus designers of courses with a grammatical basis;
- writers of materials which focus on grammar;
- trainers of language teachers on courses where an awareness of grammar is important;
- individual teachers who are interested in grammar.
- to anyone else who is involved in grammar, e.g. testers and researchers

It is concerned principally with English, but many of the insights will apply to other languages.

I.2 Why Another Book on Grammar?

Grammar is a vast enterprise. There are several hundred books with the word 'grammar' in their title, and many others involve grammar without stating it explicitly. They range from the scientific grammars of, for example, Quirk et al. (1985), to the more pedagogically oriented reference grammars, such as the *Cambridge Grammar of English* (Carter and McCarthy 2006) or the *Collins Cobuild English Grammar* (2017), or to the more practical grammars such as Swan's *Practical English Usage* (Swan 2016); from the explanatory grammars for teachers, for example, Yule (1998), to coursebooks for students of the language at university level, e.g. Greenbaum and Nelson (2009); from practice grammars for learners, such as Murphy's *English Grammar in Use* (Murphy 2004), to coursebooks for language learners designed around a grammar syllabus.

Introduction

So why another book? Because in this enterprise I have tried to do something different. All of the above books have some relevance here but none cast their net so wide; they focus on certain aspects horizontally, such as grammatical description or practice activities. Here I have attempted a 'vertical' integration of many separate areas; I have tried to 'join up the dots'. This makes the book unique, I believe.

I.3 Aims

The aim of this book is to link advances in our knowledge of grammar, from both theoretical and descriptive viewpoints, with developments in pedagogical practices, both inside and outside the classroom; in short, to connect up the whole process of grammar, vertically, as it were, from top to bottom. The book attempts to show that there is (or should be) a link between researchers in their ivory towers and the various kinds of practitioners – a link that is too often missing. As a result of this, many pedagogical practices that are popular with teachers, such as rules of thumb, or certain types of exercise (such as gap-filling), have a weak theoretical basis. However, the subtitle *Theory, Description and Practice* makes no assumption of the priority of one element over others. It is not simply a case of 'here is the theory, here are the pure scientific facts, now deal with it'. Pedagogy can, in this model, well be the instigator of scientific activity, though this is not often enough the case.

There is much that is problematic in the world of grammar and grammar teaching. By looking at it from every angle the book attempts to be critical of the status quo, but at the same time to offer solutions to all concerned. The second part of the book contains four case studies of certain important areas of English grammar in which the insights of the earlier chapters are applied, whether to arrive at new understanding and descriptions or rules of thumb.

References

Carter, Ronald and Michael McCarthy. 2006. *Cambridge Grammar of English*. Cambridge: Cambridge University Press.
Collins Cobuild English Grammar. 2017. 4th edn. Glasgow: HarperCollins.
Greenbaum, Sidney and Gerald Nelson. 2009. *An Introduction to English Grammar*. 3rd edn. Harlow: Longman.
Murphy, Raymond. 2004. *English Grammar in Use*. 3rd edn. Cambridge: Cambridge University Press.
Quirk, Randolph, Sidney Greenbaum, Geoffrey Leech and Jan Svartvik. 1985. *A Comprehensive Grammar of the English Language*. Harlow: Longman.
Swan, Michael. 2016. *Practical English Usage*. 4th edn. Oxford: Oxford University Press.
Yule, George. 1998. *Explaining English Grammar*. Oxford: Oxford University Press.

1 The Place of Grammar

1.1 Introduction

This chapter seeks to lay a foundation for the rest of the book by questioning the relevance of grammar, in particular as it applies to the teaching of English as a Foreign Language (EFL). It investigates how grammar is viewed by the various groups of people who are involved with it in some way: L1 speakers and L2 learners, linguists and applied linguists, researchers, grammarians, syllabus and textbook writers, and, above all, teachers. Given the controversial status of grammar among some of these, the central question is this: What is its place in teaching? Is it useless, as some researchers and educators in the past have claimed, or useful in a number of possible ways for both learners and teachers? If it is useful, then how? The arguments of educators and research findings from second language acquisition (SLA) studies will be examined critically. The chapter will conclude with a brief consideration of one area where the place of grammar has never really been in doubt: teacher language awareness.

1.2 Attitudes to Grammar

'Grammar' is a word that evokes different reactions in different groups of people. For linguists it refers to a particular area of linguistic study: an area which comprises a combination of syntax and (inflectional) morphology. This would be the end of the story were grammar merely the province of experts, as is largely the case with major concepts in other academic or scientific fields. For example, jurisprudence is the province of the legal profession, surgery the fiefdom of the medical profession. But grammar is unlike these; there are several constituencies that claim an interest, even expertise, in it. Everyone, it seems, has something to say about grammar (and a different conception of it).

For speakers who regard English as their first language, grammar is something of a hot potato. Debates about it are inevitably connected to the idea of correctness, as some forms are unjustly stigmatised, leading some speakers to become nervous about their usage. Issues such as the splitting of infinitives (see the distinction between descriptive and prescriptive grammar in Section 2.6.2) can become a battleground. Whenever L1 speakers ask what I do and I reply that I write books on English grammar, I am met with one of two reactions: a statement along the lines of 'good, we need more of that' from those who are confident in their usage on such matters, or a shifty look that says 'I'd better be careful' from those who aren't. The subsequent reaction, when I tell them that I am only concerned with learners of English, whose problems with English grammar and 'correctness' are immensely more extensive than theirs, is either disappointment or relief.

The main constituency of interest here is of course teachers of English as a Foreign Language (TEFL). For them grammar evokes a number of attitudes and reactions. In this there are two major subconstituencies, namely those who regard English as their first language and those who do not (a distinction which is gradually being eroded nowadays). For both groups there is one major determinant: the experience of grammar they themselves have gone through as language learners and trainees. These experiences may produce different attitudes.

To take the first group of teachers, L1 speakers are unlikely to have encountered formal grammar to any great extent in school or university (even if they are English graduates). Those with some form of TEFL qualification will have undergone a limited course in grammar, largely pedagogic in nature (see Section 2.6.3). And despite the increased professionalism of the EFL industry, there are still many parts of the world where teachers are recruited 'off the street' purely as a result of their 'native-speaker' status, and who will have to learn about grammar 'on the hoof', if at all.

As a result, such teachers may feel somewhat uncomfortable dealing with grammar in the classroom. And their experience of learning other foreign languages at school may also have put them off grammar, especially if they were taught in a highly formal manner. Nevertheless, they should possess confidence in their pronouncements on the grammaticality of learner utterances (based on their 'primary grammar' – see Section 2.6.1), even though they may not be able to explain their judgements, if asked.

In comparison, L2 teachers may have more traditional attitudes to grammar in the classroom, in particular if they themselves learnt or studied English in a traditional way. For them, grammar can be seen as an indispensable part of leaning a language (Berry 2001). Moreover, explicit grammar teaching may serve as a crutch to rely on if they are unsure of their own proficiency in the language. On the other hand, some may see grammar as a distraction from, or even a substitute for, the real task of learning a language. The majority would appear to be somewhere in between these two attitudes, thinking of grammar and its associated terminology as a way of structuring their syllabus or as a tool to help them in making generalisations. (See the example of this from Tsui 1995 in Section 4.8.) Again, it partly depends on their previous experiences.

Another reason why they may be hesitant to tackle grammar on a general level is that, lacking the level of intuition of L1 teachers, they may have doubts about their ability to make pronouncements about the grammaticality of their learners' utterances. At the other extreme they may – based on incorrect rules of thumb or misleading terminology – even reject perfectly grammatical utterances; Maule (1988) gives an example of a teacher who rejected a perfectly formed sentence because it did not correspond to the three-conditional pattern that she had been indoctrinated with.

EFL learners usually encounter grammar most prominently as a selection of simple, isolated rules of thumb, which they may or may not be able to utilise in real-time language production, followed by exercises in which they are supposed to apply these rules. (See the distinction between convention and creativity in Section 2.4, as well as the deductive/explicit options in Section 1.3.) However, should they proceed to study English as a subject at university on English Studies programmes they will be faced with an extensive and bewildering, albeit systematic, set of grammatical concepts, rules and tendencies – not to mention the associated terminology – which may or may not assist in their learning of the language (this not being the aim).[1]

We should also make mention here of grammarians of various hues: scientific grammarians who write massive authoritative descriptive tomes stretching nowadays to 2,000 pages (e.g. Quirk at al. 1985), and pedagogic grammarians such as Michael Swan (2016) who attempt to make sense of this vast data for teachers and learners. (For an examination of the difference between scientific and pedagogic grammar, see Section 2.6.3.)

Other constituencies may be cited, for example EFL textbook writers (for whom grammar may still be the best organising principle for their syllabus), as well as language-test designers and language-acquisition researchers (who are interested in the role of formal instruction). This last group is considered in Sections 1.4 and 1.5.

1.3 Grammar in Methods and Approaches

The role of grammar teaching has for many years been highly controversial in EFL pedagogy. Throughout the second half of the twentieth century, different methods rose and fell with sometimes bewildering regularity; methods which were largely defined by their attitude to grammar – whether it should be taught, and if so how. To understand the differences and similarities between these methods, it will be helpful to consider three distinctions that underlie the various approaches to grammar.

(a) **Deductive vs inductive.** This distinction applies to teaching and thought in general. It basically concerns whether the direction of instruction is from the general to the specific (deductive) or vice versa (inductive). As regards grammar teaching, the deductive approach involves the presentation of a rule or explanation followed by examples or practice; in contrast, induction involves activities leading up to the formulation of the rule, either by the teacher or by the learners themselves; the latter may involve some guidance from the teacher.

(b) **Implicit vs explicit.** This involves whether learners are made aware of the grammatical point (explicit) or not (implicit). An implicit approach, while still involving grammar at some level, does not bring the grammatical point into focus. It is perfectly possible, for example, for such a point to be 'hidden' in a text and for a lesson to proceed without comment about it. On the other hand, both deductive and inductive approaches are necessarily explicit; the grammatical point is obvious to learners.

(c) **Proactive vs reactive.** Again, both deduction and induction are inevitably proactive approaches in that the grammar is preordained, regardless of how it is arrived at. In a reactive approach, however, the grammatical point is not predetermined; it may be anything that arises in the course of a lesson which the teacher chooses to deal with (e.g. a difficult structure in a text or a learner question). Clearly this approach has serious implications for teachers; they need to be knowledgeable about and confident with grammar in order to be able to handle the unexpected.

All of these distinctions assume the role of grammar in some shape or form. But of course we must allow for the absence of any form of grammar. Thus we need to mention a fourth distinction:

(d) **Experiential vs studial**. (Howatt [1984] uses the terms 'natural' and 'rationalist'; I prefer the former terms since the latter are used in other contexts.) This distinction refers to whether a language is learnt intuitively as part of the learner's life experience or whether it is taught in a formal situation involving some form of declarative knowledge. This is similar to the explicit/implicit distinction above but it is not the same; an implicit approach may well be reliant on grammar in some way, while an experiential one could not be. In essence, the question is: Should L2 learning be like L1 learning or not? Educators have long remarked on the total success achieved in L1 learning compared to the very varied success rate in L2 learning. This observation has given rise to a number of so-called natural approaches, which claim to reflect L1 learning as much as possible. However, there are two obstacles to this attempt at imitation. The first is the 'unnatural' situation where learning takes place: the classroom with the assistance of a teacher. The second is the fact that learners already possess at least one language before embarking on an L2. The issue is whether the L1 facilitates L2 learning or hinders it. The answer to this question has altered over the years; nowadays the facilitation option seems to have the upper hand. Of course, it is not only grammar that may be affected in this way; other areas of language may be as well. Equally, it is not true to say that L1 learning proceeds without any formal instruction; parents do correct their children's grammar (and are often ignored).

Three other factors in evaluating methods and approaches are:

- whether they stress writing or speech as paramount;
- whether they believe that comprehension precedes production or that the two proceed in unison;
- whether the use of the learners' L1 is permitted; clearly if it is then explanations can be more frequent and elaborate.

With this 'toolkit' in place, we can evaluate some of the distinctive methods and approaches that have been cogently articulated by educators over the last fifty years or so (even if in the actual execution they were less than 'pure'). All are studial to some extent (despite what their proponents might claim), and all are proactive unless otherwise stated (see Richards and Rogers 2014 for a full account).

The much-maligned **Grammar-Translation Method** was supremely explicit and deductive: rules were presented, paradigms memorised, and then applied; explicit knowledge of grammar was deemed to be a legitimate aim, as was the concentration on the written form at a time when opportunities for oral communication were limited; this condition still obtains in some parts of the world. Instruction was carried out in the L1 and practice consisted mainly of translating texts from the L1 into the L2.

The variously termed **Oral/Situational/Structural Method** (see Richards 2015: 63–65) also has an explicit, deductive focus. It is sometimes called PPP methodology since it consists of three stages: presentation, practice and performance. This is still to be found underlying many courses today. It differs from grammar-translation in that it stresses oral production, particularly in the performance stage, where opportunities to apply the point creatively are offered. Nevertheless, it is highly grammatical; lessons are structured around a highly explicit point; it is principally deductive (though guided induction could be used).

The **Direct Method**, largely a reaction to Grammar-Translation, is as a result inductive and implicit, at least in theory. In addition, it rejects the use of the L1 in class and stresses oral skills first of all. Nevertheless, it partly retains a role for grammar in that lessons are built around grammatical points that are exemplified by picture, pointing or demonstration ('I am writing on the blackboard').

The **Audiolingual Method**, based on a now-unpopular behaviourist view of learning, is also (theoretically) implicit and inductive; learners are not made aware of the point they are learning. However, the repetitive automatic exercises they are required to carry out in order to achieve fluency in speech – often in language laboratories – have a clearly grammatical focus derived from a structural syllabus.

Richards and Rogers (2014) and Richards (2015: 59) distinguish methods from approaches, the latter being more general and based on theories of what language is and how it should be learnt, while the former in addition are more specific on matters such as syllabus design and classroom procedures. However, we may still apply the above distinctions to different approaches. Prominent among them recently have been the Communicative and Natural approaches.

The **Natural Approach** (not the first use of the word 'natural' to apply to methodology) is also inductive and implicit, but is based on a model of language learning that is distinctly structural in nature (Krashen and Terrell 1983). Materials should be designed to expose learners to the next structure that the learners' 'acquisition devices' are ready for (as informed by SLA research).

Until now every method or approach that has been discussed has involved grammar in one way or other. But now we must confront approaches which have no place for grammar.

Communicative Language Teaching (along with its close cousin, **task-based language teaching**) is one such approach which in its purest form has no place for grammar. It is based on a theory that we learn to speak by speaking. The target is communicative competence as opposed to linguistic competence; grammar is to be picked up along the way, without any focus on form. However, it has been pointed out that learners do not need to be taught to communicate since they can already do that in their L1s. Moreover, it cannot claim to be a fully 'natural' approach in the sense described above since it stresses production at the same time as reception (in L1 learning the latter always precedes the former). Another criticism has been that by forcing learners to communicate using whatever means they have at their disposal, they may end up with grammar that is fossilised: satisfactory for communication but full of errors; fluency at the expense of accuracy.

A realisation that the 'strong' version described above was rarely implemented in its entirety led some educators (e.g. Howatt 1984: 279) to distinguish a 'weak' version of the approach. In it the same communicative activities are used but they may be followed up with a reactive grammatical focus, especially if this is prompted by learners. Similarly, task-based language teaching may have a pre-task element, supplying learners with the linguistic resources needed to complete the task, or a post-task focus on formal problems encountered. However, this requires great skill and knowledge on the part of teachers; they have no control over what linguistic point might arise.

A more recent but less distinct trend may be termed the '**Awareness Approach**'. This has been influenced by developments in L1 education in the late twentieth century. In it a focus on grammatical features, along with a limited amount of terminology, is deemed useful, not only to achieve mastery of the code but also in order to understand the ideology 'hidden' behind certain grammatical features – for example, the use of the passive or nominalisation to conceal the agent of certain actions. Critical discourse analysis has had a role to play in this approach. Methodologically there are few guidelines, though obviously receptive skills dominate, and it is more suitable at an advanced level.

Of course, we must recognise that these methods and approaches are never slavishly followed as regards their standpoint on grammar; nor are they as distinct or mutually exclusive as their proponents suggest. Even in educational systems where the introduction of grammar is banned or frowned upon, it appears that teachers have continued to use grammar, particularly in the reactive manner. After all, how is a teacher to respond to a learner who asks a pertinent question about a grammatical problem they have encountered? Surely not by saying that it does not matter. Even Stephen Krashen, that most ardent supporter of natural approaches, allowed for the intrusion of grammar into the classroom for affective reasons, via his 'affective filter' – to satisfy learners (e.g. Krashen 1985).

However, there was a time in the 1980s when the experiential/ natural trend dominated, at least in the writings and endorsements of experts, particularly as regards the communicative approach, while voices pointing out the drawbacks were hard to hear (for one exception see Marton 1988). Nowadays, however, in this post-communicative world, there seems to be less obsession with approaches and methods, and less debate about whether grammar should be included. Meanwhile, the attention of educators and researchers has passed to the role of teachers in the (grammar) teaching process: why do they teach grammar and how? The change in emphasis was noted by Mitchell (1994: 91):

> There is now a substantial educational research tradition ... which reminds us that teachers are by no means 'implementation machines', as far as innovatory methodological advice is concerned ... As far as grammar is concerned, therefore, we need to know not only what is being said to teachers, but also what they are making of this advice at any particular time, if we are to understand better the role of grammar in classroom teaching and learning.

This research programme was taken up by, amongst others, Borg (1998, 2003), with findings suggesting the aspect that was most influential for teachers was their own learning experiences.

In the meantime, the grammatical syllabus has been alive and well in coursebooks, as will be seen in Section 6.2, though often combined with other organising principles, such as tasks, functions and situations, and pronunciation. One trend has been to have separate grammar courses, which may be used as adjuncts to skills courses, such as Murphy's classic *English Grammar in Use* (various editions from 1985) and Swan and Walter's *Oxford English Grammar Course* (2011).

But now we must turn our attention to the other endeavour which struck at the very root of the notion of grammatical involvement in teaching.

1.4 Second Language Acquisition (SLA) Studies and the Role of Formal Instruction

At the same time as educators were beginning to question the pedagogic value of grammar in language teaching, researchers in the 1970s were reaching similar conclusions from a different direction, from studies carried out into second language acquisition. Early findings regarding the acquisition of basic morphemes in English suggested that

L2 learners followed the same route of acquisition of the said morphemes regardless of their L1 background, and, moreover, similar to that of L1 learners acquiring their first language.

Based on these findings, Stephen Krashen (e.g. 1985) proposed that explicit knowledge (or 'learning' in his terms) generally did not lead to implicit knowledge (or 'acquisition') and that therefore any explicit focus on form was largely a waste of classroom time. Since that time much energy has been expended on investigating the relationship between the two types of knowledge and nowadays the majority verdict seems to be greatly in favour of the 'interface' position, whereby explicit knowledge can become implicit (e.g. Ellis 1994, 2004 and 2009). Meta-analyses of research based on several individual papers have drawn the same general conclusion (Norris and Ortega 2000; Spada and Tomita 2010). For a full discussion of the nature of implicit and explicit learning and knowledge see Ellis (2004 and 2009).

With the general acceptance that 'formal instruction' (FI), as it is termed, can have a positive effect, a number of research strands have emerged, amongst which are:

- attempts to understand how formal instruction could help, for example Schmidt's (1990) concept of 'noticing'. These basically see the role of formal instruction as focusing learners on the task ahead, and then letting them get on with the actual acquisition.
- attempts to identify which grammatical items and structures are susceptible to FI, and to find some underlying trend. A recent paper has suggested, somewhat counter-intuitively, that the more complex grammatical structures are likely to profit from a focus on formal instruction (FFI):

> more complex forms (such as third-person singular and, to a lesser extent, past tense forms) [are] more susceptible than less complex forms (such as noun plurals) to explicit FFI activities (Xu and Lyster 2014: 116)

though there is no simple accepted basis for determining complexity.

All this suggests a lack of firm conclusions. But in any case, all such research is subject to other overriding factors that we now turn to.

1.5 Problems with SLA Research into Formal Instruction

Beyond the weight of evidence cited above in favour of the positive contribution of formal instruction, there are at least two serious problems that affect any opposing claims.

Firstly, there is a theoretical problem with the nature of any research finding that claims that formal instruction does not work. The point is that it is logically impossible to disprove the value of formal instruction. To any study which claims to do so, there is an obvious response: 'You weren't using the right materials, you weren't teaching it the best way. Another method/set of materials might prove successful; or the materials you used might be successful in another context, with another group of learners. So try again.'

Many studies exhibit a naïve attitude to 'learning'; in many there is little or no consideration of the pedagogic value of the materials used; they are taken as a given. The original morpheme studies that started all this 'trouble' contained no information about the instructional materials used; one could only assume that they consisted of rules of thumb – the explicit/deductive option described above – that were supposed to improve the subjects' performance between the pre- and post-tests. But the value of such an extremely explicit approach (cf. the Grammar-Translation method) has long been questioned, especially if used in isolation. There is a whole range of approaches that could be applied, according to the situation, as outlined in the four dichotomies in Section 1.3.

The second problem is the imperfect grammatical knowledge that can be exhibited by such studies. The morpheme studies again come to mind here, particularly with their reference to 'The Article', as 'one' of the morphemes under study, whereby the definite (*the*) and indefinite (*a/an*) articles were treated as alternatives of the same 'morpheme'. In Chapter 7 the case study on the articles makes it clear that these are very different beasts; they are certainly not acquired as one.

Other more recent studies of article learning make the mistake of trying to adopt a narrow theoretical framework, e.g. that of Universal Grammar, with its parameters and plus or minus settings, whereby English article usage is treated as being merely a matter of plus or minus specificity or plus and minus definiteness. But while these two aspects of reference are indeed important (see again the case study in Chapter 7), article usage in English is much subtler than this. SLA researchers should be obliged to read the account in Quirk et al. (1985) in order to acquire a deeper understanding of article usage in English. An example of such misunderstanding is given in Section 6.6.2.

In any case, in spite of all the research into SLA in formal settings, the findings do not appear to have influenced teaching syllabuses or materials (apart from a few attempts to apply Krashen's largely discredited i + 1 method). Is this the result of a healthy scepticism on the part of practitioners, or a failure on the part of SLA researchers to answer questions that would help pedagogy? Or simply a failure to communicate (the 'poor transmission' issue described in more detail in Chapter 3)?

A final, politico-pedagogic issue needs to be raised. Most language classrooms are not purely places for acquiring a particular language; they are subject to the strictures of the local education system. The prevailing educational orthodoxy, as ordained by the political establishment – however undesirable this may seem to outsiders – will overrule insights from SLA that are incompatible with its philosophy (though teachers may subvert this to some extent). Factors such as class size will have a significant effect on what methodologies are feasible, and the type of institutional tests and exams that prevail will also influence what grammatical points are stressed in the classroom (see Chapter 6 for more on this).

1.6 Teacher Language Awareness

Throughout all the above debates on the value of grammar, there has been one area that is totally uncontroversial: the need for teachers to have grammatical awareness or knowledge of the language. (The two terms seem to be used interchangeably in the literature; see e.g. Andrews 2007.) What this actually consists of, and whether it is meant to be deployed in the classroom alongside grammatical pronouncements in materials, or simply to help teachers explain their learners' mistakes, is moot. Clearly some degree of care is required in giving such knowledge to teachers, in that they may pass it on to their learners directly, as Wright (1991) pointed out.

Teacher language awareness is not always easy to separate from other skills and knowledge that teachers might desirably possess, amongst which we might include:

- their pedagogical skills, which may well be independent of their subject knowledge; for example, how to manage classroom activities such as pair practice;
- their own language proficiency (which may be stretched by some of the points they are supposed to introduce);
- their awareness of learner knowledge (often a forgotten factor), e.g. how much terminology learners know (Berry 1997).

At varying levels, teacher language awareness might comprise:

- an understanding of the way grammar works, in terms of both language in general and the specific language in question;
- the ability to describe grammatical points clearly, accurately and appropriately (i.e. to distil what they know into statements that are helpful to learners);
- the ability to identify learner mistakes (i.e. the fact that they are wrong);

- the ability to understand learner mistakes (i.e. why they are wrong);
- the ability to explain learner mistakes when appropriate (using metalanguage learners can understand).

But of course there may be a lack of time to cover all these areas to an adequate level in many teacher-training courses.

There is also the issue of testing teachers' awareness; whether and how this should be checked. This may comprise an exam at the end of any course in order to assess whether trainees should be admitted to the profession. In some cases, however, high-stakes tests may be applied to exclude practising teachers who are deemed insufficiently 'knowledgeable' or 'aware'. One such exam, the Language Proficiency Assessment for Teachers of English (LPATE), as developed in Hong Kong, is discussed in detail in Section 6.6.3.

1.7 Conclusion

This chapter has aimed to create a space for a book dedicated to 'grammar' and to delimit the subject matter of the book by excluding certain constituencies that claim an interest in grammar – some 'authorities' on L1 grammar in particular – so as to concentrate on the EFL situation and how it affects teachers and learners, which is what the following chapters concentrate on. This comprises a vast enterprise:

- the deliberations of educators and researchers as to *how* grammar is relevant in L2 education (the foregoing discussion has hopefully determined that grammar *is* relevant, but that it may be so in several different ways);
- the rather philosophical question of what grammar actually is (it may surprise some readers to see how the meaning has changed over the years, and how many different 'interpretations' of it there still are);
- the work of grammarians to produce accounts that are comprehensive, accurate and applicable – criteria that are often not compatible;
- the role of teachers in disseminating 'grammar' and the effect on learners;
- the endeavours of course designers and materials writers to devise syllabuses, classrooms activities, tests, and so on.

Hence the title of this book: the various people who are involved in *Doing English Grammar*, and the subtitle: *Theory, Description and Practice*.

Note

1 Having been engaged in this process for many years at a fairly introductory level, I understand the disillusionment they experience when they find that the rules they thought they had mastered as learners are of little use when they become students of the language as a subject.

References

Andrews, Stephen. 2007. *Teacher Language Awareness*. Cambridge: Cambridge University Press.
Berry, Roger. 1997. Teachers' awareness of learners' knowledge: the case of metalinguistic terminology. *Language Awareness* 6/2–3: 136–146.
Berry, Roger. 2001. Hong Kong teachers' attitudes towards the use of metalinguistic terminology. *Asian Pacific Journal of Language in Education* 4/1: 101–121.
Borg, Simon. 1998. Talking about grammar in the foreign language classroom. *Language Awareness* 7: 159–175.
Borg, Simon. 2003. Teacher cognition in grammar teaching: a literature review. *Language Awareness* 12/2: 96–103.
Ellis, Rod. 1994. *The Study of Second Language Acquisition*. Oxford: Oxford University Press.
Ellis, Rod. 2004. The definition and measurement of L2 explicit knowledge. *Language Learning* 54/2: 227–275.
Ellis, Rod. 2009. Implicit and explicit learning, knowledge and instruction. Chapter 1 in Rod Ellis, Shawn Loewen, Catherine Elder, Rosemary Erlam, Jenefer Philip and Hayo Reinders. *Implicit and Explicit Knowledge in Language Learning, Testing and Teaching*. Bristol: Multilingual Matters.
Howatt, A. P. R. 1984. *A History of English Language Teaching*. Oxford: Oxford University Press.
Krashen, Stephen. 1985. *The Input Hypothesis*. Harlow: Longman.
Krashen, Stephen and Tracy Terrell. 1983. *The Natural Approach: Language Acquisition in the Classroom*. Oxford: Pergamon.
Marton, W. 1988. *Methods in English Language Teaching: Frameworks and Options*. New York: Prentice Hall.
Maule, D. 1988. Sorry, but if he comes, I go: teaching conditionals. *ELT Journal* 42: 117–123.
Mitchell, R. 1994. Grammar, syllabuses, teachers. In M. Bygate, A. Tonkyn and E. Williams (eds) *Grammar and the Language Teacher*. Hemel Hempstead: Prentice Hall, 90–104.
Murphy, R. (various editions from 1985). *English Grammar in Use*. Cambridge: Cambridge University Press.
Norris, J. and L. Ortega. 2000. Effectiveness of L2 instruction: a research synthesis and quantitative meta-analysis. *Language Learning* 50/3: 417–528.
Quirk, Randolph, Sidney Greenbaum, Geoffrey Leech and Jan Svartvik. 1985. *A Comprehensive Grammar of the English Language*. Harlow: Longman.

Richards, Jack C. 2015. *Key Issues in Language Teaching*. Cambridge: Cambridge University Press.

Richards, Jack and Ted Rogers. 2014. *Methods and Approaches in Language Teaching*. New York: Cambridge University Press.

Schmidt, R. 1990. The role of consciousness in second language learning. *Applied Linguistics* 11/2: 129–158.

Spada, N. and Y. Tomita. 2010. Interaction between types of instruction and type of language feature: a meta-analysis. *Language Learning* 60/2: 1–46.

Swan, Michael. 2016. *Practical English Usage* (4th edn). Oxford: Oxford University Press.

Swan, Michael and Catherine Walter. 2011. *Oxford English Grammar Course* (3 vols). Oxford: Oxford University Press.

Tsui, Amy M. B. 1995. *Introducing Classroom Interaction*. London: Penguin.

Wright, Tony. 1991. Language awareness in teacher education programmes for non-native speakers. In C. James and P. Garrett (eds) *Language Awareness in the Classroom*. London: Longman, 52–77.

Xu, H. and Lyster, R. (2014). Differential effects of explicit form-focused instruction on morphosyntactic development. *Language Awareness* 24/1–2: 107–122.

2 What Is Grammar?

2.1 Introduction

We now return to a basic issue, one that could have formed the subject of the first chapter, since it is a prerequisite for the whole book: what actually is 'grammar'? Amongst others, Yule (1985: 69) pointed out that 'this term is frequently used to cover a number of different phenomena'.

2.2 The Scope of Grammar

The word 'grammar' is one of the hardest to pin down in linguistics and language pedagogy. Its interpretation has changed greatly over the centuries and it is clear that it still means different things to different groups of people, as the previous chapter demonstrated. Its scope has diminished radically from the days of the ancient Greeks and Romans, when it ('grammatika') seems to have covered all the linguistic endeavours of the time; Dionysius Thrax's grammar (from the second century BCE) includes areas such as correct pronunciation, figures of speech in poetry and etymology (McArthur 1983: 49), and this approach has been influential over the centuries. Even nowadays it is not unusual to find advice on style and usage included alongside the core matter in grammar books, perhaps in an appendix; see Greenbaum and Nelson (2009) for an example. Quirk et al. (1985: 12) make a similar point:

> But in the educational system of the English-speaking countries, it is possible to use the term 'grammar' loosely so as to include both spelling and lexicology.

And of course it is impossible to describe grammar completely without touching on related fields of pronunciation, spelling, discourse and vocabulary, in particular the latter, as descriptive accounts discover grammar-like behaviour in areas that traditionally have been the province of lexis.

But while a broad interpretation of grammar has been and is still current, an alternative restricted view of grammar is also expressed, as in this hypothetical learner's quote (again from Quirk et al. 1985: 12):

> Latin has a good deal of grammar, but English hardly any.

Clearly they are thinking of grammar only in terms of morphology (see the four strategies below; in this case changing the shape of words). However, it is the standpoint of this book that all languages have a similar amount of 'grammar' and that English is no 'poorer' or 'richer' in this respect than any other language, including Latin. It is just that different languages 'do' grammar in different ways. These are discussed below.

Two other views of 'grammar' can also be briefly dispensed with or set aside for the purpose of this book. The first is where 'grammar' refers to a book about grammar: Leech's 'grammar' of English. The second is where 'grammar' in a couplet with other words refers to a particular theory of grammar, of how grammatical (and indeed linguistic) description should be undertaken: generative grammar, case grammar, universal grammar, cognitive grammar, construction grammar (though some of these will figure later in this chapter in a discussion of the relevance of theories of grammatical description).

One more distinction is relevant here, for which a question is appropriate: If phonetics (and phonology) is the study of pronunciation, and semantics the study of meaning, what then is grammar the study of? One possible answer is that it is the study of (linguistic) structure: the way things are put together. But phonetics clearly has structure in the way that sounds are put together, so this will not do. The simple answer is: grammar is the study of grammar. In other words, the field of linguistic endeavour uses the same term as the object matter. But this is not really a problem here, because this book is about both: the area of study and the study itself.

2.3 Defining Grammar

So far I have discussed what grammar is not. Now it is time to attempt a definition of what it actually is, at least for the purpose of this book. We have already rejected one definition, that of linguists, that grammar is a combination of (inflectional) morphology and syntax, not because it is incorrect in any way (it corresponds exactly to the scope of grammar as understood here), but because it is unhelpful and circular. 'Grammar', as the better-known term, will be needed for an explanation of those two concepts. Moreover, we need a definition that gives some insight into the topic, telling us what its purpose is, and using language that expresses basic ideas.

2.3 Defining Grammar

There is one broad definition that I have found useful over the years:

> Grammar is what turns words into language. (Berry 2018: 4)

This is certainly simple, but is it accurate? To illustrate it let me recount a true story. In July 2015 the French Scrabble championship was won by Nigel Richards from New Zealand. The interesting thing about Nigel was that he couldn't speak French. What he had done was to memorise an entire French dictionary – a prodigious feat, and undoubtedly allied to no mean tactical skill. But he could not put those words together to communicate, apart perhaps from two-word phrases. In addition to suggesting that Scrabble is not really a test of language ability, what this tells us is that a vocabulary, no matter how extensive, is not sufficient for communication. What is lacking is grammar.

Incidentally, in so far as Nigel was able to put two words together, grammatically he was probably at the stage young children are at when they start acquiring the grammar of their first language. They may say 'eat dog' but it is not clear how the ideas expressed by these words are to be understood, how they are related to each other. It might mean 'the dog wants to eat', 'the dog is eating', 'I want to eat the (chocolate) dog'. What is needed here, of course, is grammar, and young children acquire it very quickly, effortlessly it seems.

So hopefully the above definition – that grammar is what turns words into language – can offer some insight and serve as a starting point for a formal definition. We need to refine it in a number of ways (Berry 2018: 4):

- to stress that language serves meaningful human communication;
- to show that this meaning is expressed by grammatical items (such as morphemes, words and structures);
- to demonstrate that the way these items are formed and put together is rule-governed;
- to show that these rules are systematic, that they can work together so that a limited number of rules and items can make language endlessly productive (as opposed to pedagogic rules of thumb, which operate in isolation);
- to emphasise that grammar works in both directions, that is, in comprehension, in decoding meaning, as well as in production, in the making of meaning. (Too many treatments regard it solely as the latter.)

So the final definition that I have arrived at is:

> Grammar is the system of rules that enables users of a language to relate linguistic form to meaning.

2.4 Grammar and Meaning: Convention and Creativity

More discussion is in order here about the relationship between meaning and grammar. I have implied above that grammar and meaning – or, more precisely, grammatical form and grammatical meaning – go hand in hand. Many grammarians would support this view. Clearly a change in grammar often accompanies a change in meaning and vice versa. To take one example: 'wood' as a count noun means a place full of trees; it can be pluralised and follow the indefinite article. But if we change its grammar and make it a non-count noun then it means a material from which furniture and many other things are made. Many other nouns in English make a similar 'lexical' distinction between their count and non-count versions, e.g. *work* vs *a work/works*, or *reason* vs *a reason/reasons*, a fact which is rarely mentioned in grammars. For more on this see Section 7.2.1.

It is not only the count status of nouns which illustrates a change in meaning accompanying a change of grammar. Many words take on different meanings associated with their word-class status. An extreme example would be the word *back*:

> *I'm glad we went back* (an adverb, referring to a direction).
> *Could you stand up at the back?* (a noun, referring to a position).
> *I'm not going to take a back seat on this* (an adjective referring to a metaphorical position).

As with sub-classes of nouns, sub-classes of verbs can also behave differently; changes in transitivity can be reflected in a change in meaning, as with these further examples with *back*:

> *Okay, let's back up for a moment* (an intransitive verb, indicating movement).
> *If I stand, will you back me?* (a transitive verb, meaning 'support').

However, we should ask: is all grammar meaning-oriented? For example, the rule that says subjects (usually) precede verbs in English appears to be somewhat arbitrary – in other languages it is the other way round – but it does help to disambiguate potential confusion (e.g. the classic 'man bites dog' vs 'dog bites man'). In other words, it does have a semantic role.

Even the rule that says we must add '-s' (in writing) to the present tense of a verb (when the subject is a noun phrase or a third-person singular pronoun) has a role to play. This is a well-known source of errors for learners of English, who understandably claim that third-person '-s' is redundant, that it adds nothing to meaning. However, in reply to this we can say that redundancy is a feature of all languages;

2.4 Grammar and Meaning: Convention and Creativity

witness the fact that many European languages require agreement between nouns and their adjectives. Third-person '-s' reinforces the fact that the subject of the verb is not a participant in the act of communication (as speaker or hearer). Redundancy also serves to preserve meaning when the text elsewhere goes astray. More specifically than this, third-person '-s' helps to distinguish between the present and past tenses of some irregular verbs, e.g.

> It *hits* the target vs It *hit* the target.

Other apparently meaningless grammatical items also fulfil some meaningful role. For example, the obligatory use of the indefinite article (in front of noun phrases where the head noun is countable – see Chapter 7) serves to inform the hearer that a noun phrase is imminent. Consider these two sentences, both adaptations of Chomsky's famously ambiguous sentence *Flying planes can be dangerous*:

> Flying *a* plane is dangerous.
> *A* flying plane is dangerous.

The different position of 'a' indicates different noun phrases and therefore a different meaning. (See the case study in Chapter 7 for more on the indefinite article.)

Equally, the supposed redundancy of the difference between *is* and *are* can also indicate a structural difference; to adapt Chomsky again:

> *Flying planes is* dangerous. (*This activity* is dangerous.)
> *Flying planes are* dangerous. (*They* are dangerous.)

whereby the noun phrase in the first sentence is singular (because it refers to a singular head noun 'flying') and in the second plural ('planes').

So we should beware of saying that some grammatical features are totally 'meaningless'. The implication for practitioners is that they should always seek a way of 'selling' even the most apparently redundant or meaningless grammatical features to their learners; this point is taken up further in Section 6.7.

With this proviso in mind we can attempt to make sense of this variation by applying a distinction between **convention** and **creativity**. Conventional uses have to be accepted; that is the way things are, as with the indefinite article and third-person '-s' (although as I have shown above they sometimes have a structural role to play). In creative uses the speaker/writer is free to make meaningful distinctions with the grammatical forms they choose.

The distinction is really a cline with most items situated somewhere along it. An extreme conventional example would be the forms of irregular verbs; why do we say 'went' for the past of the verb 'go', for example? There is a historical explanation, of course, but it is not relevant or necessary for contemporary accounts. At the other extreme we may consider various verb-phrase forms, for example the difference between simple and continuous/progressive forms. This is often explained as being somewhat conventional in pedagogic terms, as being automatically determined by a number of objective criteria. This is not actually the case; it is in fact highly creative and dependent on the speaker's/writer's subjective choice. For example:

> *Before we knew it, we <u>were lifted</u> high on the shoulders of the supporters.*
> *Before we knew it, we <u>were being lifted</u> high on the shoulders of the supporters.*

Both sentences could be used to describe the same circumstances. However, the second sentence, with the continuous/progressive form, drops the reader into the middle of an action/activity in progress and makes it more vivid – if that is the impression the writer wishes to convey.

However, the dividing line between these two extremes can also be seen as mobile in terms of pedagogic and scientific grammar (see Section 2.6.3 for more on this distinction). It is justifiable to treat certain factors as conventional in pedagogic accounts – for the purpose of simplification – while in scientific grammar they are regarded as creative. One example might be the injunction to avoid progressive forms with so-called stative verbs:

> *I needed a haircut* not *I was needing a haircut.*

whereas a more nuanced, scientific, creative approach would allow for 'exceptions', such as those pointed out in Section 3.2.

Choice is not enough to establish creativity; it is a necessary but not sufficient factor. Choice can also be non-creative, for example the choice between a regular or irregular verb form (e.g. *smelled* vs *smelt*), or between *somebody* and *someone* and other pairs of indefinite pronouns.

The theoretical approaches to grammar considered in Section 2.8 can be partly understood according to where they stand on the creative/conventional dimension. For instance, cognitive and construction grammar stand at the far extreme of creativity, attempting to explain everything grammatical in terms of semantic choice. In cognitive grammar (see, for example, Lee 2001: 137–145), the choice of basic spatial prepositions is seen as a matter of creativity involving how we construe a situation. Thus whether we say *on a bus* or *in a bus* depends on whether we view the bus as a surface (*on*) or a container (*in*). While this explanation may account for the historical origin of both expressions, the days are long gone when buses were open surfaces. So another plausible explanation is that people are simply repeating what they have heard from others; in other words the use of both here is now at least partly conventional. But it would be equally wrong to take this to the extreme, as is sometimes done in the classroom, whereby learners are taught that prepositions collocate automatically with nouns.

2.5 How Languages 'Do' Grammar

A basic tenet of this book, already mentioned, and supported by Bauer (1998), is that all languages have grammar but that they do it in different (as well as similar) ways. This might not seem so relevant for a book which is only about English, but it is crucial for anyone who aims to understand English grammar as regards learning the language. In this view English grammar is not some mysterious, unnatural beast designed to torment learners but a construct which merely replaces the one which already applies in their first language.

There are four such techniques or strategies for 'doing grammar' in English, as in other languages. For more on this see Swan (2005).

2.5.1 Strategy 1: Vary the Word Order

This is the classic grammatical strategy. A difference in word order can convey completely different grammatical meanings, as we saw in Section 2.4 with the classic example *The dog bit the man* vs *The man bit the dog*. Identical words but different orders indicate different meanings. All languages seem to have an underlying default word order in terms of subject (S), verb (V) and object (O); this is sometimes called the 'canonical' (fundamental) word order of a language. English is typically an SVO language (though there are exceptions), as are the Chinese languages, even though their grammar differs widely from English elsewhere. Other languages, such as Japanese, are SOV.

Another rule of word order deals with the relationship between head (the key word in a phrase) and modifier (a word such as an adjective which affects the reference of the head). In English the modifier typically comes first; in French the head. For example:

> *un homme sauvage* (literally 'a man wild') as opposed to
> *a wild man* (literally but incorrectly '*un sauvage homme*')

Word order is a powerful tool in making meaning in other ways, as in this example:

> ...they <u>too</u> were busy building up a network of property and favour.

Note the difference if we move one little word:

> ...they were <u>too</u> busy building up a network of property and favour.

2.5.2 Strategy 2: Change the Shape of Words

This can be done by adding bits (affixes) at the end (suffixes), beginning (prefixes) or less frequently middle (infixes). Traditionally, only inflectional affixes are considered part of grammar. These are affixes which do not change the word class of a word, so in *dogs* the plural suffix is an inflection, whereas in *helpful* the ending *-ful* is a derivational affix (changing a noun into an adjective). There are only a few inflections in English, and all are suffixes, or endings. Chinese also has a few inflectional suffixes for example *-men* in Putonghua to indicate the plural of personal pronouns.

2.5.3 Strategy 3: Add Little 'Function' Words

Short, frequent words can be used to show grammatical relationships or indicate the nature of related, surrounding words. In English the best examples of this are the 'prepositions' *to* and *of*. *To* has developed a distinctly non-prepositional function as a marker of an imminent infinitive, e.g. *I want <u>to go</u>*. (This is usually called the '*to* infinitive' as opposed to the 'bare infinitive'.) Although it cannot be said to have any meaning of its own (as with all the little words in this category), *to* does help to clarify the nature of the following word (or a later word, if there is a 'split' infinitive). Thus *I told her to go*, with its infinitive, can be distinguished from the imperative in *I told her 'go'*.

Similarly *of*, while still recognisably a preposition (in that it is used to relate two noun phrases), often has a purely grammatical function. To take an example from the context of this chapter, in a phrase such as *the development <u>of</u> grammar*, the word *of* has nothing of its traditionally ascribed meaning of possession, or anything similar; there is no sense of 'grammar' possessing 'development'. *Of* simply shows the grammatical relationship of subject-verb between its neighbouring words, i.e. *grammar has developed*. This process, known as nominalisation, turns what is fundamentally a clause with a verb into a noun phrase so that further statements can be made about it (*The development of grammar is...*).

2.5.4 Strategy 4: Use Suprasegmental Features

In speech, factors such as stress or intonation can be used to convey grammatical differences. Intonation in English can convey various types of interrogative. *Yes/no* questions have a rising intonation, *wh-*questions have a falling intonation. The equivalent in writing, punctuation, is sometimes said to be a poor relation. In some cases it can match some of the features of speech, e.g. in the use of the question mark. In others, such as in 'flesh-eating virus', the hyphen helps to indicate the object-verb relationship between *flesh* and *eating*). And in some cases it identifies distinctions that speech cannot make, e.g. between plural and genitive constructions: *dogs* vs *dog's*. But overall it must be admitted that suprasegmental factors in speech are more powerful.

2.5.5 Combining Strategies

Languages use these strategies in different measure, and some do not use all four. English, as has been shown, uses all four, though in differing degrees.

There is also a historical dimension to this as well, as languages, changing over time, make more use of one strategy and less of another. English, like many contemporary European languages used to make far more use of strategy 2 and less of strategy 1 than it does now. Grammatical roles originally indicated by endings, for example subject and object, are now indicated by word order rather than by noun endings. However, the use of endings has still left some very important traces in the shape of inflections on nouns (plural and saxon genitive), verbs (third-person singular, past tense, *-ed* and *-ing* participles), and adjectives (inflectional comparatives and superlatives). It is also hypothesised that the development of articles in English from demonstratives (as in other European languages) was occasioned by this move away from a relatively free word order so as to still be able to show the topic and comment in a sentence. Previously the topic of a sentence could always be placed first; regardless of whether it was the grammatical subject or object or whatever, the ending would show its grammatical role. Nowadays, it is rare but possible to find an object in first position as the topic:

The answer I already knew.

(The passive in English has a similar function of bringing to the front a noun phrase that would normally be an object following the verb.)

There are certain situations in English where two grammatical constructions seem to be in competition, for example phrasal and inflectional comparison (e.g. *more common* and *commoner*), or 'saxon' (apostrophe *-'s*) and *of* genitives (*the boy's teacher* vs *the teacher of the boy*). These can be understood as a 'battle' between two of the strategies, 2 and 3, namely the use of extra words vs inflection. Strategy 2 seems to be winning out, albeit slowly, in the case of comparison. (See the case study on this topic in Chapter 8.) This of course has long been a historical trend in English. (In traditional linguistics English has been said to have become an isolating language as opposed to an inflecting one.)

We can also use these strategies to illustrate the way grammar develops in child language by returning to the phrase in the previous section 'eat dog'. In order to communicate clearly in English the child would need to acquire a rule that places subjects before verbs ('dog eat') and a rule that add elements to the verb, both a separate word and an ending ('the dog is eating'), to express ideas such as timing and volition (i.e. tense, aspect and modality, to use the technical terms). In other words, strategy 1, and a combination of strategies 2 and 3 are applied. Children learning other first languages may not use the same rules or strategies, but they will go through the same process of learning to make meaning via grammar.

2.6 Three Distinctions

Even though we may have nailed down our subject matter, and outlined how it operates, we can still find that there are several approaches to it. These may be explained by means of three distinctions.

2.6.1 Distinction 1: Primary vs Secondary Grammar

This is a long-established dichotomy, although different terms are assigned to it. In Quirk et al. (1985) it is termed 'operational grammar' versus 'analytical grammar'. McArthur (1983: 73–75) uses the terms 'primary' and 'secondary', and these will be used here, since they imply, correctly, the primacy of primary grammar. **Primary grammar** is the knowledge we all possess unconsciously and intuitively about our first language (or any other languages we have acquired naturally). Everyone knows the grammar of their first language; it is a truism that if they did not, they could not use it to communicate fluently and correctly. But they may also possess a primary grammar of other languages they have been exposed to.

Secondary grammar is the knowledge we possess consciously about languages, whether first or second or other. This knowledge derives from attempts to capture primary grammar and may be encapsulated in the accounts of scientific grammarians, which nowadays stretch to 2,000 pages without capturing all the nuances of primary grammar. All languages have a primary grammar in the sense described, but not all have been codified and thus cannot be said to have a secondary grammar.

Learner knowledge of secondary grammar results from formal education. As well as to L2 learners, it may apply to L1 speakers, as was the case in Britain fifty or more years ago (and is the case to a lesser extent today). Secondary grammar at best is a poor imitation of primary grammar, but at worst, if unrelated to primary grammar, it can become a misleading alternative. See the descriptive/prescriptive distinction below.

Learners of English as a foreign language will have principally a secondary knowledge of grammar, in the shape of the rules of thumb that they are given, and it is this they may deploy when constructing sentences carefully, e.g. in writing. However, alongside this they may develop a primary grammar, unnoticed by the educational process, that allows them to create, especially in informal speech, sentences that are not based on anything they have formally been taught. In addition, they may develop intuitions which conflict with what they have been told about English. See Maule (1988) for such a conflict. Invariably I have found that primary grammar, even if incomplete, is a better guide for learners to accurate performance than the rules of thumb they have received.

2.6.2 Distinction 2: Descriptive vs Prescriptive Grammar

This distinction refers to whether the rules of grammar (and other aspects of language) should be ordained by authority, as described in Section 1.2, or simply described as they are used.

Prescriptive grammar is built around a number of injunctions regarding correct usage which were largely devised in the late eighteenth and early nineteenth centuries by authoritative figures such as John Dryden, based on Latin and logic. Some injunctions, though, were simply arrived at randomly, while others reflected a desire to reverse language change (see Section 3.2). While prescriptive grammar has been on the retreat for much of the last century it still has influential adherents among native speakers. As recently as 2015 Gyles Brandreth, a well-known writer and media personality, was insisting on the use of *whom* rather than *who* as an objective relative pronoun (*He's a man who/whom we can trust*), and for the use of *fewer* rather than *less* with countable nouns (*Less/fewer than 100 people turned up for the rally*) (Brandreth, *Word Play*, Coronet, 2015, pp. 249–251). The *fewer/less* controversy even found its way into the smash-hit TV series *Game of Thrones*. In one episode in Series 2, Ser Davos is chastised by Stannis Baratheon for saying he had 'four fingers less to clean' when it should have been 'four fingers fewer'. See Berry (1998) for a discussion of this matter.

Other issues that have at various times been controversial include

- split infinitives. This was based on a false analogy with Latin. Since the Latin infinitive is 'unsplittable', the reasoning went, the same should apply to the English one. Objections to it now seem to be fading, and apart from having been used by a long list of distinguished authors, split infinitives can be very useful in distinguishing different meanings, as Crystal (1984: 29) showed:

  ...*we've tried <u>to deliberately stop</u> arguing*... (the stopping is deliberate)
  ...*I tried <u>deliberately to stop</u> arguing*... (the trying is deliberate)

- the use of *hopefully* to mean *it is hoped that* instead of *in a hopeful manner*. This belief is based on a misconception about the nature of adverbs in English; they do not merely refer to manner (or place or time). Amongst other things they can be used to make a comment on a proposition, and English is full of them (*interestingly*, *curiously*, etc.). This is a usage that Humphrys (2004) decries, and yet he uses other adverbs (e.g. *sadly* and *thankfully*) in exactly the same way:

  He is, <u>sadly</u>, extinct... (p. 217)
  What they'll get <u>(thankfully)</u> is... (p. 239)

  (see Berry 2015a for more on this). Chapter 3 also gives more information about different types of adverb; see Section 3.2.1 and Note 1. This injunction still staggers on in some quarters, however. *The Times* reported in August 2019 that Jacob Rees-Mogg, on being appointed Leader of the House by Boris Johnson, had instructed his staff not to use *hopefully* (though presumably he still allows its use as an adverb of manner).
- *It is I/me*. The injunction to use *I* rather than *me* after 'be' is another example of a false analogy with Latin. Latin uses the same case, the nominative, for this role as well as for the subject. In English, however, this is a different grammatical role sometimes called the 'complement' or 'predicative', and for most speakers the form of the first-person singular personal pronoun to be used in this case is *me*. For a more detailed discussion of this see Carter and McCarthy (2006: 380–382). The case study in Chapter 9 on personal pronouns also touches on this area.

Most of the prescriptive rules that have plagued discussions of English grammar in L1 circles have fortunately not found favour in the L2

2.6 Three Distinctions

classroom. But some have. Three such rules were investigated in a study I carried out in which first-year English majors in Hong Kong were asked for their reactions to them (Berry 2015b); their responses are shown in brackets. A fuller account of the study is given in Chapter 3 where other common pedagogic misconceptions are discussed. The three were:

1 'It is wrong to start sentences with conjunctions such as *and* or *but*.' (*TRUE 85, FALSE 59, DON'T KNOW 19, PARTLY TRUE 32*)

This rule is still trotted out widely in L1 situations (e.g. by publishers). It is based on the belief that *but* and *and* should only be used as conjunctions in joining two clauses within a sentence. However, if this is a 'rule', it is one that is often honoured more in the breach than in the observance; highly-regarded authors are known to 'abuse' it. A descriptive grammar will simply note the fact that these words are commonly used to start sentences. Readers will find several examples of 'breaches' in this book. Nevertheless, it is still somewhat worrying that such a rule had so many believers outside the L1 arena.[1]

2 'In type two conditional sentences (second conditionals) it is wrong to use WAS after IF; WERE must be used instead.' (*TRUE 78, FALSE 59, DON'T KNOW 37, PARTLY TRUE 21*)

This second prescriptive rule had a remarkably similar profile in participant responses to the above one. It concerns sentences such as

If I was/were wrong I would admit it.

This 'rule' is not an accurate description of current English (if indeed it ever was). *Was* is more common in this situation even in formal circumstances, as any examination of data shows (apart from the fixed expression *If I were you*). If anything it is *were* that is marked, as a formal alternative.

While the above two 'rules' were rather (too) well-known, a third prescriptive rule had little currency:

3 'It is wrong to put prepositions at the end of a sentence.' (*TRUE 33, FALSE 126, DON'T KNOW 26, PARTLY TRUE 10*)

This rule has long been known to have no basis in actual usage. Apart from the fact that the forbidden construction is widely used in English and is of some antiquity (Crystal 1984: 61), there is one situation where it cannot be avoided, namely with the passive of prepositional verbs:

This problem will be looked into. (Try moving the preposition while retaining the passive.)

Overall, while these prescriptive rules may still exercise native speakers to some degree, it seems that the effect on learners of English is minimal, compared to the vastly more serious problems that they face.

The **descriptive** approach aims to describe the language as it is, based on what people actually say and write, rather than on what some self-appointed authority thinks they should say or write. Behind it stand the great descriptive grammars of the last thirty or forty years; namely, Quirk et al. (1985), Biber et al. (1999) and Huddleston and Pullum (2002). It infuses most current descriptions of grammar, though, as we saw, some parts of the EFL world are resistant. And of course there are situations where being prescriptive (though not in the unhelpful sense as described above) is necessary, namely in simplifying descriptions for learners. In this way, the descriptive/prescriptive debate also has implications for the next distinction, between scientific and pedagogic grammar. And in turn it is partly dependent on the primary/secondary grammar dichotomy outlined above. For modern linguistics, primary grammar is the source of descriptions, whereas in the prescriptive tradition there is no need to rely on primary grammar; secondary grammar is the source.

2.6.3 Distinction 3: Scientific vs Pedagogic Grammar

This distinction concerns the purpose of grammatical description and its intended audience. A description meant for fellow linguists and grammarians will have no limit to the level of sophistication that may be involved; this may be termed **scientific grammar**. **Pedagogic grammar**, on the other hand, may not be able to tell the whole truth since it would not be comprehensible, or relevant, to learners or teachers.

The distinction is important because it has often been the case that learners are exposed to accounts which are not suitable for them – one of the 'sins' of pedagogic grammar exposed in Section 2.7. The distinction is also, indeed especially, relevant to different kinds of terminology. (This is further explained in Section 4.3.)

The difference between the two is not absolute but rather more of a cline, and there will be more than one version of each. In the same way that there may be competing different scientific accounts of the same area of grammar according to the various theories espoused, there may be as many variants of pedagogic grammar as there are different target groups.

This distinction is not only applicable to the varying sophistication of rules, however; it can also apply to the way whole systems are conceptualised. Take the verb phrase system in English and the obvious question: how many tenses are there? If you ask learners and teachers, most (after a pause for counting) will say 'eight'. And if you ask for a list they might come up with the following:

PRESENT (SIMPLE)	PRESENT CONTINUOUS
PAST (SIMPLE)	PAST CONTINUOUS
PRESENT PERFECT	PRESENT PERFECT CONTINUOUS
PAST PERFECT	PAST PERFECT CONTINUOUS

This total of eight forms is sometimes extended by the inclusion of 'future' tenses (involving *will* and possibly *shall*; see Chapter 4 for more) and, less frequently nowadays, 'conditional' tenses (involving *would*).

However, if you check any scientific grammar, you will find the answer is 'two': only the present and the past are counted as tenses. So does this mean the other forms are not correct in English? Of course not. It simply means that the other forms are dealt with under a different concept, namely 'aspect'; this comprises the elements perfect and continuous (or progressive) and their combination (as well as their absence, i.e. simple forms). The scientific argument for the distinction between tense and aspect is that they reflect different phenomena, not only formally (tense changes the form of the word – strategy 2 in Section 2.5.2 – while aspect involves the use of extra words, namely auxiliaries – strategy 3), but also semantically. Tense is largely (but not only) to do with the notion of time, while aspect relates to subtler perspectives on the actions or states denoted by the verb, such as whether they last, whether they are completed, whether they are repeated or are continuous.

Which is right? This depends on the purpose and target audience, as outlined above. Grammarians may feel the distinction is justified, and researchers may wish to separate errors of tense from errors of aspect; not to mention teachers, who should be aware of the difference (though many, I fear, are not). But for most learners it is a great deal simpler to conflate the two and to deal with, for example, the 'present perfect' under the heading of 'tense' rather than 'tense plus aspect', i.e. to talk about the 'present perfect tense' rather than the convoluted 'present perfect verb phrase form'. But the decision can be dodged by simply referring to the 'present perfect'.

2.7 Pedagogic Grammar as Process

Many practitioners, I believe, view the concept of pedagogic grammar as a *product*, as a statement of the grammatical facts – however

What Is Grammar?

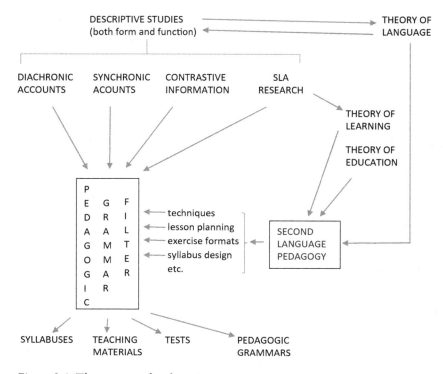

Figure 2.1 The process of pedagogic grammar
(from Berry 1999: 32)

extensive – that should be presented to learners in whatever form is appropriate. In-service and pre-service courses for language teachers entitled Pedagogic Grammar seem to stress this aspect.

However, I believe an equally valid conceptualisation of pedagogic grammar is as a *process*, with inputs and a filter as well as outputs. This approach can help in understanding some of the problems with grammar teaching. In a 1999 paper I proposed a model of this process, shown in Figure 2.1.

Thus, for example, the input from a synchronic account would be filtered through the pedagogic grammar component, where factors such as exercise format design would come into play, before contributing to an output such as teaching materials.

By applying this model we can understand some of the things that go wrong with grammar teaching – the 'sins' of pedagogic grammar, as I have called them – especially those which miss out the second language pedagogy component or the pedagogic grammar filter. One of the worst sins is where linguistic insights are passed directly on to learners, without undergoing the filter of the pedagogic grammar component; the problem with second language acquisition research mentioned in Chapter 1 can be understood in this way. Another sin is the presentation of incorrect facts about English grammar, a topic which resonates throughout this book. This occurs when descriptive studies do not feed into the pedagogic grammar filter; instead the input to the filter comes from other pedagogic accounts, producing a vicious circle.

Theories of language/grammar that might be applicable to pedagogic grammar, as well as descriptive inputs, are dealt with below. The inputs from second language pedagogy and outputs from the pedagogic grammar, such as exercises and tests, are dealt with in Chapter 6.

2.8 Theoretical Approaches to Grammar

Where might we look for a theory of grammar that can be used in language teaching? Many theories do not aim to be applied and so need no consideration. We can identify three criteria that can be used to 'weed out' such theories: their (lack of) involvement with meaning as well as form (as stressed above); their level of formalism (the use of highly technical concepts and terminology that seek to exclude all but the initiated); and, most importantly, their attitude to the nature of language.

This last factor leads to one of the great debates in linguistics, between rationalist and empiricist approaches to language. Put briefly, it is between the view that language is a mental faculty, contained within the brain, and therefore not directly visible – competence, according to Chomsky's famous dichotomy – as opposed to the view that language is something we experience in spoken or written (or signed) form – performance.[2]

It is also a debate about the source of evidence: the rationalist linguist's armchair intuitions (not always reliable) versus instances of real language (texts and conversations) that have been attested (but which may not always be 'correct'). A surely sensible standpoint would be that language is both, but extreme rationalists deny the validity of the latter. However, over the last four decades the advent of massive (and growing) computer-analysable corpora of texts has tipped the balance towards the empiricist viewpoint and enabled new theories of language, such as Pattern Grammar (e.g. Hunston and Francis 2000), to emerge.

One theory we can rule out at the start on all criteria is Chomskyan linguistics, in all its various incarnations, above all because it does not aim to be applicable. Its level of formalism, the use of formulae, make it – unashamedly – inaccessible; it was never meant to be applied to language teaching (though some have tried).

This leaves us with a number of possible candidates, sometimes grouped under the heading of functional linguistics (as opposed to Chomskyan formal linguistics). One approach that has gained many adherents around the world is Michael Halliday's systemic/functional approach, and there are others, such as cognitive and construction grammar, which also meet the meaning criterion – indeed they stress the primacy of meaning as a determinant of grammatical form. However, they may be problematic in terms of accessibility. As regards the nature of language, they do not come down on one side or the other; rather they question the validity of the distinction between rationalist and empiricist approaches, particularly between competence and performance.

However, the foregoing discussion is somewhat academic, since we already have a theory of grammar on which most pedagogy is based, though it is not always recognised as such, namely traditional grammar (in a greatly modernised form). The candidates discussed in the above paragraph all have a great deal in common with it, though they extend beyond it in several ways, for example the emphasis on the notions of rheme and theme in Hallidayan linguistics. And all the great descriptive grammars mentioned in Section 2.6.2, namely Quirk et al. (1985), Biber et al. (1999) and Huddleston and Pullum (2002), rely on it, with minor differences, especially in terminology.[3] So a critical look at it is essential.

2.8.1 Modern Traditional Grammar

Traditional grammar is based on a hierarchy of units, from the smallest, the morpheme, through the word, the phrase and the clause to the sentence. At each level a unit is composed of one or more units of the lower level. Phrases may consist of many words, or even of other phrases (the concept of recursion), but a sentence may consist of just one morpheme, for example: *Stop!* For some the sentence does not exist as a separate level: for others grammatical phenomena extend beyond the sentence.

Beyond this, traditional grammar consists basically of two areas: **word classes** and **grammatical functions**.

The former area has been developed over more than two millennia from the grammar of Greek attributed to Dionysius Thrax in the second century BCE. Originally called 'parts of speech', the more appropriate term 'word class' is applied nowadays, since that is what it is: an attempt to classify all the words in a language. The criteria for doing so have long been thought to be semantic, or notional ('a noun is the name of a person, thing or place'), but in fact have always been structural: 'a noun is a word that inflects for plural and genitive', etc.). And so on. However, the criteria are not foolproof, and while there is general agreement about the most fundamental classes (noun, verb, adjective), there are differences in the margins. Interjections and 'the article' have long been abandoned as valid classes.

In two works, I have posited the following major word classes for English:

> *noun, verb, adjective, adverb, preposition, auxiliary, conjunction, determiner, pronoun* (Berry 2015a, 2018).

Not all grammarians would agree with this. While determiners (*this, that, my,* etc.) were proposed as recently as the mid-twentieth century as a separate class, some would argue that they should be conflated with pronouns. And it is normal to regard auxiliaries (*have, be, do* and the modals) as a sub-class of verbs. I have separated them off because they are a closed class – they do not admit further members lightly, as with other closed classes (the last three on the list above). And cases can be made for other classes, numerals (*one, two, first, second*) being a case in point. At the same time there is little that holds the class of adverbs together; what do *quickly* and *yet* have in common?

While total agreement on which word classes there are will probably never be reached, a deeper issue is that of the multifunctionality of many common words in English, in that they belong to more than one word class – in some cases as many as five, as was the case with *back* in Section 2.4 on grammar and meaning. But as shown there, the word-class status of a multifunctional word can help to disambiguate the meaning. So even though the word-class approach is formally based, it is readily exploitable for meaning distinctions. And explicitly or implicitly all theories of language rely on the concept of word class.

The concept of **grammatical functions** (sometimes called clause elements) deals with the different elements at the phrase level that constitute a clause, and the different grammatical functions that they fulfil. The number varies according to the language; five basic functions have been identified for English, two of which can be subdivided:

Subject: *She hates dogs.*
Object, with three sub-types: direct (*I hate dogs*), indirect (*Have you paid them?*) and prepositional (*They laughed at us*).
Verb (not to be confused with 'verb' as a word class): *I hate dogs.*

Complement or **predicative**, with two sub-types: subject (*I am getting tired*) and object (*This weather makes me tired*).
Adverbial: *They sat quietly for a while.*

These are, like word classes, identified by formal features. Subjects, for example, are identified by their position in the clause, by the way they invert with a part of the verb phrase and the way they dictate the form of the verb (third-person *-s* or not). A common misunderstanding is to view the subject semantically, as the doer or agent in a clause, but in fact subjects cover several different semantic roles, such as experiencer (*I heard a noise*).

I have found this to be an insightful tool-kit in understanding cases of ambiguity compared to, say, phrase structure rules. Take the following sentence:

Passengers are advised to check ahead if their plane has been delayed.

The ambiguity here rests in the subordinate clause beginning with 'if'. The difference can be seen by trying to replace it with *whether*; two different types of subordinate clause result, with different meanings. In one interpretation this substitution is possible, making *whether their plane has been delayed* the direct object of *check* (a so-called nominal clause). In the other the substitution is not possible, since *if their plane has been delayed* is an adverbial (clause) talking about a condition. A phrase structure analysis would simply show a subordinate clause (or sentence); the use of grammatical functions allows us to identify the meaning of that clause via its role in the sentence. See also the Activity.

This has been a much abridged account of traditional grammar; one could also mention the different forms of phrase formation and clause combination. For a slightly fuller account see Berry (2015a). But with the addition of verb phrase formation discussed above and perhaps the omission of the more arcane aspects of grammatical functions, it forms the backbone of any pedagogical approach to grammar, and is likely to do so for the foreseeable future (but see the discussion of metalinguistic relativity in Chapters 3 and 4).

2.9 Descriptive Inputs to Pedagogical Grammar as Process

Of the four descriptive inputs to the pedagogic grammar filter in the model, one – second language acquisition research – has already been dealt with in Chapter 1 (where it has been accorded less importance than some would claim). Another – synchronic accounts – has been considered in the foregoing discussion, and will figure again at the end of

2.9 Descriptive Inputs to Pedagogical Grammar

this chapter. Now is the time to make a claim for the two other, rather controversial, areas: historical (diachronic) and contrastive accounts.

2.9.1 Historical Accounts

In this age where synchronic linguistics dominates it may seem strange to invoke a historical dimension. But an understanding of the way English got to be the way it is can explain some of the dilemmas facing synchronic accounts.

For one thing, the diachronic perspective can prevent us from seeking monolithic accounts of various idiosyncratic areas of English grammar, for example, the use of the indefinite article in rates etc.: e.g. *twenty miles an hour*. (It is in fact a reinterpretation of the preposition *on*; see the case study in Chapter 7 on articles for more on this.)

It can also help to explain various unexpected, generally formal, verb forms, as in:

> *Long live the King!*
> *Were she to come.../If she were to come...*
> *The report recommended he be reprimanded* (the 'mandative' subjunctive).

These can all be explained collectively, in scientific terms, as remnants of the 'subjunctive': an alternative system of verb forms used for hypothetical and similar situations that was widespread in Old English, but which has disappeared as a coherent system in modern English, leaving only isolated remnants; however, pedagogically it seems that the mandative subjunctive is still alive and well in current formal English (see Section 3.2).

Furthermore, as described above, a historical perspective can also help us understand why English grammar currently has in certain areas two 'competing' systems – for example, the two forms of the 'genitive' construction in English:

> *the cousin of the queen* (the phrasal or 'periphrastic' construction, i.e. involving several words);
> *the Queen's cousin* (the inflectional construction, sometimes called 'apostrophe -s').

Much research, especially involving corpora, has been carried out in order to understand the reasons why one is preferred to the other (e.g. the length of the noun phrase, which favours the periphrastic construction). But a full understanding needs to take into consideration the different origins of the two constructions. While the latter has come down to us from English's Germanic roots (should I have written 'the Germanic roots of English'?), Crystal (2017: 185) suggests that the use of the former was influenced after the Norman conquest by a French-speaking elite using a word-for-word translation of the French equivalent.

A similar explanation applies to the two systems of forming the comparison of adjectives. The competition between the periphrastic, two-word option (*more/most beautiful*) and the inflectional (*kinder/ kindest*) constitutes a major issue in pedagogic grammar and forms the subject of the case study in Chapter 8. Incidentally, the way these 'battles' between inflectional and periphrastic alternatives have continued, even stabilised, suggests that English is no longer moving towards a totally analytic state (cf. the four ways of making grammar discussed in Section 2.5).

Of course I am not saying that any of this knowledge should be passed on to any but the most sophisticated learners, if that. However, such facts may be helpful to pedagogic grammarians and teachers in understanding cases of idiosyncrasy or apparent redundancy.

Another area where two historically distinct systems are in competition is the somewhat pedagogically controversial matter of phrasal verbs, where the latter are in conflict with single-word alternatives, e.g. *hand out* vs *distribute* or *put off* vs *postpone*. In this case a compromise seems to have been reached whereby the single-word alternatives are restricted to a more formal register, while the two-word verbs have a more idiomatic flavour. The problem in pedagogy is that learners prefer the single-word forms because of their less complicated grammar and avoid the more common phrasal forms (no need to work out where to place the particle in phrasal verbs). This can result in learners sounding less idiomatic. In this case it may be justifiable to point this out to learners.

2.9.2 Contrastive Accounts

The days are long gone when contrastive information – that is, information from a comparison between the systems of the source language and the target language – was ruled out of court a priori. It is no longer feasible to maintain the belief that all learners follow the same learning route and make the same mistakes (though this is partly true). Generations of error analysts have shown how particular errors are common among learners with certain L2 backgrounds but not among others. Swan and Smith's (1987) tome, *Learner English*, is predicated on such evidence. The errors described there are uncontroversially attributable to the difference between the two languages. Thus learners whose L1 is article-less will make more mistakes, and more kinds of mistake, in this area than learners whose L1 possesses articles.

2.9 Descriptive Inputs to Pedagogical Grammar

There are two ELT constituencies, however, for whom the adducing of contrastive information is problematic. The first is the international publishers who take a 'one-size fits all' approach to the production of teaching materials (i.e. coursebooks). For them it makes more financial sense to produce a course with the same grammatical component, regardless of the L2 background of the 'consumers'. This could lead to a situation where, for example, learners of English with Mandarin or Polish as their L1 are given the same treatment on articles as speakers of Western European languages – clearly an unsatisfactory situation (cf. Chapter 7).

The second constituency is the mass (though still a large minority) of EFL teachers, mostly L1 speakers of English, spread around the world, who have little or no knowledge of the L1 of their learners (though if they are living in the homeland of their learners they will no doubt acquire an understanding of the language). Lacking even a secondary grammar of the source language (and often of the target language, i.e. English), they will struggle to help leaners with their grammar problems.

A contrastive knowledge on the part of teachers can help to prevent the wrong connections that are made too often by learners, e.g. between imperfective verb forms in Slavonic languages and progressive verb forms in English. The case study in Chapter 7 gives an example of how contrastive information can be helpful by showing how the (in)definiteness of noun phrases, marked by the articles in English, can be expressed by word order in Slavonic languages.

2.9.3 Other Descriptive Areas

A number of other areas of linguistic study – not strictly grammatical in nature – have also contributed recently to the understanding of grammatical phenomena, and have served as inputs to pedagogic grammar. They have helped to show that a narrow view of grammar is unrewarding. Only a brief account of each is possible here.

Pragmatics. There is no space here to outline here all the contributions of this fairly recent field to our understanding of grammar. One example of how a pragmatic approach to one important grammatical phenomenon, the definite article, is given in Chapter 7. Another, classic area is the mismatch between certain grammatical forms and their functions (or the speech acts they perform). A prime example of this is the imperative sentence type in English. Learners are often told that imperatives function as orders (the misleading nature of the term does not help – see Chapter 4). But of course there is a whole range of other functions implied by imperatives:

> Take a seat (an invitation).
> Multiply the width by the length... (an instruction).
> Do that and I'm out of here (a conditional functioning as part of a threat – 'If you do that...').

And so on.

Genre analysis. This shows that grammar can be (partly) accounted for by analysing the conventions of different genres, for example the use of the historic present (see Section 5.2.3) in stories: *I look out the window and see...* Sometimes it seems that, rather than reflecting the transition from one move to another inside a genre, it is the difference in grammar that creates the change, as in this example of tense usage in film reviews, which shows a switch from background information to plot description rather abruptly by means of a tense change from past (the first two underlined verbs below) to present tense (the third and fourth):

> *Fleming set three Bond novels in Jamaica, though none captured the scene as vividly as* Doctor No *(1958). After a group of assassins destroy the British Secret Service's radio station ... Bond is dispatched.*

An account of tense usage which ignored such usages could not claim to be comprehensive.

Another example of the relevance of genre is given in the activity in Chapter 10 regarding the use of direct and reported speech.

Corpus studies. As well as adding a new theoretical orientation, corpus studies have provided analysts with numerous insights into the way languages work grammatically (in addition to being a source of data for lexicography). Studies of collocations, prosodies and patterns (e.g. those triggered by verbs and nouns) have provided evidence that can be fed into the pedagogic filter, most notably the way grammar works on a lexical level. Nowadays teachers and students may access corpora (e.g. the freely available Corpus of Contemporary American English) to become their own investigators. The case study in Chapter 8 shows how the results of a corpus analysis of a particular grammatical area may have a direct bearing on pedagogy.

2.10 Conclusion

The history of 'grammar' shows it expanding and contracting as a field of study. Where the term once comprised (almost) all of the study of language, nowadays it has slimmed down somewhat, as the attempts to limit its scope and define it above demonstrate. But even if the subject matter has been successfully tied down, it should be understood that there are different ways of looking at it.

Accordingly the focus in the chapter has moved from grammar in scientific linguistics to grammar in language pedagogy. But even here – especially here – there has been a realisation that grammar, especially formal grammar, cannot be the sole input to teaching – that grammar needs to seek and accept inputs from other fields.

Activity

Look at these examples of structures using the verb *make*, one of the most versatile verbs in English (without even mentioning the numerous phrasal verbs that it occurs in, such as *make up for*). Using the concept of grammatical functions/clause elements outlined above and the (in)transitivity of verbs, can you resolve the different uses?

(a) Your bid won't make.
(b) I made a cake.
(c) I made her a cake.
(d) She made lieutenant.
(e) She'll make him a good husband.
(f) She'll make him a good wife.

Could any other system account for all these phenomena simply?

Comment

In (a) *make* is intransitive, there is no object. This is an example from a rather obscure genre, the language of bridge, where *make* means that a bid will be successful.

In (b) *make* is transitive with a direct object ('a cake'). Something has been brought into existence.

In (c) it is ditransitive with an indirect object ('her'), indicating the beneficiary of the action, as well as the direct object from (b).

In (d) *make* is a linking verb, similar to *become*, followed by a complement/predicative ('lieutenant').

The difference between (e) and (f) is that in (e) *make* is followed by a direct object ('him') and an object predicative (She will turn him into 'a good husband'), whereas in (f) it is followed by an indirect object and a subject predicative, i.e. she will become a good wife for him; a rather unusual structure.

Notes

1. In fact, this is not really a 'rule' of grammar, but rather of writing; in speech it has no relevance.
2. Later reformulated by Chomsky (1986) as a distinction between I (internalised) language and E (externalised) language.

3 Of course, there are also well-known grammars with a communicative or functional bias, such as Leech and Svartvik (2003) and Collins Cobuild English Grammar (2017), but these still rely on formal categories at some stage in their explanations.

References

Bauer, Winifred. 1998. Some languages have no grammar. In Laurie Bauer and Peter Trudgill (eds) *Language Myths*. London: Penguin, 77–84.

Berry, Roger. 1998. Determiners: a class apart. *English Today* 53: 27–34.

Berry, Roger. 1999. The seven sins of pedagogic grammar. In Roger Berry, Barry Asker, Ken Hyland and Martha Lam (eds) *Language Analysis, Description and Pedagogy*. Hong Kong: Hong Kong University of Science and Technology, 29–40.

Berry, Roger. 2015a. Grammar. In N. Baber, L. Cummings and L. Morrish (eds) *Exploring Language and Linguistics*. Cambridge: Cambridge University Press, 111–136.

Berry, Roger. 2015b. Grammar myths. *Language Awareness* 24/1: 15–37.

Berry, Roger. 2018. *English Grammar: A Resource Book for Students*. Abingdon: Routledge.

Biber, Douglas, Stig Johansson, Geoffrey Leech, Susan Conrad and Edward Finegan. 1999. *The Longman Grammar of Spoken and Written English*. Harlow: Longman.

Carter, Ronald and Michael McCarthy. 2006. *Cambridge Grammar of English*. Cambridge: Cambridge University Press.

Chomsky, Noam. 1986. *Knowledge of Language*. New York: Praeger.

Collins Cobuild English Grammar. 2017. 4th edn. Glasgow: HarperCollins.

Crystal, David. 1984. *Who Cares about English Usage?* London: Penguin.

Crystal, David. 2017. *Making Sense: The Glamourous Story of English Grammar*. London: Profile Books.

Greenbaum, Sidney and Gerald Nelson. 2009 *An Introduction to English Grammar*. 3rd edn. Harlow: Longman.

Huddleston, Rodney and Geoffrey K. Pullum 2002. *The Cambridge Grammar of the English Language*. Cambridge: Cambridge University Press.

Humphrys, John. 2004. *Lost for Words*. London: Hodder & Stoughton.

Hunston, Susan and Gill Francis. 2000. *Pattern Grammar*. Amsterdam: Benjamins.

Lee, David. 2001. *Cognitive Linguistics*. South Melbourne: Oxford University Press.

Leech, Geoffrey and Jan Svartvik. 2003. *A Communicative Grammar of English*. 3rd edn. Abingdon: Routledge.

Maule, D. 1988. 'Sorry, if he comes I go': teaching conditionals. *ELT Journal* 42: 117–123.

McArthur, Tom. 1983. *A Foundation Course for Language Teachers*. Cambridge: Cambridge University Press.

Quirk, Randolph, Sidney Greenbaum, Geoffrey Leech and Jan Svartvik. 1985. *A Comprehensive Grammar of the English Language*. Harlow: Longman.

Swan, Michael. 2005. *Grammar*. Oxford: Oxford University Press.

Swan, Michael and Bernard Smith. 1987. *Learner English*. Cambridge: Cambridge University Press.

Yule, George. 1985. *The Study of Language*. Cambridge: Cambridge University Press.

3 The Need for New Descriptions

3.1 Introduction

While Chapters 1 and 2 concerned themselves mostly with more general, theoretical issues to do with grammar and grammar teaching, which could be applied regardless of the language involved, this chapter moves on to more practical matters, specifically the description of one particular language: English. In language pedagogy there is sometimes an assumption that everything that needs to be said about English has already been said. This is not the case. Pedagogic grammars such as the *Cambridge Grammar of English* (Carter and McCarthy 2006) and *Collins Cobuild English Grammar* (2011, 2017) are constantly making accessible new knowledge about English, largely thanks to research using electronic corpora. But they cannot do everything; there is the problem of poor transmission (see Section 3.7) to be overcome.

This chapter will outline five interrelated reasons why new descriptions are needed and why old descriptions continuously need updating and revising. It will concentrate mainly on change in standard British and American English.

3.2 Reason 1: The Language Changes

The most obvious reason for needing new descriptions is language change. However, some grammarians regard grammar as an unchanging constant. Those who follow the prescriptivist tradition (see Section 2.6.2) might decry all language change, seeing it as a debasement of their beloved language, but it is an inescapable fact. We need only to look back at the history of English to confirm this, in the shape the vast changes to systems and forms that have taken place over the centuries, for example the loss of case endings and the move to a fixed word order cited in Section 2.5. Or the virtual disappearance of the subjunctive (as described in Section 2.9.1). Or the regularisation of irregular verb forms, e.g. *halp/holp* to *helped*.

Of course, it is more recent changes that are of concern here, changes that may have taken place without anyone noticing, or changes that are still in progress. For if there is something that we have learnt about language change it is that it is a gradual progress, diffusing slowly throughout the speech community (usually starting with the young) before it becomes widespread and accepted. And some changes may be halted, even reversed. We might also ask whether the pace of change nowadays is affected by mass literacy; knowledge of previous forms, as evidenced by the rather traditional spelling system of English, may impede change, but it is impossible to say how much effect it has.

There are a number of ways of detecting change in progress. Some innovations are so egregious that they can be spotted with the naked eye, so to speak. One source of such information is the protestations of the purists. While some of their targets are old enemies, others are fairly new; the popularity of *I'm like* to introduce spoken words or thoughts (sometimes called 'quotative' *like*) is one obvious example (see Chapter 10).

But the major, scientific method is the use of large-scale corpora of English usage (as described in Chapter 2). Among linguists there has emerged quite an industry involved in tracking recent changes in English. Leech et al. (2009), for example, devote a whole book to the enterprise of comparing recent corpus evidence with older material (using corpora established in 1961 and 1991). They note the following changes among others over this thirty-year period:

- A drastic decline in frequency of certain modal auxiliaries, namely *shall*, *ought to* and *need(n't)* (p. 79).
- A tendency for some modals, namely *should* and *may*, to prefer one meaning over others – weak obligation for *should* and possibility for *may* (at the expense of permission) (pp. 89 and 84 respectively).
- A loss of the difference in meaning between *may* and *might*; traditionally the latter has been said to be more tentative (p. 85).
- A revival of the 'mandative' subjunctive in British English (e.g. *They insisted that he go*) (p. 58, cf. Section 2.9.1).
- An increase in the frequency of genitive '-s', reversing a trend that was tentatively identified in pre-corpora days (by among others Otto Jespersen) towards a preference for the '*of* genitive'. (See Section 2.9.1 on historical input for competing systems.)

Of course, these are only trends, and, like any trend, they may be reversed. The short period of time available for comparison must militate against excessively firm conclusions. And the more subtle

3.2 Reason 1: The Language Changes

these corpora become, comprising as they do sub-corpora of different genres and regional varieties, the more likely one is to find contradictory trends. Moreover, it is not certain, from a pedagogical angle, what action should be taken from such results, even if they are deemed to be conclusive. Should *shall* be removed from the system of modal auxiliaries to be taught just because it is now found to be rare? Should learners be taught to use *may* only to express possibility?

One major change Leech et al. and others report on is the rise in use of progressive (or continuous) forms, as in *It was raining*. The construction is of relatively recent origin, dating from around the sixteenth century, and it seems that it is still on the rise; it 'has enjoyed a meteoric increase in frequency in the modern English period' (Leech et al. 2009: 118). In recent decades it has been given a boost by its use with so-called stative verbs – verbs implying a state, which normally would not be found in the progressive since its use implies an action, verbs such as:

HAVE: **I'm having two brothers* (but note *I'm having a bath*).
KNOW: **We're knowing this already.*
WANT: **I'm wanting a new car.*

If this is the case then how are we to account for the acceptability of sentences such as

I've been wanting to meet you for ages.
I don't like what I'm hearing.

not to mention the iconic McDonald's advert: *I'm loving it*?

These uses seem to turn a state into an action, to make the verb seem more 'dynamic' (a term that is sometimes used to describe such verbs). And before we get the impression that these are all recent uses, Crystal (2017: 190–191) cites an example from a letter written in 1917: *I can't tell you how much I'm loving it*. The use of *be* as a dynamic verb is also of some antiquity: *You're being silly*.

3.2.1 Reasons for Change

So much for just a few of the changes currently affecting contemporary English. What about the reasons for such changes? We can identify five general, interconnected trends in the causation of recent language change in British English:

(a) American influence: for instance, the rise in the use of *you guys* (see Chapter 9 for more on this), or the use of nouns as verbs, e.g. *access, impact*, as in this example from the Gatwick Airport website on 20 December 2018:

> We apologise to all of our passengers who are <u>impacted</u> today...

(One can perhaps have some sympathy for detractors here; would not 'affected' have done the job? Or does 'impacted' have more strength?) Some of these innovations draw the ire of traditionally minded commentators, none more so than *be like* (*And I'm like, so what?*). See Crystal (2017: 194–201) for more examples of American influence on British English.

(b) Creative uses: advertisers want to draw attention to their text; what better way to do this than to break a rule of grammar, so that readers or listeners remember the product? The use of the phrase *I'm loving it*, described above, is an excellent example.

(c) Informal forms, especially those representative of speech, becoming accepted in formal writing; two examples would be:
  – the establishment of *who* as an object relative pronoun (despite the best efforts of purists), as in: *I know <u>who</u> you are talking about* (with *whom* being a markedly formal alternative);
  – the increased acceptance of contractions (though there is still some reluctance in some quarters), as in: *I <u>don't</u> know who you are talking about.*

(d) New communicative needs, especially regarding the role of technology, for example:
  – the verb *attach* becoming ditransitive, with a prepositional object as well as a direct object, as in *attach a file/document <u>to someone</u>*;
  – the plural of *computer mouse* being <u>mouses</u> not *mice*;
  – changes in the count status of nouns: <u>discourses</u>, *Englishes*, in line with new approaches to the description of language;
  – *disappear* becoming a transitive verb (but only in the passive) suggesting some form of agency in the act: *Concerns are growing that some of the protesters may <u>have been disappeared over the border</u>.*

(e) Analogy. This is a universal tendency in language change. The change of irregular forms to regular is best exemplified in English in verb forms; the *helped* example above is only a distant instance. Recently I heard the regular *fleed* (rather than the irregular *fled*) from a TV presenter, though whether this innovation will become widespread remains to be seen.

Analogy does not always work to regularise verb forms; it may work in the other direction. For example, another 'innovation' I have heard is *clang* instead of *clung* for the past tense of *cling* by analogy with similar irregular verbs (e.g. *sing*, *sang*, *sung*). The forms of irregular verbs are not as fixed as some grammarians would have us believe.

While some of these changes may meet resistance, especially from older speakers, their progress is usually unstoppable; they begin with the young, and become more widespread as these become older (and pass them on to the next generation), while resistance literally dies out. The grammarian needs to be constantly on the look-out for such changes and to consider when to accept them into their accounts.

As a longer example we might consider a recent change in the use of the word *so*. *So* is a multifunctional word, used in many ways, among which the most prominent are:

- as a degree adverb (or 'intensifier', like *very* and *too*) modifying an adjective:

    I'm so happy you came.

- as a linking adverb, joining the idea in its sentence to the previous one:

    So what do we do now?

- as a subordinating conjunction to indicate purpose, answering the question *why*:

    They went into the next room so they could have some privacy. (...*so that*... is also possible)

- as a proform, to avoid repeating a long phrase:

    Is she coming? – I hope so. (= '...she is coming')

- as part of phrases: *so that, so ... that, so as to*, etc.

But then what to make of the following examples that I have heard recently?

I'm so out of here.
I'm so not going to that party.
I would be so for it (the actress Sandra Bullock on Sky TV, 18 December 2018).

At first sight it may seem that it is being employed in its degree adverb use, meaning something like: 'I'm out of here to an extreme degree'. But then are we to consider the phrases which follow it as adjectival? Surely not; we cannot (yet) say 'I'm very/too out of here'. If

48   *The Need for New Descriptions*

we identify the meaning, something like 'definitely', we can see that these examples belong not to degree adverbs, but to another type of adverb, sometimes called 'modal' adverbs (since, like modal auxiliaries, they refer to meanings such as certainty and possibility), which includes words such as *probably* and *certainly*. Surprisingly, the purists have yet to get their teeth into this one.[1]

3.3 Reason 2: Our Current Accounts Are Wrong

Here I am not thinking so much of the scientific/descriptive accounts of the previous section but rather of the pedagogic models and rules of thumb that are current in teaching but which can be easily shown to be misleading or false: the 'mythology' of English grammar. It may be argued that these are helpful simplifications, but my counter-argument would be that they simplify too much. Yet in spite of this they are held to be the absolute truth by many learners, including those who will go on to become teachers and perpetuate them. So the task in teaching is not merely to present new formulations, but also to initiate the 'unlearning' of these myths.

In a recent paper I investigated the prevalence of such misconceptions among several cohorts of first-year English majors at a Hong Kong university (Berry 2015). They were presented with a number of statements, or 'rules of thumb', which, although known to be incorrect in scientific descriptions, were thought to be prevalent in pedagogic circles (under slightly varying phrasings) – and not only in Hong Kong, as an earlier paper discovered (Berry 1994).

The respondents were offered four options: 'true', 'false', 'don't know' and 'partly true'. The last option was included in case they were aware of exceptions to the rule, as many were; the penultimate option catered for the possibility that they had not encountered any such rule because their learning experience did not include such a focus on form. Below, in order to have some confidence in the significance of these misconceptions I have extracted six statements where the number of students who chose 'true' had an absolute majority, i.e. exceeding the total of the other three options; three other statements that are of interest are also included. (Three prescriptive statements that did not meet the threshold have already been discussed in Section 2.6.3.)

1 'In negative and interrogative sentences ANY should be used instead of SOME.' (The responses were: *TRUE 119, FALSE 10, DON'T KNOW 49, PARTLY TRUE 17*)

This is a classic misconception about English grammar. In this explanation *any* – a difficult word for learners since it lacks a direct equivalent in many languages – is paired with *some*; they are treated as two variants of basically the same word; which one is to be used depends on the circumstances. There are, of course, many 'exceptions' to the 'rule'. *Any* can be found in positive sentences and *some* in both negatives and interrogatives:

> <u>Any</u> *fool can tell you this rule is wrong.*
> *We haven't stolen <u>some</u> of the money (we've stolen all of it).*
> *Did you find <u>some</u> money? Would you like <u>some</u> tea?*

A helpful, but incomplete, explanation for the last example is to say that the use of *some* in questions expects the answer 'yes'. (*Would you like <u>any</u> tea?* is hardly likely to be interpreted as a genuine offer.) A comprehensive explanation holds that the difference between the two words is one of meaning, i.e. creativity rather than convention, in that *some* presupposes or 'asserts' the existence of something while *any* does not (Biber et al. 1999: 176–177). (This concept of 'assertion' is systematic; it explains the difference between other pairs of words, for example *sometimes* and *ever*: *Have you sometimes/ever wanted to disappear?*)

2 'In reported/indirect speech, the past tense should be changed to the past perfect tense if the introductory verb is in the past tense.' (*TRUE 147, FALSE 21, DON'T KNOW 16, PARTLY TRUE 11*)

This rule of thumb forms part of a whole raft of tense-change rules, under the heading 'backshift', designed to help learners transform direct speech into reported speech (e.g. 'change present to past'). However, it is common knowledge that this 'rule' is rarely applied. In other words, a sentence such as

> '*I didn't recognise her*'

would normally retain the same tense when reported, i.e.:

> *He said he didn't recognise her*

rather than

> *He said he hadn't recognised her*

unless it is important to establish two different points in time, with the action in the reported clause occurring before that in the reporting clause. The whole edifice of backshift rules – indeed, whether we should be linking direct speech and reported speech at all – is challenged in the case study in Chapter 10.

3 'The first time you mention a countable noun you use the indefinite article (*a/an*); the second time the definite article.' (*TRUE 136, FALSE 16, DON'T KNOW 5, PARTLY TRUE 38*)

This rule is false for a number of reasons, the most important of which is that first mention with *the* is more common (because we already know what we are talking about). It attempts to make sense of two of the most difficult words in English for those learners whose first language does not possess articles. But it makes their use appear conventional when in fact it is highly creative. The case study in Chapter 7 explains the background of article usage in some detail, and offers alternatives for teaching these difficult words.

4 'The verb WANT does not occur in progressive/continuous tenses.' (*TRUE 134, FALSE 19, DON'T KNOW 38, PARTLY TRUE 4*)

This point has already been discussed in new descriptions above (*I've been wanting to meet you for ages*), from which it can be categorised as a serious overgeneralisation. However, out of all the myths discussed here, it is perhaps the most reasonable since its scope is very limited and may prevent some of the possible errors mentioned above. But in future, who knows?

5 'COULD is the past tense of CAN.' (*TRUE 119, FALSE 12, DON'T KNOW 1, PARTLY TRUE 73*)

As will be described below, the relationship between *can* and *could* (along with other so-called pairs of modals such as *may* and *might*) is very different from that between the present and past of non-modal verbs (e.g. *see* vs *saw*). *Could* is often said to be more tentative than *can*, for example:

I can do it vs I could do it.

and can refer to future time:

I could do it tomorrow, if there's time.

In addition there are restrictions on its use to refer to past time. While it can refer to general past abilities:

When I was young I could speak French fluently.

It cannot do so to specific ones:

*Last night I could eat a huge amount.

But the negative (*... I couldn't eat...*) is, somewhat mysteriously, acceptable.

6 'The continuous tenses are used for actions that last.' (*TRUE 115, FALSE 23, DON'T KNOW 14, PARTLY TRUE 43*)

3.3 Reason 2: Our Current Accounts Are Wrong

The reasons for using continuous (or 'progressive') forms rather than simple forms is one of the hardest areas in English grammar to explain. We have seen how the progressive is becoming more common and is intruding into the province of simple forms (*I'm loving it*). But as far as duration or continuation is concerned, this statement is an oversimplification. Non-continuous forms are also used for actions or states that last, for example:

> I've <u>lived</u> in Paris all my life.
> I've <u>been</u> living in Paris all my life.

If there is a difference, progressive/continuous forms seem to suggest an activity in progress which may or may not extend over time.

7 'English has three types of conditional sentences.' (*TRUE 70, FALSE 87, DON'T KNOW 35, PARTLY TRUE 3*)

This statement did not reach the threshold established above. Nevertheless, there is reason to believe that it ranks as a serious issue.

A long-established model in grammar teaching has been the variously named three types of conditional sentence:

> *If we go, we'll...* (first)
> *If we went, we would...* (second)
> *If we had gone, we would have...* (third)

English, of course, permits many more permutations of verb constructions than this three-way account would suggest, for instance combinations of the types or the involvement of modals (Willis 1994: 59):

> If you <u>had seen</u> what I saw, you <u>wouldn't be</u> so certain (a combination of the third and second conditional).

This result was seen as encouraging until one comment from a participant indicated that the statement was wrong, not because there are many types of conditional construction but because there are four, not three, conditionals (the fourth being what is sometimes called the 'zero' conditional: *If he <u>comes</u>, I <u>go</u>*). If this view was the reason behind other participants' rejection of the rule, then there is still a serious problem.

In the last century, Maule (1988) and Willis (1994: 59) both criticised the three-conditional approach; more recently Jones and Waller (2011) have done the same for the four-conditional approach. Such is progress. The activity at the end of this chapter based on concordance lines invites readers to draw their own conclusions.

Two other rules did not meet the criterion of being supported by an absolute majority of the students. Nevertheless, the findings have some value, since the number of participants that selected 'false' as an option was very low, for example:

8 'The future tense in English is formed by using WILL (and SHALL).'

TRUE 88   FALSE 5   DON'T KNOW 3   PARTLY TRUE 99

That a majority of participants showed some doubt about this statement by choosing 'partly true' was rather surprising, given my personal experience of their beliefs about tenses. However, rather than agreeing that 'the future tense' is no longer a tenable grammatical concept for English, the result merely indicated that participants were aware of alternative ways of referring to future time, in particular *going to*, as several comments made clear.

The issue here is the debatable status of the future tense in English. The identification of *will* (and in the past *shall*) as a future tense was derived, as with prescriptive rules mentioned above, from the desire to find equivalents of Latin forms. While there is little scientific support for doing so nowadays, it could be argued that a future tense is an acceptable pedagogic concept for English. However, we then have to explain away all the cases where *will* does not refer to future (*If you will stay out late at night...*), not to mention the extra meaning that it usually contains (e.g. promise, as in *I'll do it*), as well as those cases where futurity is expressed by other means. However, the strongest reason for not calling *will* the future tense is that we can simply refer to it eponymously (see Chapter 4) as 'will', and treat it like the other modal verbs.

9 'The present tense is used for present actions and the past tense for past actions.'

TRUE 75   FALSE 7   DON'T KNOW 3   PARTLY TRUE 110

This is of course a vast overgeneralisation. Admittedly, the past tense rarely refers to other times (some exceptions, where it can refer to future time, being *Would you mind if I came a bit later?* and *It's high time you started earning some money*), but claiming that the present tense only refers to present time is highly debatable because it very often refers to general statements and future events:

> It rains a lot here in April.
> Our train leaves at 10.

The problem is partly to do with terminology: the use of such a transparent term as 'present' (see Chapter 4) will inevitably encourage learners to associate it with present time. Some grammarians have even suggested calling it the 'non-past' (Quirk et al. 1985: 176–177). This is just one example of a wider problem that I call the 'time equals tense fallacy'; another aspect of it is the use of the term 'future' to apply (rather unreliably) to the meaning of *will*, as in the above misconception.

3.3.1 Reasons for Misconceptions

The reasons for the existence of such misconceptions are varied; they may result from prescriptive notions about English grammar (such as those discussed in Chapter 2) or from old misconceptions about terminology ('pro-noun' = in place of a noun, 'tense' = time); see the concept of metalinguistic relativity below. However, many seem to have come from laudable but misguided attempts to deal with difficult areas of English grammar, e.g. *some* vs *any*. In this enterprise words which are actually distinguished by their meaning (*some* asserts, *any* does not) are reduced to the status of formal counterparts; the explanation for one word (*any*, *the*) is based on another (*some*, *a* respectively). In other words, creativity is turned into convention.

But as I pointed out in Berry (2015), although they can be shown to be incorrect, they are extremely tenacious, as with any kind of myth. There are a number of reasons for this. They are always simply formulated, within the learners' comprehension; they are timely, in that they are provided at an appropriate moment when learners are struggling with a language problem; they are plausible, in that no counter-examples are (as yet) available; and they are authoritative in that they come from a trusted source – a teacher or book. I am reminded of the well-known proverb:

> 'A lie will travel half-way round the world before the truth has got its boots on.'

Rules of thumb are useful because they can provide a crutch for teachers who may be uncertain about language points themselves. And they provide learners with facts that they can memorise, just as they do with other school content-based subjects. (See Section 6.3 for more on rules of thumb.)

One last question begs an answer: Even though they are incorrect, do these rules actually cause any harm? The answer is 'yes' if learners make mistakes because of them; 'yes' if they subsequently find counter-examples which undermine confidence in their teacher; 'yes' if they are inhibited from producing forms which, although correct, are proscribed by the rule; and 'yes' if they later become teachers and pass them on to their learners as the absolute truth (even though their own competence may have progressed beyond them). However, there is an argument that such rules can be useful in focusing learners' attention on areas to be learnt (e.g. Schmidt 1990; cf. Section 1.4). One obvious response is that incorrect rules can hardly be appropriate if better, more accurate, rules are available (see Swan 1994); the case studies later in this book aim to show this.

In a recent paper I presented the results of an action research into forty-four learners' use of and reactions to incorrect rules of thumb (Berry 2014), using two of the above misconceptions (about articles and *some* vs *any*). (The full results of this study can be found in Appendix 1.) There were several interesting findings:

- as expected, the rules were well known (as with the above results), that for articles more so than that for *some/any*;
- a majority had tried to apply the rules in their production (31 and 20 respectively);
- a minority (nine out of thirty-one) had had a 'bad experience' as a result, i.e. their work had been corrected;
- nevertheless, ten said that they thought such rules could be helpful, even though they knew they were wrong; some suggested that such rules were better than nothing.

So, while some learners had suffered from these misconceptions, others thought they could be useful. But if it is acceptable to present incorrect grammatical formulations then the logical consequence would be that any statement, no matter how wrong, is fine so long as it concerns the particular forms and focuses attention on them. This area clearly needs more research.

3.4 Reason 3: New Grammatical Phenomena Are 'Discovered'

Here I am thinking, not of changes in the language that are brought to light, but of grammatical phenomena that have been around for some time without being recognised. Even though the largest descriptive grammars nowadays approach 2,000 pages in length, they cannot claim to have discovered everything that is current about English grammar – despite the use of the word 'comprehensive' in the title of Quirk et al.'s (1985) monumental work. There are other facts out there waiting to be revealed and even amateur grammarians should be encouraged to be on the lookout for such phenomena. However, they may need to free themselves from the constraints of the dominant orthodoxy on grammar in order to do so. (See the concept of metalinguistic relativity outlined in Section 3.7.1.)

3.4 Reason 3: New Grammatical Phenomena

I can personally claim to have made a modest contribution in the identification of what I called the 'pre-emptive' use of the definite article (e.g. Berry 1991); the example I used in that article was

> Mr Martin bought <u>the</u> pack of Camels on Monday night.

This is the first line of a short story, 'The Catbird Seat' by James Thurber, published in 1942, so clearly it not a 'neogrammaticism'. By using *the* in this way – when *a (pack of Camels)* would have been perfectly normal – the writer seeks to predict, rather than reflect, a state of affairs. The case study on articles in Chapter 7 (Section 7.2.2) contains more information on this use.

For a more extensive example we might take a look at the so-called semi-modal verb forms. These are forms such as *have to, had better, want to, be going to, ought to, would rather, used to*, and so on (see Berry 2018: 108–109), which parallel some of the meanings expressed by modals (e.g. obligation, possibility, permission, etc.) as well as serving, like them, in an auxiliary role with the infinitives of full verbs (*We'd <u>better</u> go*). And in some cases they fill gaps where modals are deficient (e.g. *had to* as the 'past' of *must*). However, structurally, unlike the 'proper' modals, they are an amorphous mass; some include *to* before the infinitive, although in written renderings of informal speech they are conflated into one word (e.g. *wanna*); some have their own auxiliary (*<u>had</u> better, <u>would</u> rather*), and so on.

In a thought experiment we might consider how linguists arriving from Mars today might regard these structures. They should have no trouble getting past the barrier of the accepted formal spellings shown above (as per the concept of metalinguistic relativity, see Section 3.7.1) in order to realise that they seem to be coalescing into a pattern, especially if their colloquial spoken form is used as evidence:

> *hafta, betta, wanna, gonna, gotta, oughta.*

They would treat all of these as single words. They might also note the phonological similarity whereby all consist of two syllables and end in schwa (with the intervocal 't's pronounced as /d/ as per colloquial American pronunciation). All of the above spellings have been attested and noted by grammarians in spoken English. But what about *dratha*? Or *yoosta*? I have not seen these spellings or read any discussion of these forms; and yet they are perfectly combinable with any subject pronoun: *I yoosta, they yoosta, we dratha, you dratha*, etc. (Whether these should be taught to learners is another matter, as opposed to the accepted written abbreviations: *I used to, we'd rather*, etc.)

We must be careful here not to go too far. These new forms may superficially appear to be similar. However, they do behave differently in a number of ways. The negative of *betta* and *dratha* is formed by adding *not* afterwards, while that for *wanna* and *hafta* is formed by preposing *don't* and *didn't*. And then some third-person forms are different from the rest: *she hasta* (not *hafta*) and *wansta* ('wants to') rather than *wanna*. And so on. But already we can see some convergence of the grammar in the shape of forms already attested in non-standard speech, for example *we gonna* (as opposed to *we're gonna*) and *we don't gotta*.

This revised analysis may seem fanciful, but it is not totally dissimilar to how it was realised in the past that the so-called modal verbs, words such as *can, could, may, must* and so on, should no longer be regarded as full verbs, since they only had an auxiliary function, preceding other verbs. They were called 'defective' verbs in Palmer's classic analysis (1974) since they lacked the distinctive forms of other verbs, such as third-person *-s* (**cans*, etc.), infinitive (**to can*), *-ing* participle (**canning*, etc.). Today some grammarians put them in a separate word class: 'auxiliary', alongside the similar use of *be, have* and *do*, because they behave very differently from verbs and seem to fulfil a similar function in the verb phrase as determiners in the noun phrase, that is, to modify their meaning in a fundamental way.

In addition, it was also recognised that each modal form should be considered separately, rather than being grouped in present/past pairs (e.g. *can/could* – see the myth investigated above), since the relationship between the two is unlike that between present and past of ordinary verbs: *I come here* vs *I came here*; in particular the so-called past forms could be used to refer to present or even future time (*I would come if I could get a lift*).

The Martian linguists might link the decline in the use of some such modals (as described in Section 3.2) to the increase in the use of this new system.

Setting aside this speculation, even if we reject the conclusions of the Martians, we should agree that modality in English seems to be in constant flux and therefore is in need of constant attention.

3.5 Reason 4: The Scope of Grammar – and Therefore the Phenomena Which Need Describing – Is Extended

First of all I want to consider two fairly recent trends in linguistic endeavour that have taken the study of English beyond its traditional boundaries: firstly, under the heading of World Englishes, the recognition that it is no longer the exclusive property of the original L1 nations, since it has developed roots in several parts of the world where it was originally only a colonial, foreign language; and secondly, under the heading of English as a Lingua Franca (ELF), the

3.5 Reason 4: The Scope of Grammar

realisation that more communication in English takes place between L2 speakers than it does between L1 speakers. In both cases norms independent of Standard English are developing/have developed, more so in the former than in the latter.

Three examples involving a re-evaluation of grammar caused by these trends may be cited (Mauranen 2010: 122–129 cites others in ELF):

1 Verbs which in standard English are ditransitive with direct and prepositional objects occur with indirect and direct objects. (See Chapter 2 for an explanation of different types of verb and object.)

   I explained them the problem. (...the problem to them)
   ...and suggested them a solution. (...a solution to them).
   They provided us an alternative (...us with an alternative).

   All three would be marked as incorrect if standard English is the model, but increasingly academics and teachers are recognising such forms as valid, at least in the appropriate circumstances.

2 The count status of nouns is another area which may need re-examining if we widen our perspective, especially if we are thinking of English as a Lingua Franca. Iconic uncountable nouns, such as *advice, information, research, furniture, homework, bread, milk* and *weather* are usually considered incorrect in the EFL classroom if used in the plural or in the singular preceded by *a*, for example:

   *We are missing several information<u>s</u>.
   *That's <u>a</u> bad luck.

   (Incidentally, Microsoft Word has redlined 'informations'; a similar or even worse fate will befall other words elsewhere in this book that it considers incorrect. However, it is not subtle enough to detect and stigmatise the second example above.)

   Standard English allows for such items to be counted via the use of so-called counting expressions, for example *a piece/several pieces (of information/luck)*. But some ELF speakers see no need for them; why not simply pluralise these words as with the equivalent nouns in their first languages? Mauranen (2010: 216) cites several examples for *advices, researches* and *knowledges*. Indeed, in some languages the count/non-count distinction has no place; added together, speakers from such languages may render unstable the whole system of countability in English generally. And Crystal (2017: 207) points out that some of these nouns have not always been straightjacketed countability-wise in earlier stages of English, giving citations for *researches, musics, furnitures* and *advices*. In some varieties of World English such usages may be normal. One other innovation that I am familiar with is the use in Hong Kong English of 'staff' as a countable noun, even in formal English (*a staff should...*). Other cases where formerly uncountable nouns have become countable in Standard English were mentioned earlier in this chapter (e.g. *Englishes* and *discourses*).

3 Another area where changes to English grammar have been widely influenced by worldwide varieties is that of tag questions (or question tags) as in:

The competitors knew the answer beforehand, <u>didn't they</u>?

Generations of grammatically inclined EFL teachers and textbook-writers have found employment from the complexities involved in this construction: the use of a proform in the tag question (*did* in the above case), the reversal of polarity (positive to negative in the above case), the use of a personal pronoun, etc. (not to mention the variation in intonation related to different expectations: falling, seeking confirmation; rising, seeking an answer).

However, recently attention has been drawn to simpler alternatives that have arisen in worldwide varieties (and also in non-standard British English), forms that might be termed 'universal tags', since they replace the complicated grammar described above with a single form; two such possibilities are *innit*, and *isn't it*.

They liked that, innit/isn'it?

These may jar on the ear of some speakers of English, but before we decry the use of universal tags we should bear in mind that similar tags have long been available in Standard English to turn a statement belatedly into a question, namely the informal *right*:

They hated that, <u>right</u>?

And the more formal *isn't that so?* (beloved of TV courtroom dramas):

They hated that, <u>isn't that so</u>?

It seems that everyone has some form of universal tag to help avoid the complexity of the traditional form. One wonders whether there is any currency in teaching it.

The question, then, changes from what is or is not correct/acceptable in Standard English to whether the model of English for instruction should be Standard English at all (however it is established), as opposed to an indigenous variety (exocentric vs endocentric models). An ELF grammar 'standard' is far from having been established, but this does not apply to World Englishes. Several such varieties have received very full descriptions, West African English, Singaporean English and Indian English being among the foremost, and are therefore available as models. (Discussion of them can be found in the journals *English Today* and *World Englishes*). The issue is whether the authorities are prepared to adopt them as models in the education system and beyond (e.g. in government documents). Though standard British and American English are still the target in most of the world's EFL situations – and are the model for this book unless otherwise stated – teachers need to be aware that other norms are possible.

The above fields extend the notion of grammar geographically and societally. A different approach is taken by attempts to extend the boundaries of grammar linguistically into areas that traditionally might have been thought to belong to lexis, thus emphasising the link between the two levels. Pattern Grammar (mentioned briefly in Section 2.8) in particular offers insights into the grammatical and semantic behaviour of groups of words – verbs (*Collins Cobuild Grammar* 1996), and nouns and adjectives (*Collins Cobuild Grammar* 1998) – according to the 'patterns' they occur in. (See Hunston and Francis 2000 for the theory behind this.) To take one example, they identify fifteen verbs that can occur in the pattern VERB + 'in favour of' + PREPOSITIONAL OBJECT (*Collins Cobuild Grammar* 1996: 201–203), e.g.

The majority have <u>argued in favour of</u> waiting.

These are then divided into sub-groups according to meaning. *Argue* belongs to the 'speak' group; *work* is an example of the 'discriminate' group, and *resign* of the 'stand down' group.

3.6 Reason 5: There Are Alternative Ways of Looking at Old Problems

In other words, there may be different ways of looking at the same area of grammar; the basic facts are not in dispute, nor have they changed. Such reappraisals may be motivated by pedagogical needs. As an illustration I will consider one particular area: the forms of irregular verbs in English.

Usually there are assumed to be about 250 irregular verbs (Quirk et al. 1985: 104). They are deemed to be irregular because the forms of the past tense and *-ed* participle (see Section 4.6 to understand why I prefer this last term to 'past participle') cannot be predicted from the base (infinitive), unlike the present tense and *-ing* participle. Since they are at the extreme end of the convention/creativity cline, in grammar books for learners they are usually consigned to a reference section merely as an alphabetical list (e.g. Collins Cobuild English Grammar 2011: 473–475). While there are options (usually between an irregular or regular form, e.g. *smelt/smelled* for the past tense of *smell*) this has nothing to do with meaning (apart from one curious case where the regular and irregular forms of *burn* appear to diverge in meaning and transitivity; which of the two possibilities is preferable in *The fire burned/ burnt for two hours* and *I burned/burnt my hand on the saucepan*?).

In scientific grammars, meanwhile, irregular verbs are grouped according to the sound changes involved; for example, one group would include verbs such as *sing/sang/sung*, *swim/swam/swum* etc., which have the 'i', 'a', 'u' pattern. This is an approach taken by Quirk et al. (1985: 105–114) in an attempt to be both comprehensive and put some order into the irregularity. They account for these irregularities in seven major classes, but such a classification runs into trouble because there are too many irregularities within the irregularities, too many exceptions.

Thus I felt, invoking the distinction between pedagogic and scientific grammar (Chapter 2), that it would be more appropriate for students on my grammar course (Berry 2018) to choose a middle way, by simplifying the grouping; other simplifications may of course be possible. I felt that a useful mnemonic for students would be to classify each verb according to the variations between the three parts. So while the major ordering was alphabetic (for reference, after all), a subsidiary classification comprised a straightforward five-way distinction (Quirk at al. [1985: 103] mention the same classification but do not apply it) as follows:

A Where all three forms are the same, e.g. *bet/bet/bet*; *cost/cost/ cost*, etc. (This is common with one-syllable verbs ending in *t*.)
B Where the base and the past tense are the same: *beat, beat, beaten.* (This is the only case of this type.)
C Where the base and *-ed* participle are the same, e.g. *come/ came/come*; *run/ran/run*. (This is also very rare.)
D Where the past tense and *-ed* participle are the same, e.g. *bend/bent/bent; cling/clung/clung*, etc.
E Where all three forms are different, e.g. *arise/arose/arisen*; *sing/sang/sung*, etc.

Types D and E are easily the most common, and in this way their importance will be brought to the attention of teachers and learners.[2]

This account is not more correct than any other, just different, and, according to my perspective, more appropriate for the intended audience.

3.7 Two Major Problems

The discussion above shows how we may be moving forward in our understanding of, and accounting for, modern English, so that we may obtain a satisfactory description that may be used for pedagogical purposes. But there are two factors impeding this process; they may be termed 'metalinguistic relativity' and 'poor transmission'.

3.7.1 Metalinguistic Relativity[3]

This is the belief that in attempting to understand the facts of English grammar we are constrained by history, by the concepts that we have inherited from previous generations. Several writers have supported this idea, though not under this heading – most stridently Harris (1998), who believes that the Latin–Greek tradition that has come down to us has severely constrained our ability to appreciate the more semantic core of English. The myths outlined above are excellent examples of metalinguistic relativity on a pedagogic level. Not only are they wrong, but, as pointed out, they are also extremely tenacious, having become embedded in our pedagogical culture as the absolute truth.

Another example, though more of a historical nature, would be the debate about how many and which word classes should be established for English. The Latin-based 'parts-of-speech' approach discussed in Section 2.8.1 (which originally included interjections) long held up a proper understanding of English grammar. For example, the introduction of 'determiner' as a valid class is of fairly recent origin; it has still to filter fully into the pedagogic arena (and still has some opponents on a scientific level).

English spelling, and writing in general, is a major factor in preventing a change of attitude to grammatical features that might be treated differently. Thus *no one* is as much a single entity as its related forms *nobody* and *anyone* but the awkwardness of writing it as 'noone' has held up its recognition as one word (though the similarly awkward *someone* has somehow escaped rejection). Likewise, *at all* should be written 'atall' since it functions semantically and phonetically as one unit (the aspiration of the /t/ sound showing it belongs to the following stressed syllable).

This chapter deals with metalinguistic relativity as it affects grammatical *concepts*; Chapter 4 takes this issue further with reference to *terminology*. It gives examples of terms that are inaccurate or unhelpful but which we are possibly stuck with; two examples of this, already mentioned in relation to the misconceptions above, are 'future tense' and 'past participle'. The future is not entirely bleak, however. Just as replacement terms can be introduced (e.g. 'progressive' for 'continuous') so can better concepts. This is fact is one of the aims of this chapter.

3.7.2 Poor Transmission

The problem here is basically that advances in knowledge on the scientific level do not reach practitioners. Facts which have long been in the public domain are not incorporated into pedagogic accounts. Partly this is because researchers, in whatever theoretical mode, but particularly those following the Chomskyan tradition, have passed into intellectual 'hyperspace' (as de Beaugrande 1999 calls it), from where they do not send messages back to 'Earth'.

So in the absence of assistance from research, where do pedagogic accounts originate? In Section 2.7 a model of pedagogic grammar was proposed whereby the results of various endeavours (SLA studies, descriptive accounts) should be fed into a pedagogic filter which would lead to various pedagogic outputs: syllabuses, rules, exercises, etc. What seems to be happening, however, is that the pedagogic filter and its inputs are totally missing and the only input to pedagogic accounts is... other pedagogic accounts; circularity on a grand scale. (See Section 6.3 for circularity on a minor scale.) Pedagogic accounts should be based in something more solid, and not merely recycle previous pedagogic accounts.

There is also the reverse problem: that researchers do not seem to want to answer the questions that practitioners have. An excellent example where this is *not* the case can be found in the case study in Chapter 8, concerning the comparison of adjectives, which answers the eminently pedagogical questions regarding whether adjectives form their comparative phrasally (*more common*) or inflectionally (*commoner*), and why one form is preferred to the other. But how many practitioners have read the article on which it is based (Hilpert 2008)?

The case studies in Chapters 7–10 give other examples of facts about English grammar that have been known for some time but which have not reached, or are only slowly reaching, the classroom. For example, the knowledge that the use of the past tense to replace a present tense in reported speech depends on distancing not only in time dates back to at least Lewis (1986: 69–73); another instance of poor transmission.

In the late twentieth century corpus research was seen as a saviour, as a means of bridging the gap between scientific researchers and practitioners. While there has been substantial progress, and many teachers have undertaken mini-studies of a particular area of interest using corpora, there is still a great distance between the two camps; the vast majority of descriptive, scientific papers are still not motivated by pedagogic needs, by calls from practitioners to illuminate a difficult area. And practitioners are partly to blame for this situation, because they are comfortable in their circumscribed world of simplified and inaccurate rules of thumb. The continued existence of myths about English grammar – which have long been known to be so – is evidence of this failure to communicate.

3.8 Conclusion

It is hoped that this chapter has made the case for a constant, ongoing examination and revision of the grammar that is presented to learners of English – in whatever form that presentation may be. The 'facts' need to be constantly questioned – because of language change or incorrect formulations – and extended – because of new discoveries and new fields of endeavour.

Activity: Conditional Sentences

Look at these twenty concordance lines selected at random from the British National Corpus, all containing the word *if*. Try to make some sense of them by analysing the verb forms in the main clause and the *if* clause. How many of them correspond to the three (or four) types of construction described above in Myth 9? Watch out for distractors, for example where *if* has the same meaning as *whether*. For convenience, *if* has been bolded and the relevant verb forms underlined. Note that the *if* clause may occur first or later.

1. Another rule of thumb is that **if** the act is obliged to rest their microphone stand and amplifiers on beer crates instead of the stage, it will be a good evening.
2. **If** anyone is interested in receiving more information on praying for missionaries or missionary activity please contact me.
3. **If** anyone else feels they would like to have a test to put their mind at rest they should contact us.
4. **If** you are unable to take part in your Games lesson (due to injury or illness) then you should bring a note, asking to be excused.
5. **If** there are any trees growing on the property they have the same protection as trees the subject of a Tree Preservation Order.
6. **If** the development is large or controversial, it may be worth forming an action group to give local opposition a focus.
7. **If** you asked him where a particular coin was he would be able to tell you exactly where it was.

64   *The Need for New Descriptions*

8 Now **if** this contaminated fish <u>is eaten</u> in large enough quantities it <u>can cause</u> symptoms of Minimata disease.
9 They say that **if** they <u>create</u> Regional Government they <u>will do</u> so at the expense of National Government and not Local Government.
10 I'<u>d go</u> again today **if** it <u>didn't mean</u> waiting in line till a month from Monday.
11 **If** you <u>don't know</u> <u>don't make</u> it up.
12 It's not my fault **if** you <u>don't pass</u> your exams.
13 **If** <u>it grows</u> back <u>I'll be</u> a very happy man.
14 I <u>don't believe</u> for one minute that the cattle would be any better **if** you <u>had</u> a lot of Limousines or something else.
15 Finally, then, **if** I <u>can</u> just <u>have</u> your attention for a moment.
16 To see **if** there <u>are</u> any tickets available, you <u>click</u> on the arena.
17 **If** there <u>is</u> easy access to the loft this <u>can be</u> a relatively simple job.
18 **If** this <u>is</u> the way things go, there <u>would be</u> a certain art-historical justice in it.
19 **If** there <u>is</u> not enough space on the form to describe the change, <u>attach</u> a continuation sheet.
20 Everyone'<u>s</u> entitled to throw their money away **if** they <u>like</u>.

Comment

Firstly, it should be repeated that these lines are in no way representative of the usage of *if* in contemporary English. Secondly, we should remind ourselves that there are other ways of expressing conditions: phrasal conjunctions such as *provided that, so long as, even if*; or structures involving an imperative (e.g. *Do that and you'll be in trouble*), or inversion (e.g. *Had I known...*). And thirdly, there are other ways in which *if* is used (not only as an alternative to *whether* in indirect questions); it can be used to indicate the idea of concession (like *although*) rather than condition:

She was ecstatic, if a little exhausted.

Nevertheless, the lines do offer some interesting insights into the use of *if*. Firstly, we can dispense with lines 15 and 16 since the latter is a distractor introducing an indirect question (similar to *whether*), while the former only has an *if* clause (a fairly common occurrence whereby the consequence is left unstated).

Beyond this, only six lines actually contain one of the original three conditional types: the first (numbers 1, 9 and 13) and the second (numbers 7, 10 and 14). The zero or fourth conditional (present + present) also has three examples (5, 12 and 20), but the third conditional is completely absent, reflecting its rarity. Two other structures that feature are IF + PRESENT, IMPERATIVE as in numbers 2 (*If anyone is interested ... contact me.*), 11 and 19; and especially IF + PRESENT, MODAL, with five occurrences, the modals being *should* (numbers 3 and 4), *can* (8 and 17) and *may* (6). The total for this category would rise to eight if we include the first conditional examples in it (after all, *will* is usually treated as a modal verb). This leaves the rather 'exotic' line 18, which is a mixture of first and second conditionals.

These twenty lines are only a snapshot of the way *if* is used, but if this pattern were to be repeated on a larger scale, we might reach one of two pedagogic conclusions. Firstly, we might conclude that because there are so many different conditional structures – indeed, there are many more patterns than shown above (Jones and Waller 2011) – the three or four types model has no validity at all. In fact, this is the way the situation is treated in scientific descriptions: *if* is just another subordinating conjunction, and the unexpected tense forms that are associated with it (unexpected by speakers of other tensed languages, that is) – for example, the use of the present tense in the *if*-clause to refer to future time (*If we don't hurry we will miss the train*) – are not unique to it, but also apply to other conjunctions of time, such as *when* and *before*.

Alternatively, if we accept that some sort of model is accepted as a basis for further development and that frequency should be a criterion, then we would not end up with the three or four conditional models above but with a different scheme. We would dispense with the so-called third conditional and amalgamate the first conditional into modals, leaving the following structures to be focused on:

> IF + PRESENT, PRESENT (the fourth or zero conditional): *It's not my fault if you don't pass your exams.*
> IF + PRESENT, MODAL (*will, should, can*, etc.): *If it grows back, I'll be a very happy man.*
> IF + PAST, WOULD (the second conditional): *I'd go again today if it didn't mean…*
> IF + PRESENT, IMPERATIVE: *If anyone is interested […], contact me.*

And all this is before we start to consider meanings. Indeed, two sets of terms for the three conditionals are meaning-based (see the third and fourth columns in the table below). But where then do we place the functions associated with other structures, for example, warnings and threats (*If he comes, I go*)? Or the request implied by the single clause in line 15 above:

> *If I can just have your attention…*

To drive home the problem with conditionals we can present the proliferation of terms used to describe them:

First:	type 1	real	likely
Second:	type 2	hypothetical	unlikely
Third:	type 3	unreal	impossible

The decision on which set to use is largely a matter of form (the first two columns) vs meaning (the last two).

Notes

1 See Berry (2018: 93–97) for more on different types of adverbs, in particular the way several belong to two types, with parallel changes in meaning. To take *however* as an example:

> *However much you praise her, she still lacks confidence.* (degree adverb)
> *He swore that it was true; however, no one believed him.* (linking adverb)

The problem with 'hopefully' (Chapter 2) can be understood in this way:

> *The children looked at the toys in the window hopefully.* (adverb of manner)
> *Hopefully, there won't be a problem with our claim.* (comment adverb; this use is the bane of prescriptivists)

2 Grammarians have several further difficulties in trying to encapsulate all the different possibilities. Firstly, there are derived forms, such as *overdraw, overdrew, overdrawn*; or *misunderstand, misunderstood, misunderstood*; or *underwrite, underwrote, underwritten*. Do these need to be included? Secondly, there are different levels of irregularity; some verbs only differ slightly in their forms, while others differ greatly, e.g. *bear/bore/borne*. Thirdly, there are many irregular verbs which can also be regular, e.g. *learnt/learned, quit/quitted* or *bust/busted*. Fourthly, some verbs seem to have two possible irregular forms, for example *bid/bid/bid* and *bid/bade/bidden*, which reflects both A and E types from above.

3 The term is drawn from the parallel concept of 'linguistic relativity', whereby it is theorised that the language we speak constrains our worldview. The theory has always been rather controversial, especially since some of its wilder claims, for example that the Inuit have more words for snow and are therefore better equipped to talk about it, have been challenged.

References

Berry, Roger. 1991. Re-articulating the articles. *ELT Journal* 45/3: 252–259.
Berry, Roger. 1994. 'Blackpool would be a nice place unless there were so many tourists': some misconceptions about English grammar. *Studia Anglica Posnaniensia* XXVIII: 101–112.
Berry, Roger. 2014. Learners' use of and reactions to incorrect rules of thumb. Paper given at 12th Biennial Conference of the Association for Language Awareness, Hamar, Norway, July.

References

Berry, Roger. 2015. Grammar myths. *Language Awareness* 24/1: 15–37.
Berry, Roger. 2018. *English Grammar: A Resource Book for Students*. Abingdon: Routledge.
Biber, Douglas, Stig Johansson, Geoffrey Leech, Susan Conrad and Edward Finegan. 1999. *The Longman Grammar of Spoken and Written English*. Harlow: Longman.
Carter, Ronald and Michael McCarthy. 2006. *Cambridge Grammar of English*. Cambridge: Cambridge University Press.
Collins Cobuild Grammar Patterns 1: Verbs. 1996. London: HarperCollins.
Collins Cobuild Grammar Patterns 2: Nouns and Adjectives. 1998. London: HarperCollins.
Collins Cobuild English Grammar. 2011. 3rd edn. 2017. 4th edn. Glasgow: HarperCollins.
Crystal, David. 2017. *Making Sense: The Glamourous Story of English Grammar*. London: Profile Books.
de Beaugrande, Robert. 1999. Description and analysis of language in applications to language teaching: resetting our priorities. In Roger Berry, Barry Asker, Ken Hyland and Martha Lam (eds) *Language Analysis, Description and Pedagogy*. Hong Kong: Hong Kong University of Science and Technology, 6–28.
Harris, R. 1998. *Introduction to Integrational Linguistics*. Oxford: Elsevier Science.
Hilpert, Martin. 2008. The English comparative – language structure and language use. *English Language and Linguistics* 12/3: 395–417.
Hunston, Susan and Gill Francis. 2000. *Pattern Grammar*. Amsterdam: Benjamins.
Jones, Christian and Daniel Waller. 2011. If only it were true: the problem with the four conditionals. *ELT Journal* 65/1: 24–32.
Leech, Geoffrey, Marianne Hunt, Christian Mair and Nicholas Smith. 2009. *Change in Contemporary English*. Cambridge: Cambridge University Press.
Lewis, Michael. 1986. *The English Verb*. Hove: Language Teaching Publications.
Maule, D. 1988. Sorry, but if he comes, I go: teaching conditionals. *ELT Journal* 42: 117–123.
Mauranen, Anna. 2010. *Exploring ELF: Academic English Shaped by Non-native Speakers*. Cambridge: Cambridge University Press.
Palmer, F. R. 1974. *The English Verb*. London: Longman.
Quirk, Randolph, Sidney Greenbaum, Geoffrey Leech and Jan Svartvik. 1985. *A Comprehensive Grammar of the English Language*. Harlow: Longman.
Schmidt, Richard. 1990. The role of consciousness in second language learning. *Applied Linguistics* 11/2: 129–158.
Swan, Michael. 1994. Design criteria for pedagogic language rules. In Martin Bygate, Alan Tonkyn and Eddie Williams (eds) *Grammar and the Language Teacher*. Hemel Hempstead: Prentice Hall International, 45–55.
Willis, Dave. 1994. A lexical approach. In Martin Bygate, Alan Tonkyn and Eddie Williams (eds) *Grammar and the Language Teacher*. Hemel Hempstead: Prentice Hall International, 56–66.

4 Working with Terminology

4.1 Introduction

We now switch to an issue that is inextricably entwined with grammar, and which is equally controversial, if not more so: the use of terminology in language teaching. It is of course possible to teach grammar without terminology; some methods are built around the teaching of grammar without the need to talk about it, e.g. the Direct Method, or the Audiolingual Method (see Chapter 1). Equally, it is possible, though difficult, to talk about grammar without terminology. But when terminology is used, it is grammatical terminology that comes most under scrutiny. The pros and cons of using terminology are discussed below along with other important factors.

4.2 Attitudes to Terminology

Many people are suspicious of terminology, not just learners and teachers of EFL. Legal jargon has long been a target of suspicion, as this text from an insider shows:

> 'Conference' is the industry term for a meeting. By referring to it as a conference (or 'con' for short), we succeed in our twin aims of linguistically alienating outsiders and making what we do sound more impressive than it actually is. (*The Secret Barrister*, Picador, 2018, p. 88)

Here the (anonymous) author shows how terminology can be used to distance the public and promote the expert – a cause of mistrust that is shared by many on both sides of the EFL classroom. This chapter will attempt to understand some of the negative attitudes about terminology and perhaps arrive at a measured evaluation of its role in EFL.

Since this is a book about grammar, I am basically thinking about grammatical terms here, but it is interesting to note that other areas of classroom terminology, e.g. to do with methodology or pronunciation, do not arouse such passions; nobody questions the use of terms such as 'pair-work', or 'consonant' and 'vowel' (in fact, they are hardly regarded as terms).

4.3 Understanding Terminology

Before looking at the role of grammatical terminology in teaching we should perhaps try to understand some basics about it; this will have significance later on.

All technical subjects have their terminology, some more than others, and acquiring it is necessary as a rite of passage into the technical community. Doctors, academics and other professionals need hundreds of terms before they can practise. Language learning/teaching is somewhat different in that the learners in general are not attempting to enter any profession, and of course it is quite possible to acquire a language without any terminology. And even if they do, in the course of formal language education, they are perfectly at liberty afterwards to forget whatever terms they have learned.

The first issue to confront is the relationship between terms and concepts (Pearson 1998: 10; Berry 2010: 21–22). We can regard concepts as primary and terms as arising out of them. However, it is not easy to conceive of concepts, and more importantly to converse about them, without terms. But the more abstract a concept is (as opposed to, say, a physical object) the more uncertainty there may be over what to call it and what the term actually refers to; many linguistic concepts are by nature abstract. Thus there is the possibility of terms whose reference is not clear or even terms which refer to empty concepts.

There are number of important distinctions that we can tease out from the nature of terminology. The first is the difference between terminology itself and metalanguage. Many writers appear to use the words interchangeably, as in this quote from Ellis (1994: 714):

> Metalingual knowledge is knowledge of the technical terminology needed to describe language.

However, I feel a useful distinction is being missed here, namely, between all of language that is used typically to describe language, i.e. metalanguage, and the technical terms that are used in such descriptions, i.e. terminology (Berry 2005). Setting aside the logician's desire for a unique 'metalanguage' (which would be quite distinct from human language), we can recognise that metalanguage, i.e. 'language about language' (Johnson and Johnson 1998), insofar as it applies to the description of grammar, consists of three levels (see Fortune 2005 for a slightly more nuanced classification):

- The everyday language that is indistinguishable from the words used to construct any text.
- The sub-technical language of content words that, though not specifically terminological, is frequent in linguistic description because it refers to concepts that are innately linguistic, for example, words such as 'action', 'state', 'process' that are needed for the description of verb forms and their meanings. This level is discussed in more detail in Section 5.5.
- Terminology, where words have a special, technical, meaning. In other words, terminology is (part of) the lexis of metalanguage. Some words such as 'word' itself and 'sentence' may belong to this level as well as to the previous one.

Another, perhaps the most important, distinction concerning terminology is that between pedagogic and scientific terminology. The distinction mirrors that in grammar, described in Section 2.6.3, between that which is suitable for learners and that which is the product of scientific endeavour, with no limitation on its complexity. This distinction is sometimes attributed to Chomsky (1966: 10), who justifiably wanted to make clear what kind of linguistics he was doing (though he used the terms 'pedagogic' and 'linguistic'). But the distinction goes back further; Corder (1973: 330) observed that, amongst others, Henry Sweet was aware of it at the turn of the twentieth century. This quote from Howatt (2004: 80), referring to grammar in general but relevant to terminology, demonstrates how grammar was essentially practical and pedagogic until the advent of linguistic theory:

> Broadly speaking, the grammars, dictionaries, and other manuals of the seventeenth and eighteenth centuries took the form they did, and exhibited the priorities they did, because they were addressed to an audience that had a practical need of them. The modern notion of an objective, scientific description of language as a self-justifying activity in its own right did not take root until the development of philological studies in the nineteenth century.

So what is the difference between pedagogic and scientific terminology? Two important attributes of scientific terminology are precision and distinctiveness (Berry 2010: 36–42). By 'distinctiveness' I mean that the term should be recognisable as a metalinguistic item and not as an ordinary lexical item. Some terms are entirely exclusive to language description and so are in themselves distinctive: for example, the names of the major word classes such as **noun**, **verb**, **adjective** and **adverb**. Other terms are not so easily distinguished, but in writing distinction can be achieved by the use of certain conventions: italics, bolding or inverted commas.

4.3 Understanding Terminology

Distinctiveness is not exclusive to scientific terms; thus **past** as a term referring as a tense can be distinguished from 'past' as a word referring to time by the above conventions. However, in speech, the distinction would not be clear and so it is sometimes advisable to resort to entirely different forms. This explains why we are confronted by pairs of 'synonyms' such as **countable** (pedagogic) and **count** (distinctive and scientific). **Countable** is not distinctive in speech since it is also a perfectly acceptable word in common usage; for example, you can say that 'money' is countable ('one, two three pounds') but to be distinctive you would need to say that it is **non-count** (i.e. you cannot say 'one money').

The other attribute, precision, though desirable (and achieved in other technical fields), is sadly lacking in scientific metalinguistic terminology. It refers to whether the term has one and only one referent (Pearson 1998: 11). Unfortunately, there are many exceptions to this; **number** would be a good example since it refers not only to two classes of words (**ordinal** and **cardinal numbers**) but is also the hypernym of **singular** and **plural** (in addition to being frequently used in language description ('There are a number of verbs which take...') and as a term in mathematics ('prime numbers'). Usually precision goes hand in hand with distinctiveness; thus **numeral**, the scientific alternative to **number** (when it refers to ordinal and cardinal) has both qualities. But there are cases where terms, such as **verb** or **predicate**, are distinctive but not precise, having (in some circles) more than one meaning. **Verb**, for instance, as well as being a word class, can also be an element in clause structure (see Section 2.8.1).

Aside from these rather theoretical considerations, the distinction between scientific and pedagogic is important in practical terms. One of the main problems with terminology in language learning – as we shall see below – is its overuse, and the main culprit in overuse is scientific terminology, namely, the use of terms that are far beyond the learners' comprehension, let alone their need.

Wright (1991: 68–69) gives an explanation for this:

> One great danger of acquiring specialist knowledge about language is the possible desire to show learners that you have this knowledge.

Since training appears to be at fault here, it should be training that provides the solution: by showing how and why terms which are suitable for the training of teachers may not be appropriate for classroom use.

A word of caution about the distinction between pedagogic and scientific terminology is in order here. It should not be thought that the borderline between the two is always hard and fast; rather it should be seen as a cline. Some terms are more or less pedagogic/scientific; some may sit in the middle. Also, the same term may have a different status in different situations (for example **predicate**, which, as my research discovered, is very much a pedagogic term in Austria – see Section 4.6). Thus pedagogic terminology will be as varied as the number of situations in which it occurs, just as the grammar that is taught needs to be tailored to suit its audience.

The final distinction that I would like to make concerns three (or four) types of term according to the nature of the relationship between the term and its referent: whether it is meaning- or form-based (Berry 2010: 45–61). These are:

- **transparent** terms, 'where the terms attempt to give some indication of the meaning of the concept', for example, **past** and **present** when applied to **tense**;
- **opaque** terms, which give no such indication, such as the term **tense** itself;
- **iconic** terms, which use some formal aspect of the item itself, such as *-ed* (preceding **adjective** or **participle**).

An extension of the last category may be termed **eponymous**, in that it is not just a part of the grammatical item that is used; rather it is the whole item itself which becomes the term. Thus if we want to refer to 'used to' as a grammatical item, we do not call it the 'habitual past semi-modal'; we refer to it simply as **used to**. Similar cases are **would rather** and **(be) going to**. The most persuasive argument against calling 'will' the 'future tense' (cf. the discussion about misconceptions in Section 3.3) is that there is a perfectly uncontroversial eponymous way of referring to it, namely as **will** (especially since now 'shall' has been detached from it); why say 'do not use the future tense here' when you can say 'do not use "will" here'? In fact, the vast majority of terminological items are eponymous; it is just that we do not notice them as such. This in essence is the concept of reflexivity (Sinclair 1991; Lyons 1995: 7): our ability to use language to refer to itself (and so avoid using a totally distinct metalanguage). In no other field of intellectual endeavour is this possible.

In some cases, eponymous terms are in competition with rivals. The best examples of this are the articles 'a' and 'the'. Do we refer to them as the (somewhat scientific, albeit not totally distinctive) **indefinite** and **definite articles**? Or simply eponymously as 'a' and 'the'? Apart from pronunciation problems (how do you pronounce 'a' and 'the' in isolation?), the eponymous choice would seem to be more pedagogic (and learner-friendly). However, there is an inbuilt problem with eponymous terms in that they cannot refer to their own form; whereas you can say 'the future tense is formed using *will*', it is tautologous to say '**will** is formed using *will*'. In the case of 'a' as a term this is complicated by the fact that there are two possible forms: 'a' and 'an'; **indefinite article** then serves as a cover term. (In fact, this applies to the 'the' as well, but only in pronunciation.)

Many terms are mixed types in terms of the above classification. Take for example **third-person -s**: the first two elements are opaque (who knows what 'third-person' refers to?) while the final element is iconic. Another example, this time of an eponymous-opaque combination, would be *to* **infinitive**.

Each type of term has its advantages and drawbacks. Transparent terms are easy to come by and learn, but may be misleading. Opaque terms, on the other hand, are never misleading but are harder to come by and learn. Iconic terms are limited and not capable of self-reference formally, as pointed out above. A fuller discussion of the pros and cons will be found in Section 4.4 and the Activities.

We can use this classification to analyse trends in the use and popularity of terminology. Thus the most common terms, referring to the word classes, are opaque (and distinctive, as per above): **noun**, **adjective**, **verb**, etc. However, following this the tendency is for transparent terms, in referring to verb or noun forms or categories: **past** and **present**, **countable** and **uncountable**. A further application of this classification is useful in examining the development of terms; iconic terms seem to be gaining in popularity among grammarians, a case in point being combinations with *-ing* and *-ed* (for example, ***-ing* nouns** in preference to the opaque **gerund**).

4.4 The Pros and Cons of Terminology

Why is terminology so controversial for some? A number of educational arguments against it can be cited but these basically boil down to three (Berry 2010; see also Borg 1999).

The first is what Carter (1995), playing devil's advocate, calls 'excess baggage': the extra load it imposes on learners. The use of terminology by teachers implies the learning of terminology by learners. This takes time and, unlike ordinary vocabulary learning, results in learners knowing words that are unlikely to be of use outside the classroom. Indeed, when the learning process is done, these words will be of no value for most.

However, we should ask how extensive this load really is. I previously suggested that, even for advanced learners, between fifty and a hundred terms would be sufficient (Berry 2010: 123). Over a learning life of perhaps ten years, this implies an average of between five and ten terms per annum, which does not seem excessive. In comparison with the number of vocabulary items that learners acquire during the same period it is miniscule, especially if we concentrate on the user-friendly iconic and transparent terms, as described above. The learnability of terms is discussed later in the chapter (Section 4.7) along with other criteria for choosing terms.

Another major argument against terminology – and grammar teaching in general – is that it can distract from the goals of language teaching; indeed, it can even become the target of language teaching, a charge levelled readily at the grammar-translation method (Mohammed 1995). Learning a foreign language is not easy. Terminology and other forms of explicit knowledge about language (such as rules of thumb) offer learners a simple alternative which mirrors the learning of other school subjects (which also uncontroversially have their own terminology). No current theory of language learning would support this position, but my research found that some teachers still believed in an 'integrative' motivation for terminology, that it is an indispensable part of learning a language (Berry 2001).

The third argument is that terminology and other forms of explicit knowledge about language do not improve proficiency (Mohammed 1995). The evidence here is somewhat inconclusive; there are studies supporting both this viewpoint and the opposite. Alderson et al. (1997) found no link between the metalinguistic knowledge of university students of French and their proficiency in that language. However, metalinguistic knowledge is a much broader concept than terminology; in fact it can be accessed without terminology, as this quotation from Macaro and Masterman (2006: 299) indicates:

> A difficulty also resides in measuring knowledge about language, in that learners cannot be said to lack explicit knowledge simply because they do not possess the required metalinguistic competence to articulate it.

In addition, the heavy emphasis on learning about language that would have been predominant in the secondary school classes of Alderson et al.'s (1997) subjects (cf. the integrative motivation cited above) makes the results unsurprising and at the same time inapplicable to other learning situations.

On the other hand, in two studies (Berry 1997 and 2009), I found a significant correlation between Hong Kong learners' knowledge of terminology and their proficiency in English as measured by the school-leaving exam at the time (the Use of English). This is not to claim a causal relationship between the two factors, of course; there is no suggestion that teaching more terminology would increase proficiency. It is quite possible that a superordinate factor is at work, such as a higher level of terminology among students who studied in English-medium (as opposed to Chinese-medium) schools, where the teaching methods are more traditional and the learners more proficient in the first place. We must also consider the wider picture, already discussed in Chapter 1, in which the consensus is for the importance of a focus on form. In any case, this argument is perhaps moot if we accept that the use of terminology serves other functions, such as saving classroom time (for use in other activities).

Against this we can set perhaps four arguments in favour of terminology. The main argument is that it allows teachers to make generalisations. A learner who writes 'I wish I know' and is told to change 'know' to 'knew' learns nothing and is not prevented from making the same mistake with another verb; but if the teacher tells the student, 'after *wish* we use the past tense' then they can apply this to other situations. In this sense terminology is a form of shorthand, avoiding the use of extensive circumlocution (Carter 1990). It is of course possible to talk about grammar without using terminology but it would be a laborious process ('after *wish* we use words that end in -ed but not the ones that have *have* or *be* in front of them').

Another argument in favour of terminology is that some learners expect it. In his study of teachers' beliefs and attitudes, Borg (1999: 109) quotes one of his subjects:

> Some students like and feel comfortable with grammatical labels. This needs to be respected.

This is similar to Krashen's so-called affective filter (1985: 3–4), which, in his Natural Approach, allowed some limited focus on form in order to keep students who liked grammar teaching happy. Whether it is grammar or terminology in question, learner expectations are important as a motivational factor, and teachers, regardless of their principles, need to respond to them.

A third argument is that teachers do not exist in isolation; no matter how much they believe that using terminology is wrong their learners will come across terminology in various pedagogic materials elsewhere and they need to prepare them for it. It may occur in a limited form in their textbooks or in self-access materials. And of course if learners consult reference grammars they will encounter it frequently. Indeed, a knowledge of terminology is a prerequisite for access to reference materials.

A final, more controversial argument (mentioned in Borg 1999, but attributed to Faerch 1985) is that talking about language may facilitate acquisition; terminology is almost indispensable in such an endeavour.

4.5 What Goes Wrong with Terminology?

Beyond the principled pros and cons outlined above there are several problems in the application of terminology which are not the fault of terminology per se but of faulty linguistic or pedagogic practices associated with it. The discussion below is adapted and extended from a list from Berry (2010: 241–242).

The problems can appear on various levels. Firstly, as noted above, there can be an issue with the concept referred to. Thus **future tense** as a term is problematic for English because the concept is an empty one, as most grammarians agree.

Then there is a whole range of problems with the nature of the terms themselves. Prominent among these is their form; many terms, especially scientific terms with their Latinate origins are lengthy and easy to confuse (Berry 2010: 148). Cases of confusion that I have come across in my research (using the Metalinguistic Terminology Survey, see Section 4.6) include **verb phrase** and **phrasal verb**, **progressive** and **possessive**, **past tense** and **past participle**. Pairs of complementary terms also cause confusion: the reference of **definite** and **indefinite article**, **comparative** and **superlative adjective** can easily get reversed. Some terms are simply mixed up with similar non-terminological items, e.g. **perfect** with 'prefect'.

The semantics of terms also poses problems since many are polysemous and synonymous, as this complaint from the authors of a dictionary of EFL terminology shows:

> Different grammarians are entitled to analyse language in different ways, and fresh viewpoints may call for new terms. But while grammarians sometimes explain what they mean by a new or unusual term, it is rarer for them to point out that they are using an existing term in a new way. This is a cause of real confusion. Another problem is that new terms may in the end turn out to be alternatives for an old concept – a synonym in fact (e.g. *progressive*, *continuous*). (Chalker and Weiner 1994: vii)

Another common case of synonymy is **reported speech** and **indirect speech** (discussed in the case study in Chapter 10). Other examples would be **past participle** and **-*ed* participle**, or **genitive, possessive** and **apostrophe -*s*** (for the form of nouns in *dog's*), not to mention the various competing nomenclatures for types of conditional sentences as mentioned in the Comments section of Chapter 3. In some cases, the two terms may be the same apart from word order: **present simple** and **simple present**, **tag question** and **question tag**. See the discussion points at the end of the chapter.

There are also pairs where one member is pedagogic in nature and the other scientific, for example:

past tense vs **preterite**
countable vs **count** (nouns)

4.5 What Goes Wrong with Terminology? 77

In the scientific arena there is a proliferation of competing terms, usually related to different theories or approaches, for example:

middle vs **ergative** (verbs)
light vs **delexical** (verbs)
noun phrase vs **noun group**
headers and tails vs **left and right dislocation**
main vs **independent** (clause)

The list goes on. (See Bralich 2006: 63; and Berry 2010: 92 for more.)

These terms are not directly relevant to learners, of course, but they still pose a problem for pedagogic grammarians and are a major factor interfering in the process of pedagogic grammar (see Section 2.7), rendering scientific insights less accessible to pedagogy. At the very least, as Bralich suggests, linguists should cross-refer to alternatives, or even better (but improbably) decide on a single term. (He does not raise the embarrassing possibility that they are ignorant of each other's work.)

A major issue with synonymy occurs when transparent terms (see above) are juxtaposed with their non-terminological use. In most cases this will not happen; the two uses will not occur together. But sometimes in grammars it is unavoidable, as shown by these examples from Murphy (1994), identified in the METALANG corpus (see Chapter 5, Note 1, for a description):

To talk about the present use the **present simple**... (p. 36).

Of course, this is the whole point of transparent terms. But sometimes ambiguity may arise:

For the past we use 'must have'... (p. 56).

Does 'past' here refer to past time or the **past tense** (of *must*)? The issue is that of distinctiveness, or rather lack of it, as described above. In such cases, typographical conventions (italics, inverted commas) can be used to achieve distinctiveness in writing – in grammars and textbooks (although this is not always well done), but in speech, as was pointed out earlier, no such distinction is possible in the classroom.

As for polysemy a much-overused word is **complement**, though it is more relevant in scientific terminology. A pedagogic example would be **phrasal verb**; in one approach it indicates both of the structures in the sentences below; in another only the second (whereas the first would be called a **prepositional verb**):

I looked after my sick sister (cf. *I looked my sister after).
I looked up the answer (cf. I looked the answer up).

The above issues concern the nature of terminology, but there are equally issues with its use. In materials such as textbooks and grammars terms are sometimes used without principle (see later in this section), and non-terminological uses are mixed in with terminological ones (as described earlier in this section).

In the classroom there may be a number of problems with terminology, largely but not exclusively associated with teachers. Some may use terminology for the wrong reasons, such as to impress learners, or to shore up their authority in the classroom. Many practitioners do not understand the distinction between pedagogic and scientific terminology. The overuse of scientific terminology can even affect teachers, as in this quote from Andrews (2006: 8), discussing a teacher's attitude to terminology:

> Teachers around me seemed to have a big vocabulary for grammar, especially my panel head. He couldn't read or write, but he was very good at throwing those grammatical terms every time we had a meeting. I had to read some grammar text books before I knew what they were actually talking about.

In an introductory course for students of English Grammar I used to relate the fictional account of a teacher who is confronted by a learner with an example of a sentence which contradicts a rule that she has presented to the class: 'We demand that he be sacked.' 'Why is it not "is sacked"?' asks the learner. The teacher starts to sweat, aware that the leaner has a point which she cannot answer and which will cause a loss of face. But then from the depths of her training a term comes to her rescue. She draws herself up to her full height and announces dismissively 'That is a subjunctive!' All the class is amazed and satisfied (though some may still be slightly confused).

One can certainly question the pedagogic validity of this exchange, such as: was the term absolutely necessary? And could the teacher not have explained why an unusual form was used? However, one cannot be totally unsympathetic with the fictional teacher's action. By using the term, albeit without explanation, she maintained the respect of her class. One would hope that she would go away and study this use, the better to explain it to her learners the next time.

Notwithstanding such inventions, the overall impression that I have received from my research is that too much terminology is used in teaching, and that terms may be used by teachers without consideration for what their learners know, or without an awareness of the differing levels of terminological knowledge of their learners. The research findings in Section 4.6 report more on this.

A final classroom issue applies to transparent terms. Although they are generally user-friendly, learners may assume that they are god's truth, that for example the **past tense** always refers to past time. This is the issue of accuracy, which is discussed in more detail in Section 4.7.

The obvious solution to the overuse of terminology, or to the use of inappropriate terms, lies in better training for teachers (and for materials writers). Unfortunately, many courses are too short to cover English grammar satisfactorily, let alone inculcate appropriate attitudes to the use of its associated terminology.

4.6 Researching Terminology

While the above factors seek either to encourage or discourage the use of terminology, both sides in the debate have something in common: they seek to prescribe one or other pedagogic approach to terminology. I have argued for a more dispassionate attitude, for what might be termed a descriptive approach, which involves studying the use and knowledge of learners and teachers as a prerequisite for the formation of attitudes towards terminology (Berry 2010: 135). In various papers this approach has yielded interesting and useful results (Berry 1997, 2001, 2008, 2009), which, since most are based on Hong Kong teachers and learners, must not be overgeneralised. Some of the questions raised were

1 *Why do teachers use terminology?* In a survey of seventy secondary and tertiary EFL teachers in Hong Kong I found that many were aware that their (over-)use of terminology was inconsistent with the largely communicative syllabus in favour at the time (Berry 2001). The evidence suggested that personal factors played an important role, such as their own learning experience. I concluded that 'teachers whose own teachers had used a lot of terminology tended to be frequent users themselves'.

2 *Are teachers aware of what terminology learners know?* In a study of 372 first-year Hong Kong business students on a course in (English) Business Communication, using the Metalinguistic Terminology Survey (MTS), a selection of fifty grammatical terms (including a few of a rather scientific nature), I found that there was a large gap between what the learners actually knew and what their teachers thought they knew (Berry 1997). This in itself might not be a problem but it becomes one when teachers act on their belief and use terms that learners do not know. The mean level of knowledge among learners was 22 out of 50, i.e. 44 per cent. (Participants were required to tick the terms they knew and exemplify them; if the example was incorrect the term was counted as unknown.) Their ten teachers' overall estimate of

their knowledge was fairly similar, averaging 49 per cent, but this hides some drastic discrepancies regarding individual items. In many cases teachers wildly overestimated learners' knowledge and when this was allied to a desire to use the term, the result could have been confusion. For instance, half of the teachers thought their students would know the terms **indefinite article** and **relative pronoun** (and in each case seven out of ten wanted to use them), but in fact only 16.9 and 6.5 per cent of the students respectively did know the terms. In other cases teachers underestimated learners' knowledge, a case in point being **comparative adjective**, which was known by just half of the students but estimated to be known by only one teacher.

Overestimation among teachers might be particularly acute at the point of transition from secondary to tertiary education, when learners are expected to bring analytic abilities to bear on their studies. (Cummins' distinction between BICS and CALP is relevant here; for more on this see Cummins 2000). Thus the finding of a teacher/learner gap might be exceptional, and the results cannot be generalised to other situations or jurisdictions. Nevertheless, it does reinforce the notion that learners' knowledge of terminology needs to be checked and, if found to be wanting, should be addressed.

3 *Which terms do learners generally know?* In two studies the Metalinguistic Terminology Survey (MTS) identified two areas of grammar where learners were happiest: the major parts of speech and verb tenses (Berry 1997, 2009). In the earlier study the exponents of these two areas were known by 80.2 and 76.3 per cent. In the later study (involving 296 students from Hong Kong, Austria and Poland) the most well-known terms were **noun, verb, plural, future tense** and **adjective**, all with a figure above 90 per cent.

The MTS also contained pairs of synonyms. The earlier study confirmed what would have been expected, that **present continuous tense** (94.6 per cent) was much better known than **present progressive tense** (7.8 per cent). The later study confirmed this in all three jurisdictions, though not to the same extent.

4 *Are there differences between learners in different situations?* In the later study I compared the terminological knowledge of learners in three countries using the MTS: Austria, Poland and Hong Kong (Berry 2009). The subjects were university English majors at the start of their first year, i.e. before they had begun any formal study of grammar. Overall the means (out of 50)

were quite similar: for Hong Kong 22.55 (n = 123), Poland 23.87 (n = 98) and Austria 21.33 (n = 75). The higher score for Poland might be explained by the higher metalinguistic awareness of the students, while the lower one for Austria was possibly attributable to the more communicative syllabus in force at the time. Likewise, the results for individual terms contained many similarities: **noun, verb, future tense, adjective** and **plural** appeared in all three top-ten lists. There were, however, notable differences in knowledge of individual terms. Two egregious examples were **indefinite article**, known to only 29 per cent of the Hong Kong students (presumably because they were familiar with the iconic *a*) but to 95 per cent of the Polish students; and imperative, known to 71 per cent of the Austrian students but to only 5 per cent of the Hongkongers (presumably because the transparent but inaccurate term 'order' is used instead). Clearly, different pedagogic cultures are operating here.

5 *Are there differences within groups?* The answer to this is a definite 'yes'. In the three groups mentioned above there were vast differences between the highest and lowest scores: for Hong Kong the range of correct answers (out of 50) was 9–35, for Poland 7–40, and for Austria 5–36. The standard deviations were equally large: respectively 5.32, 7.27 and 7.23. That for Hong Kong was noticeably smaller, perhaps because of the more cohesive nature of its society and education system, but all three ranges and standard deviations indicate wide discrepancies and suggest that some students will be entering university to study English with hardly any of the terminology that their teachers might assume to be known, while others will have extensive knowledge. This emphasises the need for checking terminological knowledge mentioned above in point 2).

6 *How is terminology treated in textbooks and grammars? Is their use of terminology consistent and principled?* The answer to the latter question is 'not very'. A study of a series of textbooks – six, used across three years for secondary schools in Hong Kong (Berry 2010) – revealed extensive use and several forms of inconsistency. Overall seventy-two different terms were used, though often in different patterns. For example, both **pronoun** and **present participle** occurred twelve times, but the former was spread over five of the books, while the latter was present in only one. Only three terms – **verb, adjective, noun** – appeared in all six books. Well over half of

the terms used (forty-five out of seventy-two) appeared in only one book. Most worryingly, twelve terms appeared only once overall; these included the pedagogic **subject** and **object** as well as the scientific **subject clause** and **object clause**. One may ask, if a term only appears once, whether its use is necessary. Of course, the pattern of usage in this rather grammatically determined syllabus is not necessarily typical of all textbooks. The use of terminology may be far less in books which do not have a formal grammatical syllabus. Nevertheless, it illustrates the danger that terminology is used on an ad hoc basis rather than a planned one.

As regards grammar books, one would expect the extensive use of terminology and therefore a far more principled approach. This was generally the case with the grammars in the METALANG corpus, but there were occasional inconsistencies. For instance, the term **imperative** appeared only once in Murphy (1994). One interesting phenomenon found sometimes in the corpus is the presence of 'meta-metalanguage', i.e. comments about terminology, usually to explain terms that only occur once or which have synonyms:

> 'These nouns are called different things in different grammars: **gerunds, verbal nouns,** or **'-ing' forms**. In this grammar we call them **'-ing' nouns**' (Collins Cobuild English Grammar 2011: 24).

By way of conclusion from this research, one may suggest that greater awareness on the part of teachers and materials writers is important – awareness of the fact that they may be using terms inconsistently, or terms that learners do not know. In either case, terms need to be chosen on a principled basis, perhaps using the criteria in the next section.

4.7 Evaluating Terminology

In a 2008 article I proposed a number of criteria for evaluating terms similar to those applied to general vocabulary in general (Berry 2008).

1 Learnability. This involves a number of factors amongst which length and potential for confusion will be important. If the word is already known to learners as a regular word then its form will not a problem. But such transparent terms may be problematic to distinguish semantically from the counterpart meaning, for example 'past' vs **past**, which leads to the next point.

2 Accuracy. Many transparent terms, for all their learnability, have a problem with this, as pointed out above. '**Continuous**' forms (already discussed in Sections 3.2 and 3.3) do not necessarily refer to something 'continuing'. Amongst others, they can refer to something repeated: *They've been calling me all week.* And the so-called **past participle** has nothing past about it; when it appears in verb phrases referring to the past, the 'pastness' is supplied by other forms. Of course, the question is: does it matter? Are learners really misled by such terms? Common sense would say 'yes'; I have often encountered cases where learners are reluctant to use forms in situations where the meaning contradicts the term, for example, the use of the **present continuous** to refer to the future (*We're leaving tomorrow.*) But much more research needs to be carried out into this area.

3 Theoretical validity. This refers to whether terms are consistent with the theory of language and education espoused. This often explains why there are two competing terms for a similar concept. For instance, whether a lesson is built around **conditionals** or *if* **sentences** should depend on the approach: formal for the latter, semantic for the former.

4 Productivity. Productivity revolves around whether a term can appear as part of several phrasal terms, thereby making the overall learning load lighter. For example, once we start using the iconic element *-ing* we can apply it not just to **participle** (*They are coming*), but also to **noun** (*His crying worried me*), **adjective** (*It was exciting*) and even, on a scientific level, to **clause** (*Knowing what I do now...*).

5 Systematicity. This refers to the fact that terms cannot be chosen in isolation; they usually form part of a system, and the selection of one term raises the issue of whether to introduce related terms. For instance, when introducing the term **passive** it is difficult if not impossible to avoid introducing its partner **active**. (In linguistic terms these are co-hyponyms and their relationship is called hyponymy; their superordinate term – the hypernym **mood** – is far less necessary and likely to figure only in scientific accounts.) A similar example would be **plural, singular** and **number**.

6 Utility. Rather obviously, this asks whether the term is likely to be used frequently in the classroom. In turn, this depends partly on how the focus on form is structured. Certain terms

may be introduced for one lesson but then ignored, while other terms, such as **verb** and **plural**, may crop up throughout the course of learning and therefore are high in utility, as the survey of textbooks indicated.

7 Familiarity. Not all of the above criteria will be applicable to every term, but there is one overriding factor that may work against any conclusion, namely: are the learners already familiar with the term? This is not quite as straightforward as it may seem, for, as the discussion above showed, even basic terms are not always understood by the entirety of a cohort, even if they have a similar educational background. (This supports the claim made in Section 4.6 that teachers need to do more to understand their learners' level of terminological knowledge.) A lack of familiarity may work against other factors, such as accuracy; thus **continuous** may still be retained over the more accurate (or less inaccurate) **progressive**. If a term is not already known then strong arguments from the other criteria, in particular utility, need to be found for introducing it.

4.8 Changing Terms

The question here, given all the problems discussed above, is: are we stuck with these grammatical terms? Standard English grammatical terminology is well established and very conservative. In a survey of William Cobbett's *A Grammar of the English Language* published in 1819 I found that the great majority of terms used would be easily recognised in the classrooms of today (Berry 2010: 68–69). (One example that would not is 'noun of multitude' for **collective noun**.) But then one can ask: why should it not be so?

There are certainly some who would say it should not, as in this quote from Lock and Tsui (2000: 24–25):

> Teachers, coursebooks and learners inevitably tend to talk about those aspects of grammar that they have some shared metalanguage to talk about. This means that areas that ESL grammars have traditionally dealt with in detail tend to get a lot of attention while other areas of the grammar barely get a mention. For example, TEG [traditional English Grammar] provides an extensive battery of terms for labelling the tenses of English ... there is hardly any metalanguage in TEG for talking about the textual systems of theme/rheme and given/new, which means that these systems are not taught in any systematic way.

4.8 Changing Terms

Walsh (2003: 134) describes a similar problem when talking about a training course for teachers that stressed interaction:

> One of the concerns at the beginning of the study was the absence of a metalanguage both to describe interactional processes and comment on changes in them. If teacher-participants are to become more conscious, more 'mindful' ... of the interactional architecture of their classroom, they must have a metalanguage to facilitate reflection, evaluate interactive actions and prompt reaction.

These complaints point to a wider concern that I have called in Section 3.7.1 'metalinguistic relativity' (Berry 2010: 64). This refers to the notion that the terms we use are not only limiting our appreciation of grammar, they are actually distorting it. Much in the same way that the notion of *linguistic relativity* (or the 'Sapir/Whorf hypothesis') supposes that our worldview is influenced by the particular language we speak, the idea of metalinguistic relativity suggests that our descriptions of grammar (and language) may be constrained by the framework of terms and concepts that we have inherited – largely from the Latin tradition. Harris (1998) claimed that if we were to start with a completely clean slate, uninfluenced by the Greek and Roman grammarians, we would end up with a very different description of English grammar, one that focused above all on meaning.

As with linguistic relativity it is impossible to prove whether or not we are so constrained; we must confront what we have inherited, i.e. what I call Standard English Grammatical Terminology (SEGT). Attempts to make radical changes, such as the limited system for verb forms suggested by Lewis (1986: 160), have met with little success. (Amongst other changes, he suggested 'durative' as an alternative to **progressive/ continuous** and 'retrospective' instead of **perfect**. Both suggestions are eminently sensible (especially in terms of accuracy) but have not caught on.

However, there are signs that SEGT is not a totally fixed monolith. Firstly, there are the differences between language-learning communities around the world, as noted above. Then there are the new or improved terms that occasionally appear, not to mention the terms that are needed to describe new phenomena, as discussed in Section 3.4; but they all have a hard time gaining acceptance and finding a place in teaching. One small victory may be that in time **progressive** comes to supplant **continuous**. A change that is currently taking place is the acceptance of **determiner** as a pedagogic term (to describe words such as *this* and *that*) so that *my* and *your* etc. may be correctly labelled **possessive determiners** and not **possessive adjectives**.

86 Working with Terminology

4.9 Using Terminology Effectively in the Classroom

The classroom exchange below, reported in Tsui (1995: 33), shows how terminology can be effective if used appropriately. In it a teacher is discussing errors in a student writing assignment; he cites a student's sentence which involved the incorrect use of verb forms after modals:

T: <u>You can write programmes, play a game, doing calculations, drawing a picture, etc.</u> I like the idea very much, you've got some concrete examples, but it's not quite balanced so far as grammar goes. OK, what is the modal in that sentence?
Ss: Can.
T: <u>Can</u>. OK, and we see here the modal (points at the previous sentence on the board), now, what's the infinitive after should in this sentence?
Ss: Learn.
T: <u>Learn</u>, this is the infinitive. <u>Should learn</u>. If you've got one modal in a sentence, all the verbs which follow it must be infinitives...

(underlined text represents text being cited)

This exchange seems to meet many of the requirements for the effective and appropriate use of terminology in the classroom:

1 The use of terminology is consistent with aims of the lesson, namely, to discuss learners' composition errors.
2 The terminology is an integral part of the grammatical explanation; it would be extremely difficult if not impossible to achieve this without its use.
3 The terms – **modal, infinitive, verb** – are simple, pedagogic terms that the class is clearly familiar with.

Other requirements for effective use that we cannot witness in this brief exchange would include

4 that there are opportunities for the limited use of these terms in other lessons;
5 that they are part of an inventory of terms that have been selected, perhaps according the criteria mentioned above;
6 that the learners are sufficiently sophisticated to be able to handle terminology.

4.10 Conclusion: Towards the Appropriate Use of Terminology

The main causes for the unpopularity of terminology in some quarters may be its (unnecessary) association with the discredited grammar-translation method and its overuse by some teachers (regardless of method). However, the current trend seems to be to support its moderate use, as the following quotes show:

> A limited amount of metalinguistic terminology can help to facilitate learning, provided that it does not become a substitute for it. (Berry 2001: 103)

> Very often a limited knowledge of linguistic terminology can make explanations easier. (Woods 1995: 89)

> Introducing unnecessary jargon into the classroom is intimidating and unhelpful, but the careful introduction and regular use of a few well-chosen terms can be helpful and save a lot of time over the length of a course for both teacher and learner. (Lewis 2000: 129)

All three quotes include the idea of limited use of terminology and refer to its role in helping/facilitating learning. Lewis also stresses the desirability of terms being well-chosen (which of course is rarely the case) and their regular use. All of these points have been major themes in this chapter, leading to the conclusion that terminology can be helpful if it is done well.

Finally, to finish this chapter, here is a quote from Bloor and Bloor (2004: 17) which may be seen as a riposte to the scepticism in the quote from *The Secret Barrister* in Section 4.2:

> Some people argue that it is not necessary to use technical terms for language because we can use language efficiently enough without describing it in this way. It is true that people may have an excellent command of their mother tongue and know little about the analysis and labelling of the language that they speak; it is even possible to learn a foreign language without conscious recourse to such considerations. The fact remains that if you wish to talk about language you must have a vocabulary for doing so. After all, it is not inconceivable (though it does not often happen) that people might manage to repair car engines, play musical instruments or even perform an appendectomy without acquiring related technical terminology, but, in order to systematically discuss these matters, they would have to acquire or invent the appropriate language for such discussion. No one questions this obvious truth in mathematics, medicine, music or motor-vehicle maintenance; it is only in the field of language ... that this happens.

Activity

Reflect on and discuss the following questions and tasks:

1 What has your experience of grammatical terminology been, both as a learner and as a teacher? How much terminology do you yourself use in class?

88 Working with Terminology

2 Are there any terms that you personally do not like, and why?
3 If you had to limit your use of terminology to ten terms, what would they be? Compare your choice with a colleague's.
4 Analyse these three terms using the distinction between pedagogic and scientific. (NB Different answers are possible.)

   subjunctive, clause, conjunction

5 Analyse these three terms using the three-way distinction between transparent, opaque and iconic terms discussed in Section 4.3.

   preposition, comparative adjective, -*ing* participle

6 Consider the pairs and groups of terms that were identified as synonymous in Section 4.5. Which one in each case do you prefer (if either/any)? Evaluate them in terms of the seven criteria above (not all will be applicable to each case).

   reported speech and **indirect speech**
   past participle and **-*ed* participle**
   genitive, possessive and **apostrophe -*s***
   different systems for **conditional sentences**
   present simple and **simple present**
   tag question and **question tag**

Comments

4 **Subjunctive** is clearly a scientific term (as well as a concept), while **conjunction** is pedagogic for most (though some would prefer the more transparent **linking word**). **Clause** is debatable; while rather technical, it is useful at a higher pedagogical level.
5 **Preposition.** This is largely opaque but may give some clue to advanced learners (though it is not the only word class that can be 'pre-posed').
   Comparative adjective. This is a combination of transparent and opaque.
   -*ing* participle. This a combination of iconic and opaque.
   Try to analyse some more compound terms, such as those in Point 6 above.
6 **Reported speech** and **indirect speech.** In terms of familiarity, both are widely known and used, so it may be necessary to familiarise learners with both. In terms of systematicity, I would argue that using 'indirect' creates a false connection with **direct speech** and that thus **reported speech** is preferable.

   Past participle and **-*ed* participle.**

Here we have a transparent plus opaque term versus an iconic plus opaque one. The former is clearly the more familiar in pedagogy, but this should be outweighed by its lack of accuracy. The use of the transparent 'past' is plainly wrong; when it used in passive forms it has nothing to do with past time or the past tense; the time is denoted by other elements (*He will be arrested.*). As a term, **-ed participle** is also slightly inaccurate formally in that some such forms are not formed by the addition of '*-ed*' (or '*-d*'), and of course the past tense also uses this suffix. In transformational/generative parlance it is referred to as '*-en*', which is far less encompassing. (Interestingly, Cobbett in 1819 called it the 'passive participle', which is closer in terms of accuracy but not totally so as it excludes its use in perfect forms.)

Genitive, possessive and apostrophe -s.

In terms of familiarity, **possessive** is clearly the winner. However, in terms of accuracy it falls down, since 'possession' is fairly low down on the list of meanings indicated by this form (e.g. *Murray's victory*; a fuller explanation is given in Section 9.9.3). But the other two terms are highly opaque, and **apostrophe** has learnability issues from its length and unusual pronunciation. Personally, I prefer genitive, but only at an advanced (i.e. scientific) level.

Present simple and simple present.

There is little to choose between the two; both seem to be current, but in terms of systematicity, the former is to be preferred as it patterns with **present perfect** and **present continuous**; it would be strange to say 'perfect present' or 'continuous present'.

Tag question and question tag.

Likewise in terms of systematicity, the former is to be preferred as it patterns with *wh-* **question** and *yes/no* **question**. But the issue is moot if we remove this point from the canon of English grammatical structures (as suggested later on in Section 6.2).

References

Alderson, J. C., C. Clapham and D. Steel. 1997. Metalinguistic knowledge, language aptitude and language proficiency. *Language Teaching Research* 1: 93–121.

Andrews, Stephen. 2006. The evolution of teachers' language awareness. *Language Awareness* 15/1: 1–19.

Berry, Roger. 1997. Teachers' awareness of learners' knowledge: the case of metalinguistic terminology. *Language Awareness* 6/2–3: 136–146.

Berry, Roger. 2001. Hong Kong English teachers' attitudes towards the use of metalinguistic terminology. *Asia Pacific Journal of Language in Education*, 4/1: 101–121.
Berry, Roger. 2005. Making the most of metalanguage. *Language Awareness* 14/1: 3–20.
Berry, Roger. 2008. Talking terms: choosing and using terminology for EFL classrooms. *English Language Teaching* 1/1: 19–24.
Berry, Roger. 2009. EFL majors' knowledge of metalinguistic terminology: a comparative study. *Language Awareness* 18/2: 113–128.
Berry, Roger. 2010. *Terminology in English Language Teaching*. Bern: Peter Lang Verlag.
Bloor, Thomas and Muriel Bloor. 2004. *The Functional Analysis of English*. 2nd edn. London: Arnold.
Borg, Simon. 1999. The use of grammatical terminology in second language classrooms: a qualitative study of teachers' practices and cognitions. *Applied Linguistics* 20: 136–146.
Bralich, Philip A. 2006. The new SAT and fundamental misunderstandings about grammar teaching. *English Today* 22/3: 61–64.
Carter, Ronald. 1990. The new grammar teaching. In Ronald Carter (ed.) *Knowledge about Language and the Curriculum*. London: Hodder and Stoughton, 104–121.
Carter, Ronald. 1995. How aware should language-aware teachers and learners be? In David Nunan, Roger Berry and Vivien Berry (eds) *Language Awareness in Language Education*. Hong Kong: Department of Curriculum Studies, University of Hong Kong, 1–15.
Chalker, Sylvia and Edmund Weiner. 1994. *Oxford Dictionary of English Grammar*. Oxford: Oxford University Press.
Chomsky, Noam. 1966. *Topics in the Theory of Generative Grammar*. The Hague: Mouton.
Cobbett, William. 1819, reprinted 2003. *A Grammar of the English Language*. Oxford: BCA.
Collins Cobuild English Grammar. 1990. 3rd edn 2011. Glasgow: HarperCollins.
Corder, S. Pit. 1973. *Introducing Applied Linguistics*. Harmondsworth: Penguin.
Cummins, J. 2000. Putting language proficiency in its place: responding to critiques of the conversational/academic language distinction. In J. Cenoz and U. Jessner (eds) *English in Europe: The Acquisition of a Third Language*. Clevedon: Multilingual Matters, 54–83.
Ellis, Rod. 1994. *The Study of Second Language Acquisition*. Oxford: Oxford University Press.
Faerch, Claus. 1985. Meta talk in FL classroom discourse. *Studies in Second Language Acquisition* 7/2: 184–199.
Fortune, Alan. 2005. Learners' use of metalanguage in collaborative form-focussed L2 output tasks. *Language Awareness* 14/1: 21–38.
Harris, R. 1998. *Introduction to Integrational Linguistics*. Oxford: Elsevier Science.
Howatt, Anthony P. R (with Henry G. Widdowson). 2004. *A History of English Language Teaching*. 2nd edn. Oxford: Oxford University Press.
Johnson, Keith and Helen Johnson. 1998. *Encyclopedic Dictionary of Applied Linguistics*. Oxford: Blackwell.

Krashen, Stephen. 1985. *The Input Hypothesis*. Harlow: Longman.
Lewis, Michael. 1986. *The English Verb*. Hove: Language Teaching Publications.
Lewis, Michael. 2000. Language in the Lexical Approach. In Michael Lewis (ed.) *Teaching Collocation: Further Developments in the Lexical Approach*. Hove: Language Teaching Publications, 119–134.
Lock, Graham and Amy B. M. Tsui. 2000. Customising Linguistics: developing an electronic grammar database for teachers. *Language Awareness* 9/1: 17–33.
Lyons, John. 1995. *Linguistic Semantics: An Introduction*. Cambridge: Cambridge University Press.
Macaro, Ernesto and Liz Masterman. 2006. Does intensive grammar instruction make a difference? *Language Teaching Research* 10/3: 297–327.
Mohammed, Abdulmoneim. 1995. Grammar instruction in language development. *Language Awareness* 4/1: 49–58.
Murphy, Raymond. 1994. *English Grammar in Use*. 2nd edn; 3rd edn 2004. Cambridge: Cambridge University Press.
Pearson, Jennifer. 1998. *Terms in Context*. Amsterdam: Benjamins.
Sinclair, John. 1991. *Corpus, Concordance, Collocation*. Oxford: Oxford University Press.
Tsui, Amy M.B. 1995. *Introducing Classroom Interaction*. London: Penguin.
Walsh, Steve 2003. Developing intercultural awareness in the second language classroom through teacher self-evaluation. *Language Awareness* 12/2: 124–142.
Woods, Edward. 1995. *Introducing Grammar*. London: Penguin.
Wright, Tony 1991. Language awareness in teacher education programmes for non-native speakers. In Carl James and Peter Garrett (eds) *Language Awareness in the Classroom*. London: Longman, 62–77.

5 Issues in Grammatical Description

5.1 Introduction

This chapter examines the choices that grammarians, whether pedagogic or scientific, face when describing grammar. Chapter 4 discussed one of these issues, namely the selection of terminology – how much to use and which terms to use when explaining grammar. In this chapter further choices are discussed, including:

- whether and to what extent to be prescriptive (as per Section 2.6.2);
- how extensive to make the account;
- what style to adopt, and how to involve readers;
- how to deal with formality and acceptability;
- what sort of examples to use.

The chapter is largely based on a series of studies which examine these factors. It ends, by way of illustration, with a comparative study of comparable extracts from two grammars, one scientific and one pedagogic. This is clearly more relevant to the professional writer. However, all the issues discussed relate as much to the use of spoken language by classroom teachers; whether, for example, to say 'you use X to...' or 'X is used to...'. Such decisions may seem trivial, but they are not, as will be seen.

The starting belief is that there are no 'neutral' accounts (as per metalinguistic relativity in the previous chapters); some of what a grammarian is allowed to say has already been ordained. But more than this, the chapter aims to explore the reasons why one grammar would describe a certain grammatical phenomenon in one way while another would arrive at a very different (though not necessarily contradictory) description, even if they are aiming at the same audience and relating the same basic facts. It may not seem obvious, but there are many choices that grammarians and teachers make, perhaps unconsciously, on the way to their final product, hence the

5.2 Basic Issues in Describing Grammar

characterisation of it as an 'art'. By investigating aspects of grammatical description that grammarians themselves rarely reflect on, the chapter may serve as guidance for any would-be grammarian.

It may be thought unusual to turn the spotlight on grammatical description, and it is indeed rare to do so (Berry 2009a). But linguists have already investigated every genre under the sun – academic writing, conversation, journalese, political speeches, advertising, etc. – so why should grammatical description be sacred? And as we will see, important insights can emerge from such a study.

5.2 Basic Issues in Describing Grammar

A major issue in grammatical description facing writers, the nature and use of terminology, has already been discussed in detail in Chapter 4. Another, which is closely related to it, namely the use of sub-technical vocabulary, is discussed in Section 5.5, along with other established factors. These are dealt with in the following sections.

5.2.1 Depth and Refinement

One of the most important issues affecting grammatical description is that of 'depth' or 'refinement': how deeply should the analysis go, how refined should it be? The response of some scientific grammarians would be 'always as deep as possible'; nothing less is acceptable. But such an approach would result in accounts on a very limited range of topics that are only for the eyes of other scientific grammarians (and which are partly responsible for the problem of poor transmission described in Section 3.7.2). It is stating the obvious to say that the depth of description will depend on the level and maturity of the target audience.

On a practical level, the issue comes down to how many distinctions to make for a particular phenomenon. A more sophisticated account will include more uses than a less sophisticated one. A similar dilemma affects lexicographers in their writing of dictionaries; how deep should they go in distinguishing different meanings? For example, the *Collins Cobuild English Dictionary* (HarperCollins, 1995) gives ten uses/meanings for the word *yet*; the Google Dictionary (online) gives only four (though one has three sub-divisions). Which one is right? Neither, necessarily; they are both applying different levels of refinement, according to their understanding of the topic and the assumed target audience.

In grammatical description the parallel issue is: how many uses/meanings to identify? Here we encounter a long-standing debate between two groups with opposing attitudes to grammar, between the 'splitters' and the 'lumpers'. The former would seek to split up the subject matter and identify as many uses as possible (i.e. taking refinement to the maximum), while the latter would seek an overriding, underlying reason for the use of the feature.

On the one hand I feel that we should not assume that all the uses of one particular grammatical feature can be lumped together at any expense – this is not the way language works. The following examples demonstrate this. On the other hand, I find some of the minuscule distinctions that are teased out excessive. In some cases the perceived distinctions are the result of other factors. To take the perfect progressive as an example, there is an argument that, in addition to a continuous interpretation, there is the possibility of an iterative (repeated) interpretation. Thus

> He's *been calling* me all day.

would have an iterative interpretation as opposed to a continuous one, whereas

> He's *been working* all day.

would be continuous. However, this misses the point. The possibility of an iterative interpretation arises not from the nature of the present perfect progressive but from the meaning potential of the verb *call*. 'Calling' is (usually) of short duration (especially if the phone goes unanswered) and so if the relevant time period is lengthy, as implied by the verb form or some adverbial ('all day'), the conclusion will be that the action is repeated; this is not the case with *work*.

5.2.2 Distinguishing Uses

There are a number of ways in which grammarians can evaluate whether the grammatical item or structure they are studying is uniform or not. One method is for them to use their own intuitions, however unreliable: do the two meanings seem so apart as to be worthy of separate mentions?

Another method is to look at the structures they appear in. A third is to apply known synonyms. As an example of both, take these two sentences containing *if*:

> We'll miss our connection *if* our plane's late.
> Nobody seems to know *if* our plane's late.

On the surface these seem to have an identical structure: a main clause and then a subordinate clause starting with *if*. Our intuitions may well suggest that there is a difference in meaning between the two uses of *if*. However, a surer method is to apply a potential synonym to the two sentences, and there is one such synonym: *whether*. This leads to the following results:

> **We'll miss our connection <u>whether</u> our plane's late.* (But add
> ...*or not* and it is acceptable.)
> *Nobody seems to know <u>whether</u> our plane's late.*

The substitution only yields an acceptable sentence in the second case. This 'test' can assure us that there are two (at least) broad uses of the word *if*: one in conditional sentences, as described in the Activity for Chapter 3, and the other to introduce indirect questions (as in Chapter 10). In fact, their structure also disambiguates the two. In the first case the *if* clause functions as an adverbial in the sentence; in the second it is an object of the verb *know*. But this is harder to establish.

For a fourth way of how to decide whether a particular grammatical form has more than one use or meaning, we can turn to a perhaps surprising area, namely that of language play, especially jokes and advertisements. Here are four examples which can help us to determine whether distinctions are valid; if the point did not work, the distinction would be invalid:

1 The present perfect. In one of the Marx Brothers films (*Duck Soup*) Groucho Marx is leaving a party (to which he has not been invited) and says to the party-giver, as he exits: 'I've had a wonderful time.' The party-giver beams. But then Groucho adds: 'But this wasn't it!' The joke relies on the distinction between an experiential use of the present perfect ('In my time I've had...') and a recency interpretation ('I've just had...'). The hostess assumes the intention is the latter meaning, and is upset when the punchline affirms the former.

2 The reference of *we*. In eastern Europe, before the fall of communism, many jokes circulated subversively regarding the selfishness of officials and the economic shortages that those countries suffered from. In one the Prime Minister of a country invites the Economics Minister to his office and asks him a number of questions:

> *How much food do we have left?*
> *Enough for a month*, the Food Minister replies
> *And what about petrol?*
> *It will run out in a week.*
> *That's terrible. How will the people survive?*

The Food Minister looks puzzled and replies:

> *Excuse me, Prime Minister, when you said 'we' I thought you were talking about you and me.*

This joke clearly validates the varying reference of *we*; in this case the difference between the inclusive use (speaker and hearer) and the 'all-inclusive' use. (See Chapter 9 for more on these distinctions.)

3 Converting uncountable nouns to countable. At a rugby tournament, Heineken came up with a clever advert to promote its beer. The advert showed a horde of thirsty rugby fans approaching a bar where a nervous waiter was holding a single bottle of beer – obviously the last one. Up came the slogan: 'One game, one tournament, one beer.' The language play revolves around the fact that there are two regular ways of converting an uncountable noun such as *beer* to countable: firstly, to refer to units of the substance (bottles, glasses), and secondly to refer to types. The first interpretation is one *bottle* of beer, but in fact the slogan is referring to one (unique) *type* of beer. The advert shows that these two uses are in fact distinct.

4 The meanings of *can*. The following joke plays on two meanings of *can*. A woman is talking to her friend about a health problem. 'My doctor has told me I can't play football.' The friend replies: 'Oh, has she seen you play?' The first statement implies (lack of) permission, but the reply, as with all jokes, surprises us with another interpretation: (lack of) ability.

Unfortunately, language play is not available to all aspects of English grammar to help us decide where distinctions are valid. But grammarians should be on the watch for such instances since all areas of English grammar may be subject to language play.

5.2.3 An Example: The Present Simple

To exemplify the issue of refinement we might consider a very important area of English grammar: how the present (simple) tense is used. (See also the list of specific uses of the definite article in Section 7.2.2 as an example.) The English tenses (I am including aspect here) in English are probably the most important area in teaching and similarly one of the hardest to explain.

So how does the present simple fare in the debate between lumpers and splitters? The extreme 'lumper' view would be that the present simple tense refers exclusively to 'presentness'. This notion is the source of the myth discussed in Chapter 3 that 'the present tense is used to refer to present time'. While there is a grain of truth in this idea of 'presentness', in that the present moment can be discerned as a factor in the reference of the simple present, most uses involve other points in time

5.2 Basic Issues in Describing Grammar 97

(including both future and past). That this must be so can be shown by the fact that, unless there is modality (i.e. the modal auxiliaries), all complete sentences must choose between a present or past tense, since tense is an obligatory feature in English. As I said,

> dividing the whole of human experience into two basic time options would be very limiting. What about experiences that cross this division? (Berry 2018: 98)

So how far do we go in 'splitting up' the meanings of the present simple? There are few clues from the structure or from synonyms (or from language play), so the grammarian is obliged to rely on introspection into the meanings, especially the time references involved. In my book for university students of English I identified eight uses/meanings after a careful consideration of numerous accounts (and my own intuitions):

1) States, as in *The earth is round*. This clearly involves both past and future time as well as present.
2) Repeated event or habits, as in *Bill drinks heavily*. Again this also involves past and future.
3) Timeless happenings, as in the plots of books and films, e.g. *At the end they fall in love...*
4) Declarations of feelings or intentions, as in *That sounds great!* Clearly the time is not limited to the present.
5) Instantaneous events, as in commentaries or descriptions of processes: *Kane shoots, and it's a goal*. Of these eight uses only this one can be said to be purely 'present'.
6) The so-called historic present, as in *And then she looks at me and says...*, whereby a past event is made more vivid.
7) Scheduled events, as in *The train leaves at 10*. This is a classic case of how present time is involved, even though the actual reference is non-present. The event predicated is in the future, yet the schedule exists now. Even grammarians make use of this, as in *We look at this in the next chapter*.
8) Future events in subordinate clauses following *if* [see Chapter 3 on conditionals] and temporal conjunctions, as in *We'll be there at the airport when your flight arrives*. (Berry 2018: 98–99)

While this may unavoidably appear to readers as an authoritative, exhaustive account, it is not. A splitter may want to divide meaning (5) into two, since the event described in commentaries is of necessity slightly in the past, whereas descriptions of actual processes, e.g. recipes, can be totally contemporaneous: *I pour the liquid into...* As regards meaning (4), a lumper may question its validity and merge it perhaps with (1).

Is this a standard picture? To investigate this we can examine and compare how many uses or meanings are given in other accounts. Michael Swan (2016: 30–32), in his popular reference grammar, gives only four distinct uses (plus two situations which specify when the present simple should *not* be used – see Chapter 6). Another classic reference grammar for learners, Thomson and Martinet (1986: 159–160), gives nine uses, while a more recent one aimed at a lower level gives five (Leech et al. 2001: 426–428). Which one is right? The answer is 'none'; they are simply applying different levels of refinement according to their intended audience. Even if two accounts have the same number of uses, but different ones, this can be justified by saying that they prioritise different uses, or cut up the 'same' cake in different ways. Nothing in the scheme of present simple usage is absolute. Nevertheless, we can still examine critically any such account to question whether it unnecessarily splits one use into two, or lumps two uses into one (or even misses one use completely). One of the activities at the end of this chapter invites readers to do just that by comparing two accounts.

5.2.4 Formality

Formality is a difficult concept for grammarians to handle. It is clearly an important factor in describing grammar and in advising what forms learners should use; many forms can be characterised according to it. Yet what does it actually mean? Why is it said that *whom* is formal and *who* informal in *Who/whom did you see*? Why is *much* categorised as formal in

> There is <u>much</u> to be done.

but not in

> You've done so <u>much</u> for us.

Two other determiners, namely *few* and *little* (Berry 1998), are also regarded as formal in similar situations, whether as pronouns or determiners:

> There is <u>little</u> hope.
> <u>Few</u> countries have accepted this claim.

'Not much hope' and 'not many countries' would be the alternatives here. Why formality should be an issue affecting such determiners is not clear.

Quirk et al. (1985: 25–27) arrive at a five-way distinction (while pointing out that it is in fact a cline):

> very formal – formal – neutral – informal – very informal

However, in most pedagogic descriptions of formality, a simple dichotomy between formal and informal is applied. I believe this is wrong; while I accept that a two-way distinction is appropriate, I believe the major opposition in most cases in describing modern English is not between formal and informal language but between formal and *non-formal* language. Thus, whatever the case may have been in the past, it is nowadays incorrect to characterise *who* as informal; it is non-formal (or 'neutral' as Quirk et al. would describe it), while it is *whom* that is marked for formality. The same applies to the determiners exemplified above: rather than characterising the alternatives to *few* and *little* as informal they should be regarded as non-formal. This is not to say that there are no cases of clearly informal grammar, particularly spoken forms and their written representation, e.g. *gonna*, *wanna*.

To conclude, the problems with formality are

- Firstly, in identifying it – what is informal for one person may sound normal for another.
- Secondly, in explaining it – why have *much*, and to a lesser extent *many*, not to mention *few* and *little*, acquired formal status in certain contexts?
- thirdly, in expressing it. How can advice be given when its effects on use are so hard to quantify? And do we have an adequate pedagogic metalanguage to describe it? It is not enough to talk only of formal vs informal, as my use of 'non-formal' above indicates.

5.2.5 Acceptability

Acceptability is closely linked to formality; what is informal for one person may be unacceptable for another (or non-standard for a third). But while structures characterised in terms of formality are still nevertheless considered correct, there is another area of usage where correctness is at issue. Acceptability is a term preferred here to 'correctness' and 'grammaticality', since, while the latter terms refer to some absolute quality, 'acceptability' implies the involvement of subjective judgement.

As was made clear in Chapters 1 and 2, grammar is not just a question of what is right or wrong, although many L1 speakers – influenced by the prescriptive tradition – think that the main role of 'grammar' is to decide on matters of correctness, for example to rule on the use of *less* ('incorrect') and *fewer* ('correct') with plural countable nouns. Take this example:

> There were <u>less protesters</u> at last night's demonstration than before.

Purists may object to this, saying that it should be 'fewer protesters'. However, the use of *less* in this situation goes back centuries (Swan 1999); the insistence on *fewer* is an eighteenth-century invention. And when *less* is separate from the noun, there does not seem to be a problem:

> *There were <u>less</u> than 100 <u>protesters</u> at last night's demonstration.*
> (Though *fewer* is also possible.)

So what do descriptive grammarians say to learners about this issue? Do they simply ignore the prescriptivist injunctions and merely note that the so-called correct option is in fact just a formal alternative to the non-formal form? Surely not; the beliefs and expectations of language users are in some way valid, even if they are unsupported linguistically. Thus there is a case for arguing that grammarians need to advise learners that certain uses may have an adverse effect on L1 hearers (or even, especially, on their non-L1 teachers). But how is this to be expressed without sounding prescriptive? Typical statements go something like this:

> But some people do not approve of this usage/consider this incorrect.

(I admit to having said something like this myself.) What are learners to make of such statements? Who are these 'some people'? The importance of acceptability and how to express it constitute another problem for grammarians.

Eastwood (1994: 283), quoted in Swan (1999: 61), gives the following, rather strong, advice regarding the use of the of *less* with plural count nouns:

> It is safer for the learner to avoid this usage.

Alternatively, rather than paying heed to prescriptive injunctions, should pedagogic grammarians take the lead in rejecting them? Here is Michael Swan (2016: 90) on split infinitives (see Chapter 2):

> Split infinitive structures are quite common in English, especially in informal style. There is an old rule which says that split infinitives are incorrect. This is not true.

Let us take as example an issue which is not clouded by the prescriptive/descriptive debate. Look at these examples taken from Kazuo Ishiguro's *The Buried Giant* (Faber and Faber, 2015):

> *It's this man alone destroyed the fields.*
> *There's something else puzzles me.*

These would be counted as incorrect by some on the grounds that the subject relative pronoun is missing (...<u>who</u> destroyed..., ...<u>that</u> puzzles...).

Relative clauses with the *object* missing (sometimes called contact clauses) are, of course, non-formal or neutral (*That's the pen (which) I lost.*), though they too may have been considered incorrect once upon a time.

This usage receives little attention in the literature. One exception is Biber et al. (1999: 619), where it is characterised as 'marginally non-standard'. They also note that it is common with existential *there*:

> Th<u>ere</u> aren't many people say that nowadays (…who say…).

In his examples Ishiguro may be trying to capture a non-standard or dialectal tone. However, if we decide that it is informal/non-standard/unacceptable, what are we to make of the following example, uttered by David Cameron, former British Prime Minister (when describing to his cabinet colleagues the reaction to his announcement of the royal wedding between Prince William and Kate Middleton)?

> *There was a great cheer went up.*

Surely this cannot be counted as unacceptable. But what are we then to say? Is this construction on its way to acceptability, and should our description of it reflect this? Many diachronic changes start out as 'unacceptable', then become acceptable, though at first informal, and then non-formal.

We now turn to two issues which are generally not considered when grammatical accounts are considered: the modality and 'personality' involved in grammatical statements.

5.3 Modality

Modality refers to whether and how a statement may be qualified to show that its author wants to modify its truth value. Its most obvious exponents are the modal auxiliaries (also called modal verbs) such as *can*, *should*, *may*, etc. which modify the meaning of verbs, but other word classes can encompass its meaning: adverbs (e.g. *generally*), adjectives (*it is <u>possible</u>*) and nouns (*the possibility…*). In academic writing it is sometimes referred to as 'hedging'. For example:

> Some verbs are <u>generally</u> not used in progressive forms… (Swan 2016: 33).

In grammatical description modality has great relevance, since writers may not be able to present the whole truth (and nothing but the truth) for a number of reasons:

- There isn't enough space in the limited number of pages that their publishers have accorded them.
- The writer (along with perhaps everyone else) does not know the 'whole truth'.

- The readers may not be mature enough or linguistically advanced enough to comprehend it, even if there is space and knowledge.

In order to investigate prominent exponents of modality I set up a corpus of grammatical description composed of well-known grammars of English: METALANG[1] (see Berry 2009a). The first part, METALANG 1, consisted of brief matching samples of eleven grammars. The second part, METALANG 2, consisted of three well-known grammars in their entirety: *English Grammar in Use* by Raymond Murphy (1994), referred to below as MURPHY, *Practical English Usage* by Michael Swan (1995), henceforth SWAN, and the Collins Cobuild English Grammar (1990), henceforth COBUILD.

The exponents of modality selected for investigation were:

- modal auxiliaries: *can* and *may*;
- modal adverbs of usuality or frequency: *usually, normally, generally, often, sometimes.*

(Exponents of personality are discussed in the next section.)

Here are examples of each of these, taken from Berry (2009a) but originating from Swan (1995):

> We <u>can</u> use the future perfect to say something...
> In some structures we <u>may</u> put the prepositional object...
> 'Indeed' is <u>often</u> used after an adjective or adverb...
> Sometimes we leave out 'if I were you' and just use 'I should'...
> We <u>usually</u> put the marker 'to' before the infinitive...
> We <u>generally</u> use 'in' and 'on' to talk about the position of things...
> Passive infinitives are <u>normally</u> made by putting 'not' before the infinitive.

Of course, these are not the only exponents of modality in grammatical description. Other adverbs and modal auxiliaries are possible. Nor am I claiming that these words are identical in meaning and therefore interchangeable; the fact that they sometime co-occur (*We can usually*...) demonstrates this.

Note this rather unusual use of *must* in Thomson and Martinet (1986: 160):

> It [the simple present tense] <u>must</u> be used instead of the present continuous with verbs which cannot be used in the continuous form, e.g. *love, see, believe* etc.

Such strong assertions are rare in grammatical description, perhaps because of the danger that they may turn out to be wrong, as is certainly the case with this rule, as the examples in Chapter 3 (*I'm loving it*, etc.) demonstrate.

Equally, not all statements contain modality, far from it. Here are two examples:

> Modals are used in 'question tags'.
> We say a friend of mine/yours/his.

However, the results from METALANG 1 showed that overall modality is much more common in grammatical description than in normal language. Here are the individual frequencies:

can 769   *may* 234   *usually* 173   *normally* 98
generally 47   *often* 181   *sometimes* 171

As can be seen, *can* was by far the most common choice in the survey, but this is only to be expected; it is more common than the others in general usage. However, what is significant is that all these exponents of modality were far more frequent in grammatical description than in the language as a whole. To show this, these results were compared with the Cobuild Direct corpus and its four sub-corpora.[2] In all cases the seven exponents were more frequent, compared to the overall size of the corpora. To take two examples: *can* was between 7.77 and 2.57 times more frequent in METALANG than in Cobuild Direct (depending on which sub-corpus is used for comparison), while at the other extreme *usually* was between 43.97 and 8.87 times more frequent. The full table of results is contained in Appendix 3 (Table A.1).

One other particular finding was of interest. While, as expected, *can* was more frequent than *may* in the ten pedagogic grammars included in METALANG 1, in the eleventh, a scientific grammar (Quirk et al. 1985), it was the reverse: *may* was actually more frequent than *can* (119 to 100 instances). This is presumably because of their choice of authorial style, preferring the more formal *may* over *can* for expressing possibility and permission, for example:

> The non-finite clause *may* be with or without a subject (Quirk et al 1985: 993).

Presumably *can* would have sufficed for less scientific grammars (though they would have expressed the same proposition differently, or not at all).

The results from METALANG 1 are rather crude figures. In particular, *can* and *may* have more than one meaning, notably possibility and permission (as well as ability for *can*); these are not differentiated above. Thus in the second part of METALANG one of the focuses was on contexts where the modality involved hedging, that is, the writer pulling back from a full commitment to the proposition.

In Hyland (1998) hedging has a number of functions which may be reduced to two broad motivations (Berry 2009a):

- epistemic, to do with the knowledge content;
- interpersonal, to do with the relationship between reader and writer.

In academic writing both apply. In other words, academic writers hedge not only because they are uncertain of the facts, but because – contrary to beliefs that academic writing should be assertive – they do not want to force the facts upon their audience, and because they want to allow them room to disagree. In this case the audience consists of their peers, so it is understandable that they would not want to appear confrontational or excessively authoritative.

However, in grammatical description, except at the most scientific level, the relationship between writers and readers is asymmetric; the writers are the authority and the readers are the 'pupils'. So one would expect to find that only the epistemic motivation for hedging occurs, that writers would hedge only because of uncertainty about the facts, or because for some reason they cannot present the whole truth.

I called this issue the 'pedagogic grammarian's dilemma' (Berry 2009a). This was based on a paper by Widdowson (1997) in which he pointed out that, since descriptions of language necessarily involve abstraction, there is bound to be imperfection. As examples of this he cited two texts from pedagogic grammars about the past tense (Widdowson 1997: 1890–1892), the first from Alexander (1993: 288):

The simple past tense describes events, actions or situations which occurred in the past and are now finished. A time reference is usually given or strongly implied.

Widdowson pointed out that there is a problem with this abstraction:

the implication is that the use of the simple past in English to describe events, actions and so on is distinctive of this tense. But clearly it is not. The past continuous and past perfect are also used in this way. Nor is it the case that the simple past is used only in reference to past time. It occurs commonly in conditional expressions. (Widdowson 1997: 1891)

The second text is from Swan (1980: 470–471); the comments in bold in parentheses were added by Widdowson:

*The past tense is the one most often (**but not always**) used to talk about the past. It can (**but need not**) refer to short, quickly finished actions and events, to longer actions and situations, and to repeated happenings (**i.e. it can refer to almost anything**).*

5.3 Modality

Pedagogic grammarians seem to have two choices, to paraphrase Widdowson:

- to be specific and risk being wrong, as in Alexander above (though it should be noted that Alexander's second sentence is not specific);
- to be so general as to risk saying nothing, as in Swan above, i.e. to 'hedge'.

Widdowson's verdict on these two attempts is perhaps a little harsh, for the task facing pedagogic grammarians is actually more complex than this. It involves issues such as space and learner factors as well, as suggested earlier in this section. Moreover, writers may simply be responding to their readers' expectations. As Chalker (1994: 36) pointed out:

> 'Learners on the whole want language made easy ... They also want prescriptive guidance',

which reminds one of the partial link between prescriptive and pedagogic accounts posited in Chapter 2. Chalker's comment would seem to suggest that learners would prefer the first option above: specificity at the risk of being wrong. But do the writers of grammars respond to this?

This trade-off between pressures of space (you can't say everything), learner level (they wouldn't understand it anyway), accuracy (are you allowed to simplify if it could make what you say prescriptive and/or wrong?) and certainty (can you appear uncertain by hedging?) is what constitutes the pedagogic grammarian's dilemma. So what do the writers of pedagogic grammars do? Do they use the kind of modality highlighted by Widdowson or not? And is the epistemic function the only reason for hedging?

The result from METALANG I that certain kinds of modality were far more frequent in grammars than in English generally was reduplicated for the three grammars studied intensively in METALANG II; once cleaned, there were 1,539 tokens of *can* in SWAN (1.2 per cent of the total), 1,647 in COBUILD (1.6 per cent) and 265 in MURPHY (1.3 per cent). (*May* was not included in this stage as it was far less frequent, but the adverbs were retained.)

In order to ensure a more specific context the search at this stage was restricted to the use of modality with the verbs *use* and *say*; in the case of *use* both passive and active forms were sought ('we can use'/'can be used'); for *say* the passive not an option (i.e. only 'we/you can say'). Cases where *say* was clearly referring to speech as opposed to writing were not included. The results are shown in Table 5.1.

Table 5.1 Incidence of can and main adverbs with use(d) and say

	SWAN		COBUILD		MURPHY		TOTALS	
	use(d)	say	use(d)	say	use(d)	say	use(d)	say
a verbs: raw total	2,754	282	2,718	500	575	313	6,047	1,095
b with *can*	661	18	924	115	137	86	1,700	219
c with *usually*	77	11	82	6	6	11	165	28
d with *often*	255	4	101	1	42	1	398	6
e with *sometimes*	79	2	103	2	18	–	200	4
f with *generally*	62	2	3	–	2	–	67	2
g with *normally*	154	–	37	3	37	–	228	3
h total (b)–(g)	1,288	37	1,250	127	242	98	2,756	262
i percentage (h) in (a)	47%	13%	46%	25%	42%	31%	46%	24%

Again, *can* was by far the most frequent form of modality in these contexts, but all the exponents were comparatively common. Overall, as can be seen from the bottom line, in association with *use(d)* they made up almost half the tokens of that verb in each grammar.

Of the two verbs, as can be seen, *say* is much less frequent, perhaps because *use* offers both the active and passive options. However, it is relatively more common in MURPHY, where the passive with *used* is rare (presumably because the author of this less advanced grammar considers it more difficult for learners to decode than the active). Overall, *say* with *can* is much less common than *use(d)* as a carrier verb, notably so in SWAN, where it is hardly used at all. And with the adverbs of frequency and usuality *say* is very rare. Overall it occurs less than one tenth as frequently as *use(d)* – 262 vs 2,756 occurrences.

In answer, then, to the issue of the pedagogic grammarian's dilemma, a very frequent response in these grammars, perhaps surprisingly, is to hedge. Why is this so? Is it from a fear of being inaccurate? Or is it because they know the truth but it is too complicated for their readers? It is difficult to say. Perhaps it is out of a desire not to seem prescriptive, which would seem to contradict Chalker's comment earlier in this section.

The next question is: Is the hedging in METALANG 2 solely epistemic (to do with the facts) or is there an interpersonal element? As described above, the unequal relationship between writer and reader would suggest that the latter should not be present. The next section investigates this.

5.4 Personality[3]

We now turn to a factor in grammatical description that is perhaps less obvious than hedging but which is just as important an element in the style of grammarians, and which has an interesting relationship with modality: 'personality'. This term, taken from Goatly (2000) and Berry (2004, 2005 and 2009a), refers to the systemic choice facing writers about whether (and how) to place themselves in the text, and whether (and how) to address readers. The concept can easily be applied to other genres, for example academic writing; e.g. should single authors refer to themselves with *we*? According to Hyland (2001) the use of *I* is becoming more common. (See Chapter 9 for more on the use of pronouns.)

In grammatical terms it boils down to the choice between **personal constructions** (and then among personal pronouns):

we use X (personal, first-person plural)
you use X (personal, second person)

and **impersonal constructions** (and then between passive and active forms):

> X *is used* (impersonal, passive)
> *it is normal to use* X (impersonal, active, including modality)

A number of variations on these choices exist, particularly for the impersonal active option, for example to use the word in question as the subject:

> *'Enough' normally goes before nouns.*

Other languages have other possibilities, such as reflexive verbs. In French one can say 'le passé s'utilise...', literally 'the past uses itself', wherein *s'* represents a reflexive pronoun.

Until recently the dominant options would have been the personal *we use/say* or the impersonal passive. In Thomson and Martinet's *A Practical English Grammar* (1986) the style is mostly impersonal with a sprinkling of *we*; there is no use of *you*. Both *we* and the passive are somewhat problematic: the latter because it more complex structurally and therefore thought to be unsuitable linguistically for some learners, the former because it can smack of a didactic expert, remote from the reader: the so-called exclusive use. (See Chapter 9 for more on this.) In the first edition of Murphy's *English Grammar in Use* (1985), however, *you* is quite common (though it is mixed with *we*). It was the insistence on *you* in Cobuild publications, starting with the *Dictionary* (first edition 1987), where it was a reaction to traditional lexicographese, and continuing with the *Grammar* (first edition 1990), that really promoted the use of what I have called 'youser-friendly' metalanguage (Berry 2000):

> You use 'must' to show that you believe something is the case...

The use of *you* is intended to bring the writer and reader closer together, to sound more friendly. It is not without problems, though (in particular because of the generic as well as specific interpretation of *you*; see Chapter 9 for more on this), but it has proved influential and has been adopted in other grammars. In some it is mixed with *we*, where no doubt the author also intends the inclusive interpretation, i.e. a joint enterprise, rather than the exclusive interpretation, as in this example from Murphy (1994: 8):

> We often use *can* + *see/hear/smell/taste*. [Example omitted]. But you can use the continuous with *see*... when the meaning is "having a meeting with".

However, I found that an exclusive interpretation among readers is possible if *we* is juxtaposed with *you* (Berry 2005: 94). I concluded that by mixing *we* and *you* in close proximity pedagogic grammarians take the risk that their readers will create some opposition between a group that the writer belongs to which has positive characteristics and a group to which they as readers belong which has negative characteristics. Writers of pedagogic grammars should consider avoiding personality mixing, especially that between *we* and *you*, unless it is clear that different reference is intended.

Above it was hypothesised that hedging in pedagogic grammars is inappropriate because of the distance between writer and readers. However, if writers choose to get close to their readers by using *you*, an interpersonal motivation for hedging is also feasible; they may wish to avoid sounding prescriptive and authoritative. Some evidence for this was found; see later in this section.

As regards METALANG 2, and the choice of pronoun in personal constructions, there is a clear distinction: COBUILD uses *you* exclusively, and SWAN, with a few exceptions, *we*. (Though in both the impersonal passive and other constructions are common.) MURPHY uses both, though in different ways as will be seen (and doesn't use passives).

Table 5.2 shows a comparison between the SWAN and COBUILD, starting with the overall incidence of 'use' and 'used' as verbs and then refining it to see how likely *CAN* is to occur in the context *PRONOUN* ___ *use*.

As can be seen on the top line of Table 5.2, the incidence of *use(d)* was remarkably similar in the two grammars, but when the passive constructions were omitted in order to focus on personal pronoun use with the verb, there were rather more instances of *use* (as an active verb) in COBUILD (1,051) than in SWAN (831); this difference was still maintained when its uses as infinitive and with other subjects were removed (leaving 964 and 731 instances). The main difference,

Table 5.2 Incidence of pronouns with CAN and USE in SWAN and COBUILD

	SWAN	COBUILD
Total USE(D) (verb)	2,754	2,718
Total USE (verb)	831	1,055
as infinitive and with other subjects	100	91
we (...) *use*	731	4
you (...) *use*	–	960
___ *can use*	176 (*we*)	413 (*you*)
% *can* with *we/you*	24% (*we*)	43% (*you*)

110   *Issues in Grammatical Description*

highlighted, is that in SWAN *we* was used exclusively in the context of *use*, while in COBUILD *you* greatly predominated (960 out of 964; the four instances of *we* seem to have 'slipped through'). This difference is obviously a question of the style chosen by the authors.

These instances of *we use* and *you use* were then further investigated to see how often *can* occurred, i.e. *we can use* and *you can use*. As can be seen, as a proportion, *you can use* was far more likely to occur in COBUILD (43 per cent) than *we can use* in SWAN (24 per cent). In other words, it would seem that hedging is more common when a more personal approach is taken via the use of *you*. However, if we add in the selected adverbs a different picture emerges. There were 178 cases of *we* + adverb + *use* in SWAN as opposed to only 57 in COBUILD. If these are added to the figures above we obtain this calculation:

SWAN: 178 + 176 = 354, OUT OF 731
COBUILD: 413 + 57 = 470, OUT OF 960

This results in almost identical percentages: 49 per cent for COBUILD and 48 per cent for SWAN. In other words, both would appear to hedge the same amount when they use *use* with a pronoun, but they do it differently; in SWAN the 'formula' is *we* + ADVERB + *use*, while in COBUILD it is: *you* + *can* + *use*.

Another interesting finding regarding the link between personality and modality involved the third, smaller, grammar: MURPHY. In this case, it concerns examples of 'double hedging', that is where both an adverb and modal *can* are combined (somewhat redundantly, perhaps), as in *We can sometimes use*/*You can sometimes use*. As would be expected, double-hedging (rare in all three grammars) only occurred in SWAN with *we* and in COBUILD with *you*. However, an interesting finding came from the results for MURPHY, as shown in Table 5.3. This grammar used both pronouns (though *we* was more common) but it used them in different contexts. With the adverbs *we* only occurred without *can*, while *you* only occurred with it. There were no cases either of *we* + *can* + ADVERB + *use* or of *you* + ADVERB + *use* (without *can*). In other words, the two pronouns were in a kind of complimentary distribution. A modest finding based on low numbers, perhaps, but it is not impossible that the choice of pronoun was related to the amount of hedging; i.e. the modality and personality were linked.

So, what recommendations regarding personality can be made for writers of grammatical description? What style should they adopt? The evidence cited above suggests we should be wary of the personal options, in particular the mixing of *we* and *you*. I feel that the passive ('X is used') is not as problematic as is sometimes claimed. Against its

Table 5.3 Adverbs correlated with pronouns and can *in MURPHY*

	we ——— use	we can ——— use	you ——— use	you can ——— use
usually	1	–	–	2
often	33	–	–	3
sometimes	12	–	–	3
generally	2	–	–	–
normally	29	–	–	1
TOTAL	77	–	–	9

syntactic complexity we should set its generic appropriateness (learners expect such a formal style of writing) and its referential simplicity (learners do not have to work who is being referred to/addressed). They may react to the use of *you* ('Why am I being addressed? I simply want to know what L1 speakers say') or *we* ('Am I being included/excluded?'). The use of the passive avoids these issues. Having said this, the expected proficiency of readers may play a part in discouraging the use of the passive at lower levels; and the need for modality may encourage the use of the personal *you*, as suggested above. But we should not forget that personality is not a simple three-way choice; there are other impersonal options that are available (*It is normal to use...*, etc.).

Further research is needed into the style of pedagogic grammars, into what effect the different choices have on their readers, and into the link between personality and modality. This makes the point that research into grammar should not only concern the improvement of grammatical knowledge, but should also involve applied matters: how that knowledge is transmitted to learners. The language of grammatical description should not escape attention, any more than any genre should.

5.5 Sub-technical Vocabulary

In Chapter 4 a distinction was made between terminology – the specialised, technical terms that are distinct from ordinary language – and metalanguage: the entirety of language used to describe language. Grammatical terminology was discussed there as a particular problem in language teaching (unlike the terminology used in other formal areas of language, say, phonetics), but it constitutes only part of the vocabulary of grammatical metalanguage. If we exclude terminology and, at the other extreme of technicality, the everyday language that is found in any text, we are left with an interesting area of words that, though not specifically terminological, are common in linguistic description because they refer to concepts that are inherently linguistic; they are useful precisely because they retain their usual meaning. I am thinking of words that are used in the describing the meaning of

- verb structures: words such as action, activity, event, process, state, situation;
- nouns: thing, person, name;
- adjectives: quality, attribute.

Take this example from Swan (2016: first page of section 1):

> "*Tenses*" are verb forms that show the times of <u>actions</u> and <u>situations</u> (my underlining).

I often come across generalised descriptions of verb forms where their meanings are referred to as 'actions' alone (and I may have been guilty of this myself). This, of course, is not accurate; verbs refer to much more than actions, as Swan's use of 'situation' above shows. This relates back to the issue of how to describe word classes – by formal or semantic criteria (Section 2.8.1). But there is a temptation to avoid repeating lengthy circumlocutions every time the meaning of a verb form is referred to. Then there is the rather philosophical question of whether such 'simple' concepts are adequate to characterise such profound phenomena. Are 'action' and 'situation' enough to cover all the possible meanings of verbs? Should we not also mention events or happenings (*It rained*)?

Beyond this, we are sometimes lacking in metalanguage to describe certain concepts, and it may be necessary to resort to inventing words, though hopefully transparent ones, as I have done with 'presentness' in Section 5.2.1 on depth to refer to meaning of the present tense; or the use of 'wanting' as a noun to describe the past tense of the verb *want* in *I <u>wanted</u> to speak to you*, when its reference is clearly to present time; this can be phrased as 'the <u>wanting</u> is clearly now'.

5.6 Exemplification

We now turn to an area which has caused some debate: the role of exemplification. Examples are an essential part of any book on grammar, just as they are in dictionaries. No matter how good the explanation, an example will bring the point home to the reader and make the language real. The main issue in the choice of examples is whether they should be authentic or contrived.

5.6 Exemplification

Ever since the publication of the first Cobuild dictionary in 1987, quickly followed by related publications on grammar, there has been a trend towards the use of authentic examples to illustrate grammatical points. This was largely made possible by the introduction of large-scale corpora of authentic texts which could be searched systematically for natural usages. Of course, authentic examples had been used before; the various editions of the *Oxford English Dictionary* depended on them, and in terms of grammar Quirk et al. (1985) had access to a sizeable corpus – though, as Sinclair (1991: 100) pointed out, they relied heavily on contrived examples; the corpus served mainly for analysis.

However, since the Cobuild 'revolution', and the advent of massive searchable databases of text, the assumption has been that authentic examples are the preferred option, that there is something wrong with the contrived examples of earlier years. But before making a judgement about the authentic/contrived controversy we need to examine the arguments rationally – arguments which are usually made with reference to vocabulary, but which also apply to grammar.

5.6.1 Advantages of Authentic Examples

Firstly, and most importantly, because they are real evidence they sound natural, as though someone actually could say or write them, as the introduction to the second edition of the *Collins Cobuild English Dictionary* (1995: viii) puts it:

> [This work] made us aware that all the details of a natural use of a word are essential and cannot be faked. We realized that we would have to use real examples, in the tradition of the great English lexicographers, rather than make them up.

Contrived examples can sound ridiculous because they do not contain normal collocations or colligations. For instance, a contrived example for the phrasal verb *break out*, in the general sense of 'begin suddenly', might fail to observe that the subject of the verb is usually something bad, such as war or disease, as in this example from the *Cobuild English Dictionary* (1995):

> *I was in a night-club in Brixton and a fight broke out.*

Certain grammatical words, such as linking adverbs, are almost impossible to exemplify purely from the writer's intuition because of the complexity of the propositions, involving as they do at least two sentences. Here is how Carter and McCarthy (2005: 257) exemplify *besides* from their corpus of spoken English, capturing neatly its informal nature (but at the same time taking up much space):

> *And I should have told you about things here, I often thought about it, then I thought no, it's too complicated. I didn't want to involve you.* **Besides***, you don't tell me much these days. It's not like it used to be.*
> [original formatting]

Conjunctions are similar in that they require a lengthy co-text.

A second argument sometimes heard is that, because they come 'warts-and-all', they are memorable. However, this might apply equally to iconic *contrived* examples, such as

> *The postilion has been struck by lightning.*

which, although they are no longer used in teaching (one hopes), have somehow achieved a status independent of their original grammatical intention (to exemplify the passive, one assumes, in the above case). Another such example is provided by Guy Cook in the title of a 2001 article:

> The philosopher pulled the lower jaw of the hen.

But he is arguing for the benefits of such contrivances, in terms of their memorability and potentially personalised nature.

Thirdly, authentic examples can have a didactic purpose. By providing a model of natural usage they can help learners to acquire the item exemplified and use it accurately. (This is somewhat at odds with the memorability argument.)

5.6.2 Disadvantages of Authentic Examples

Against this we may set some problems to do with completely authentic examples from corpora:

- their length, as with the example above from Carter and McCarthy;
- comprehension problems – there may be difficult vocabulary or cultural items;
- distasteful topics – war, crime etc.;
- cases of direct reference to named persons or organisations;
- the difficulty of interpreting spoken examples because they are meant to be heard, not written down; their essence can be lost in the transition from speech to writing.

These can usually be overcome by judicious selection; after all, in most cases only one instance of the search item is required.

A different type of problem arises when grammatical structures, i.e. items composed of more than one word, are being sought. The component parts may not be next to each other; they may be separated by several words. Complex verb phrases, for example, may have adverbs inserted into the so-called middle position, for example:

I have, somewhat carelessly, left my wallet behind.

Some structures are hard to spot, requiring a corpus that has been tagged (to show the grammatical status of each word) before they can be identified. Even tagging may not be sufficient to distinguish some uses, for example between the verbal use of *-ed* participles and their adjectival use, as in this example:

The door was <u>closed</u>.

Is this a state (= adjective) or an action (a passive verb)? It will be necessary to refer to the context to decide. The context is also important for certain uses of the definite article; a whole text may be necessary to establish what kind of reference is indicated (see Chapter 7 on articles).

None of these problems is insuperable. The large number of instances available to the searcher will furnish numerous possibilities, and usually the main difficulty is picking out the best one. This in itself can be a problem; how far does one go in looking for the best example? There may be a better one just round the corner.

One other problem with authentic examples is that there may be more than one instance of the required word or structure in the selected text. This is particularly true with common items such as the articles or prepositions, so great care needs to be taken to ensure that there is no confusion. Take this example from the Cobuild text discussed in Section 5.7:

The article focuses on how to protect the therapist rather than how to cure <u>the patient</u>.

In this authentic example there are three instances of *the*, but only one, the last one, is highlighted in order to draw the reader's attention to the use under discussion, namely, formal generic reference with singular nouns. However, the second one exhibits the same use and so should also be underlined, whereas the first one is clearly an example of specific reference to a particular already mentioned article. (In fact, this would make a perfect example of the difference between the two types of reference.) The appropriate use of underlining (or other convention) is important.

5.6.3 Adapting Examples

The main solution to all of these issues is to 'edit' the example, by cutting out irrelevant intervening material (such as relative clauses), by replacing long noun phrases and personal references with pronouns, by leaving off the start and end of sentences. This is a route taken by most users of authentic sources of examples. However, it needs to be carried out with great care.

As a rule, as far as possible the remaining text should still constitute a finite clause (if the original was the same) and the proposition should not be changed (e.g. from negative to positive). Changes must be marked: replacements with square brackets and omissions with dots. Take this sentence chosen at random from the British National Corpus; it was obtained in a search for the keyword 'some':

> *It is hoped that the inclusion of these items will give you, the public, the opportunity to understand why and how craftsmen create such beautiful and, in some cases, controversial items.*

The key phrase 'in some cases' is a perfect example of the way *some* is used, but the whole sentence is too long and complex to be used in full. It can be shortened, but however this is done the main clause will be lost. Probably the best place to start, in order to give as complete a picture as possible, is 'the opportunity'; if 'craftsmen' is thought to be problematic, it could be replaced by 'they'. This would result in the following text:

> *...the opportunity to understand why and how they create such beautiful and, in <u>some</u> cases, controversial items.*

It would be wrong to start from 'why and how they create...' because the reader might be expecting a direct question ('why and how <u>do</u> they create...'). This shows how great care is needed with adaption/abridgement.

There is always a risk in doing too much to the original text; the example may end up being totally lifeless, having the same characteristics that may be used to identify contrived examples, namely brevity, vagueness and simplicity of vocabulary. Of course, unadapted examples may also have these qualities.

5.6.4 The Purpose of Exemplification

One important issue that can be lost in the contrived/authentic debate is: what is the purpose of exemplification? A didactic function was identified in Section 5.6.1. Three other basic functions of linguistic examples may be put forward:

- to illustrate and give support to the main text. To misquote the proverb: 'An example paints a thousand words.'

- to give extra information, for example about the grammatical structures and collocations that the item is used with. This is the case with the *break out* example in Section 5.6.1.
- to make a grammatical point, in which case a carefully contrived example is irreplaceable.

This last function may occur in a number of situations; the following examples are all from Berry (2018):

- when disambiguating structures which are superficially identical:
  She'll make him a good husband. ('She will turn him into a good husband.')
  She'll make him a good wife. ('She will become a good wife for him.') Cf. the Activity for Chapter 2.
  They played a little football with a little football. (*A little football* is determiner + non-count noun in the first case and determiner + adjective + count noun in the second.)
- when explaining ambiguity:
  She has a duty to perform. (*Perform* may be intransitive, or transitive, with *duty* as its hidden object.)
  (Cf. Chomsky's *Flying planes can be dangerous.*)

Such examples may also form an awareness-raising introduction to a point, and are more suitable for students of language than for learners. But they tick the memorability box. To find such succinct examples by authentic, corpora-based means would prove time-wasting and almost impossible.

5.6.5 Authenticity Revisited

Beyond all the practical issues described above in Sections 5.6.1–5.6.4 there is a wider theoretical issue, to do with the nature of authenticity in general in language teaching. What exactly do we mean by 'authentic'? To follow the argument made by Widdowson (1978), any utterance taken out of its context is no longer authentic (though it may be termed 'genuine' for its purely linguistic nature, rather than its communicative function). Widdowson is thinking of texts used with language learners here, but the same argument applies equally to examples. Simply by virtue of the fact that they are taken out of context and do not have the original communicative purpose they become inauthentic.

The problem with contrived examples, as we have seen above, is that they often sound unnatural, untypical or ridiculous. But there is surely a compromise: contrived examples which attempt to sound 'authentic' (in the same way that contrived texts can be constructed), using the native-speaker intuitions of what sounds natural.

5.6.6 A Third Approach

There is another type of exemplification, which in a sense lies between the two extremes, in that it may be 'contrived' – but not for the purpose of exemplifying language. I am referring to isolated examples from literary works which strike the (grammatically aware) reader as apposite. Over the years I have found numerous examples to be very useful in illuminating grammatical issues that I was working on.

In an article on the generic use of *you* (Berry 2009b), I presented the following telling examples:

- from Pete McCarthy (*McCarthy's Bar*, Hodder & Stoughton, 2000, p. 36):
    You can tell you're not Irish.
    where the two uses of *you* are not co-referential, the first being generic (similar to 'one') and the second specific (referring to the addressee).
- or from John Updike's *Terrorist* (Hamish Hamilton, 2006, p. 271), where the reference slips from the specific, involving the addressee, to the generic, excluding the addressee:
    A. *In a war, if a soldier beside you falls ... do you run and hide, or do you march on...?*
    B. *You march on.*

Writers seem to have the knack of teasing out interesting grammatical points; such effective examples would not be thrown up by a corpus, even if the original text were included in it. We might call them 'super-natural' examples. Here is one more telling example, from former Prime Minister Tony Blair, quoted in *Broken Vows: The Tragedy of Power* by Tom Bower (Faber & Faber, 2016):

When you are someone like me...

Chapter 9 deals specifically with personal pronouns and generic uses.

5.6.7 Contrived vs Authentic: A Summary

This section has taken a somewhat reactionary approach to the issue of grammatical exemplification, going against a trend that has been under way for the last thirty years, by suggesting that authentic examples are not the answer to every need for exemplification and are not, in a sense, totally authentic anyway. Where appropriate, according to the purpose or function, carefully contrived examples are acceptable, indeed at times preferable.

Nevertheless, the introduction of corpus-based examples has led to the following progress:

- We can now access a wide range of possible sources for examples.
- Writers of contrived examples are aware of the danger of them sounding unnatural and unrepresentative, and can aim to create realistic example.

5.7 Comparing Texts

To illustrate the above points we may make a comparison between two sample texts, from different grammars but on the same topic. The topic chosen is the use of the definite article to make formal generalisations, as in 'The lion is a...'. (See Chapter 7 for more on the uses of the articles.) The two texts, chosen for their different levels, are from: *A Comprehensive Grammar of the English Language* (Quirk et al. 1985: 282–283) and the *Collins Cobuild English Grammar* (2010: 49).

Here are the texts, firstly *Cobuild* (with the original underlining):

Nouns referring to plants and animals can be used in the singular with *the* when you are making a statement about every member of a species. For example, if you say *The swift has long narrow wings*, you mean that all swifts have long narrow wings.

The primrose can grow abundantly on chalk banks.
Australia is the home of the kangaroo.

Similarly, a noun referring to a part of the human body can be used with *the* to refer to that part of anyone's body.

These arteries supply the heart with blood.
... the arteries supplying the kidneys.

The is sometimes used with other nouns in the singular to make a statement about all the members of a group.

The article focuses on how to protect the therapist rather than how to cure the patient.

These uses are fairly formal. They are not common in ordinary speech. Usually, if you want to make a statement about all things of a particular kind, you use the plural form of a noun without a determiner.

Secondly, from Quirk et al. (1985, including original capitalisations), headed 'with singular noun phrases':

> *The* is rather limited in its generic function. With singular heads, it is often formal or literary in tone, indicating THE CLASS AS REPRESENTED BY ITS TYPICAL SPECIMEN:
>
> > A great deal of illness originates in *the mind*.
> > No one knows precisely when *the wheel* was invented.
> > My colleague has written a book on *the definite article in Spanish*.
> > Marianne plays *the harp* very well.
>
> As the last example shows, names of musical instruments and also dances usually take the definite article:
>
> > *play the violin* [but: *play baseball*], *dancing the samba*.
>
> When the noun refers to a class of human beings, the typifying connotation of generic *the* can sound inappropriate:
>
> > ?*The Welshman is a good singer*. [cf. *Welshmen are good singers*.]
> > ?*The doctor is well-paid*. [cf. *Doctors are well-paid*.]
> > ?*As the child grows, it develops a wider range of vocabulary*.
>
> It is more appropriate when used to identify the typical characteristics of a class in terms of personality, appearance, etc.:
>
> > He spoke with the consummate assurance and charm of *the successful Harley Street surgeon*.
>
> [Note omitted]

5.7.1 Analysis

Quite apart from the 'facts' contained in these two accounts (and some could be challenged) there are some interesting differences, as well as similarities. They do not cover exactly the same material (see later in this section) but the length, surprisingly, is identical: 173 words. One would have expected Quirk et al. to spend much more space on this topic, given its extra size.

Depth. Given the length it is hard for Quirk et al. to have more refinement, but it does seem to be more concise and cover a wider remit. For example, it cites three problematic examples in order to show the limits of this use. The Cobuild text is rather repetitive, perhaps in order to drive home the main point:

'every member of a species'/'all the members of a group'/'all the things of a particular type'.

But it does include a comment about generalising with plural nouns without *the*, which is mentioned elsewhere in Quirk et al.[4]

Formality and acceptability. Both rather downplay the formal nature of this use and there is no mention of its written, academic/scientific, nature. The limits of acceptability of the use are brought into question in Quirk et al. by the employment of words such as '(in)appropriate'.

Modality and hedging. Ironically, both qualify the formality of this use: 'rather formal' in Cobuild and 'often formal' in Quirk et al. Apart from these cases there is qualification in both: 'usually', 'rather' and 'can sound' in the latter, and 'can be used' (twice), 'is sometimes used' and 'usually' in the former. As suggested above, hedging is found in a scientific grammar like Quirk et al., even though it might be thought that it would detract from its authority, but it uses different forms.

Personality. As would be suspected, the two grammars take a different approach. Cobuild uses *you* as well as the passive; as shown above, hedging with *can* only occurs with the passive, not with *you* (though this is common elsewhere). Quirk et al. is completely impersonal, but only uses the passive once, in a non-finite clause ('when used').

Sub-technical metalanguage and terminology. Cobuild uses fairly basic pedagogic metalanguage: 'singular', 'plural', 'nouns' and 'determiner' for terminology, and words such as 'statement' for sub-technical vocabulary. In Quirk et al. the metalanguage is quite different, as shown by the use of vocabulary such as 'class', 'specimen', 'typifying connotation' and 'names' (for referring to nouns), as well as scientific terms such as *generic, heads, take* (with distinct terminological meanings). More than anything it is this metalanguage which indicates that this grammar is intended for fellow linguists, whereas Cobuild is for teachers and perhaps advanced, grammatically schooled learners.

Examples. Making up examples for this use is a tricky business, as the three dubious examples in Quirk et al. demonstrate; it would be easy to overstep the line and create something unidiomatic. (Incidentally, I have my own doubts about these three examples; the third one is perfectly acceptable to me, given the right circumstances, whereas the second could only have a specific interpretation.)

In Quirk et al. all the examples but one sound contrived – the vagueness, simplicity of language and brevity indicate this. The last example sounds more authentic; the length and the phrase 'consummate assurance' suggests that no simplification has taken place. As for Cobuild, there may be a problem for learners with a word such as 'primrose'; surely they could have found an example with 'rose'. But in general the examples sound authentic, if abbreviated.

5.8 Conclusion

This chapter has tried to cover the many factors that are involved in the making of grammatical statements: the many choices that face grammarians and the decisions that they make, although sometimes unconsciously. It is not enough to get the facts right; it is important to present them appropriately. This is a vast and complicated enterprise, and an important one in that the way grammar is written (and spoken) affects how learners react to the text. This chapter has only scratched the surface and much more investigation is needed.

Activity

Compare my account of the uses of the present simple above in Section 5.2.3 with that in Swan (2016: 30–32), much adapted and abridged, and with letters replacing the numbers. Judging from the level of complexity, what are the different audiences that these accounts are aimed at? How do the uses in one map onto the other? Are any uses missed or too general?

(a) General time, timeless truths, as in:
   It always <u>rains</u> in September.
   Alice <u>works</u> for an insurance company.
(b) Non-progressive verbs, as in:
   I <u>like</u> this wine.
(c) Talking about the future in schedules:
   His train <u>arrives</u> at 11.46.
And in subordinate clauses:
   I'll kill anyone who <u>touches</u> my things.
(d) Series of events: demonstrations, commentaries instructions, stories, as in;
   First I <u>take</u> a bowl and <u>break</u> two eggs into it.
   Lydiate <u>passes</u> to Taylor...

Comment

As regards level of complexity, at first glance Swan's account may seem to be simpler because of the fewer uses. But as will be seen below, each use is quite complex and covers a fairly wide area. As regards the correspondence between the two accounts, there are a number of similarities and discrepancies. Firstly, Swan's (a) seems to correspond with my (1) and (2). It may well be that states and repeated events are merely two ends of a cline of usuality, and that therefore lumping the two into one is justifiable. Similarly, Swan's (c) seems to cover my (7) and (8), but while these two both have futurity in common, I would argue that they are distinct uses. Swan's (b) seems to be absent from my list, but in fact it corresponds to my (4), although it is expressed in formal rather than semantic terms; expressions of feelings or intentions are typical meanings of stative verbs. Finally, Swan's (d) seems to include my (5) and (6), but I would suggest that the two uses need to be distinguished because of the structural difference. Only use (3) in my account would seem to be absent from Swan's, but it could easily be incorporated into one of his uses. So overall, while the two accounts seem to cut up the cake in slightly different ways, it is still the same cake that they are cutting up.

Notes

1 METALANG 1 contained matching samples of eleven grammars, ten of which were pedagogic in nature, and one scientific (Quirk et al.'s *Comprehensive Grammar of the English Language*, 1985); the total size was approximately 85,000 words. A full list of the grammars can be found in Appendix 2.
METALANG 2 consisted of three pedagogic grammars in their entirety; together they amounted to approximately 245,000 words. There have been further editions of these grammars, but the style remains the same.
2 The Cobuild Direct Corpus was at the time a general corpus of approximately 57 million words.
3 The term 'personality' should be not to be confused with another application in psychology.
4 In fact, Quirk et al. do discuss generalisation in the following section in the context of plural nouns but it is not specifically formal, and Cobuild also talks about generalisation elsewhere.

References

Alexander, L. G. 1993. *Longman Advanced Grammar*. London: Longman.
Berry, Roger. 1998. Determiners: a class apart. *English Today* 53: 27–34.
Berry, Roger. 2000. 'Youser-friendly' metalanguage: what effect does it have on learners of English? *International Review of Applied Linguistics* 38: 195–211.
Berry, Roger. 2004. Awareness of metalanguage. *Language Awareness* 13/1: 1–16.
Berry, Roger. 2005. Who do they think 'we' is? Learners' awareness of personality in pedagogic grammars. *Language Awareness* 14/2–3: 84–96.
Berry, Roger. 2009a. The pedagogic grammarian's dilemma: modality and personality in grammatical description. *Studia Anglica Posnaniensis* 45/1: 117–135.

Berry, Roger. 2009b. 'You could say that': the generic second-person pronoun in modern English. *English Today* 23/3: 29–34.
Berry, Roger. 2018. *English Grammar: A Resource Book for Students*. 2nd edn. Abingdon: Routledge.
Biber, Douglas, Stig Johansson, Geoffrey Leech, Susan Conrad and Edward Finegan. 1999. *The Longman Grammar of Spoken and Written English*. Harlow: Longman.
Carter, Ronald and Michael McCarthy. 2005. *Cambridge Grammar of English*. Cambridge: Cambridge University Press.
Chalker, Sylvia. 1994. Pedagogical grammar; principles and problems. In Martin Bygate, Alan Tonkyn and Eddie Williams (eds) *Grammar and the Language Teacher*. Hemel Hempstead: Prentice Hall International, 31–44.
Collins Cobuild English Dictionary. 1995. London: HarperCollins.
Collins Cobuild English Grammar. Various editions. London: Collins.
Cook, Guy. 2001. 'The philosopher pulled the lower jaw of the hen': ludicrous invented sentences in language teaching. *Applied Linguistics* 22/3: 366–387.
Eastwood, John. 1994. *Oxford Guide to English Grammar*. Oxford: Oxford University Press.
Goatly, Andrew. 2000. *Critical Reading and Writing*. London: Routledge.
Hyland, Ken. 1998. *Hedging in Scientific Research Articles*. Amsterdam: Benjamins.
Hyland, Ken. 2001. Humble servants of the discipline? Self-mention in research articles. *English for Specific Purposes* 20: 207–226.
Ishiguro, Kazuo. 2015. *The Buried Giant*. London: Faber and Faber.
Leech, Geoffrey, Benita Cruickshank and Roz Ivanič. 2001. *An A–Z of English Grammar*. Harlow: Pearson Education.
Murphy, Raymond. 1994. *English Grammar in Use*. Cambridge: Cambridge University Press.
Quirk, Randolph, Sidney Greenbaum, Geoffrey Leech and Jan Svartvik. 1985. *A Comprehensive Grammar of the English Language*. Harlow: Longman.
Sinclair, John. 1991. *Corpus, Concordance, Collocation*. Oxford: Oxford University Press.
Swan, Michael. 1999. How much does correctness matter? In Roger Berry, Barry Asker, Ken Hyland and Martha Lam (eds) *Language Analysis, Description and Pedagogy*. Hong Kong: Hong Kong University of Science and Technology, 53–63.
Swan, Michael. 2016. *Practical English Usage*. Oxford: Oxford University Press.
Thomson, A. J. and A. V. Martinet. 1986. *A Practical English Grammar*. London: Oxford University Press.
Widdowson, Henry. 1978. *Teaching Language as Communication*. Oxford: Oxford University Press.
Widdowson, Henry. 1997. Metalanguage and interlanguage. In R. Hickey and S. Puppel (eds) *Language History and Linguistic Modelling (Volume II: Linguistic Modelling)*. Berlin: Mouton de Gruyter, 1887–1899.

6 *Grammar in Operation*

6.1 Introduction

This chapter brings together many of the insights in the preceding chapters by looking critically at implications for practices inside and outside the classroom. However, grammar in practice or operation is a vast field; a whole book could be devoted to it. So of necessity the chapter will take a number of snapshots of a selection of important areas:

- syllabuses;
- rules of thumb;
- exercises and activities (with a focus on gap-filling exercises);
- error correction;
- tests;
- attitudes and innovative approaches.

The case studies in Chapters 7–10 have more concrete examinations of how certain grammatical areas are dealt with in practice.

6.2 Syllabuses

In Chapter 1 we looked at a number of methods which espoused the idea of a grammatical syllabus, whether explicitly or not. Faced with the problem of how to structure a course, given the vast enterprise that constitutes learning a language, designers have always sought some guiding principle on which to base their lessons. Notions (time, etc.), functions (agreeing, disagreeing, etc.), situations (at the post office, etc.) and tasks (writing or implementing a recipe) have all been proposed at various times. But none has come close to rivalling the idea of a grammatical syllabus as the guiding principle. Why is this so? Because the grammatical syllabus has a solid backing in linguistic theory; the grammatical nature of language has been comprehensively explored. In contrast, where is the theoretical support for functions or notions? A theory of communication is nowhere near complete. Syllabuses of notions and suchlike tend to comprise purely a list with little rationale for ordering or inclusion.

This is not to say that the grammatical syllabus is without problems. This should not surprise us, given the vast amount of knowledge about grammar that is available. Since only a small part of this can appear in a course (even one lasting several years) there are bound to be debates about what to include and how to structure it. But again the issue of poor transmission arises (Section 3.7.2). The items for inclusion in most grammatical syllabuses seem to have been chosen with little regard for the scientific knowledge, especially recent developments, for example in verb and noun complementation. A recent study of ESP materials used in Hong Kong suggested that

> 'both textbook and grammar book writers need to pay more heed to the insights presented in the influential and authoritative descriptive grammars of recent years'. (Lee and Collins 2009: 51)

Then there is the problem of how to order the selected items. It is impossible to avoid introducing more advanced items alongside simpler items. For example, in the syllabus list below determiners (12) precede nouns (14) in their order of introduction. But as a word class determiners are more complex than nouns; in fact, it is impossible to introduce the one without the other. It is a chicken-and-egg situation.

We can identify a number of criteria to apply when selecting items and structures for inclusion and for their ordering (similar criteria have already been seen in Chapter 4 on terminology):

- Frequency: an obvious criterion, but one that needs to be treated with caution (see later in this section).
- Simplicity: certain structures are very complex (e.g. cleft sentences: *It's the humidity that I can't stand*), which raises the issue of whether to exclude them entirely on the grounds they are too difficult or to include them since they cannot be acquired otherwise.
- Systematicity: are rare structures nevertheless needed to complete a grammatical pattern or system, for example, the past perfect (it is extremely rare)?
- Contrastiveness: how different is the structure from the learners' L1?
- Utility: certain items may not be frequent but can they stand in for something else? For example, given the complexity in the use of *much* and *many*, *a lot of* can stand in for both.

6.2 Syllabuses

- Communicative value: will they be understood if misused? For example, retaining inversion in indirect questions (e.g. *Do you know where <u>is he</u>*) will not be misinterpreted. (Such forms are becoming normal in English as a Lingua Franca.)
- Idiosyncrasy within English: structures which, though rare, will cause difficulty for all learners regardless of their backgrounds (e.g. the past tense in *It's high time we <u>left</u>* or the irregularity of *aren't I* as a tag question; it should be *amn't I*).

As an example let us take one structure and apply the above criteria (where appropriate), namely to continuous/progressive forms. Although growing in frequency, as was pointed out in Section 3.2), they are still much less frequent than simple verb forms as well as being more complex syntactically (mistakes are common, such as the omission of the auxiliary: *I coming*), and yet they get a similar amount of space in syllabuses. However, this can be explained in terms of their systematicity – they are necessary for the completion of the verb system – and their contrastiveness; even closely related languages do not possess a similar form. They do not have a high utility or communicative value; the simple verb forms can stand in for them.

As an example of a syllabus we may take a look at one particular book from a widely used grammar course – Swan and Walter's *Oxford English Grammar Course, Volume 1: Basic* (2011). It is divided into twenty-two 'sections' (rather than 'units', since they are on average fifteen pages long and each has several focuses), namely:

1. *be* and *have*;
2. present tenses;
3. talking about the future (NB. There is no mention of a 'future' tense);
4. past tenses;
5. perfect tenses (i.e. the concept of 'aspect' is not introduced, as per Chapter 2);
6. modal verbs;
7. passives;
8. questions and negatives;
9. infinitives and *-ing* forms;
10. special structures with verbs (e.g. phrasal verbs);
11. articles: *a/an* and *the*;
12. determiners;
13. personal pronouns; possessives;
14. nouns;
15. adjectives and adverbs;

16 comparison;
17 conjunctions;
18 *if*;
19 relative pronouns;
20 indirect speech;
21 prepositions;
22 spoken grammar.

Overall this represents a fairly unexceptional selection and ordering of items, beginning with verbs and associated matters and then moving on to other word classes. We might note that almost half the book is devoted to verb phrases (Sections 1–10), with verb forms also figuring largely in Sections 18 and 20). This conforms to most approaches to description in that the verb phrase is seen as central to the construction of basic utterances.[1]

Progressive verb forms do not get a section to themselves, which is to be expected. Here as elsewhere they are subsumed under the headings of other verb forms (which might make for repetition or a lack of generalisation, but this cannot be avoided one way or other).

We can perhaps question the status of *if* (i.e. conditional sentences) as constituting a whole section and indirect speech as a category at all (see Swan's own comment in the case study in Chapter 10). Conditional sentences in descriptive theory are no more than one type of subordinate clause and follow the same rules as other conjunctions, especially those referring to time; the use of the present tense for future time reference is therefore nothing exceptional: *If he comes.../When he comes...* In addition, the sometimes-called 'third conditional' (*If I had...I would have...*) hardly merits inclusion, on the grounds of infrequency.

The main reason for including this structure (and perhaps reported speech as well) in syllabuses seems to be historical; 'that's the way it has always been done'. A 'canon' of grammatical items has been established and course designers depart from it at their peril, because teachers expect to find them in any course. Tag questions, another part of the canon, constitute another problematic area whose inclusion could be re-evaluated, as suggested in Section 3.5. If we were to invoke the principle of metalinguistic relativity, as discussed in Chapters 3 and 4, and were to start over again, we might end up with a somewhat different syllabus, though at a basic level it would probably be similar.

At a more advanced level, a case could be made for including the following structures, which currently get little mention in teaching materials:

- Certain 'unexpected' uses of personal pronouns, namely generic *you*, and *they* as singular, as described in the case study in

Chapter 9. Neither of these is included in the first volume of Swan and Walter (2011) but the former makes an appearance in the second volume, and the latter in the third volume. Given their frequency and distinctiveness in contrastive terms, an argument could be made for introducing them earlier.

- The ergative (also called 'middle voice', as opposed to passive and active voices). This is where a normally transitive verb is used intransitively but with the transitive object becoming the intransitive subject. For example, *your essay reads well* or *the door opened*. This structure can be used with many verbs and is quite common in English. It may confuse learners who are used to the normal transitive use of such verbs (especially speakers of European languages, where the equivalent may be a reflexive verb). This structure does not appear at all in Swan and Walter. A story exemplifying its value appears in Section 6.7.

6.3 Rules of Thumb

In general parlance a rule of thumb is a rule that is derived from experience rather than scientific knowledge and which may help to make simple decisions (e.g. as with the use of a thumb for measuring). In grammar teaching, rules of thumb are used by many teachers as a way of simplifying difficult points (though they may not always be aware of the extent of simplification). Rules of thumb are applied in various ways; they may begin a lesson on grammar – the deductive, explicit option mentioned in Section 1.3 – or they may be used to sum up – the inductive alternative. In those cases they are being used proactively, but they may also be used reactively. However, as Chapter 3 showed (Section 3.3), regardless of how they are used, many popular rules of thumb are based on shaky linguistics. So is there a place for them in teaching?

In a 1994 paper Michael Swan outlined six principles or criteria for the design of pedagogic language rules:

1 Truth: what we tell learners should be true or accurate. This was a charge levelled at several popular rules in Section 3.2 (for instance, 'In negative and interrogative sentences *any* should be used instead of *some*'). As a further example, see Thomson and Martinet (1980, cited in Swan 1994: 55):

> When the main verb of a sentence is in the past tense, verbs in subordinate clauses must be in a past sense also.

He notes that this statement is 'only true of certain kinds of subordinate clause in certain kinds of structure' (Swan 1994: 55). But, as he concedes, this criterion is likely to conflict with others, necessitating compromise.

2 Demarcation: the limits of usage of a particular item must be clearly shown. It is quite possible to be truthful about something but still be misleading. As an example Swan (1994: 55) again quotes Thomson and Martinet (1980):

> The present perfect continuous tense ... is used for an action which began in the past and is still continuing, or has only just finished.

This is undoubtedly true, but it is too general; it does not point out that other tenses (e.g. the present continuous) can be used in this way. The rule does not specify how the two tenses should be distinguished. Failure to demarcate structures properly can have negative consequences. I have personally encountered cases where rules for the use of continuous (progressive) forms have led to their overuse by learners whenever they were introduced to them.

3 Clarity: rules should obviously be clear to/easily understood by learners. While obvious, this is somewhat at odds with other criterion. See the discussion of circularity and complex language later in this section.

4 Simplicity. Again this is obvious, but both simplicity and clarity can be at odds with each other, as well as with accuracy. In Section 3.3 it was suggested that too much accuracy was being traded with some prominent rules in order to achieve simplicity, in particular the rule that says 'use *the* the first time you mention something and *the* the second time'.

5 Conceptual parsimony: rules should use the concepts and terms learners are already familiar with, if possible; this is why a term such as '-*ing* noun' is preferable to 'gerund', because 'noun' will already have been encountered, as well as -*ing* in the context of verb forms and adjectives.

6 Relevance: rules given should respond to the particular needs and situation of learners. Swan gives the following examples of invented errors by learners from different L1 backgrounds which on the surface might seem to be identical:

> *My sister lives in Belgrade. She is hairdresser.*
> *My sister Marie-France lives in Lyon. She is hairdresser.*

In both cases the correction would be to insert 'a' in front of 'hairdresser'. But a rule of thumb that is helpful to the respective learners would be different. In the first case, with a Serbian speaker (whose L1 does not possess articles), the explanation would cover the fact that singular countable noun phrases need a determiner (and if no other is available then 'a' must be used), while in the latter, with a French learner, the much more focused rule would say 'articles are used when describing someone's profession'.

Two particular problems which would fall under Swan's headings of clarity and simplicity may be mentioned here: the use of over-complex language (i.e. don't use language more complex than the phenomenon being described); and circularity, whereby the structure being described is actually used in the description.

As regards the latter, two of the hardest areas to describe without falling foul of circularity are: the forms of comparative and superlative adjectives (Chapter 8 on this area gives an example), and continuous/progressive forms, as in this description (or similar) that I have heard many times:

> The present progressive refers to something that <u>is going</u> on.

Clearly the learner must already be able to understand the present progressive in order to understand the definition. So what is the point of the definition? (Not to mention the fact that the present progressive doesn't always refer to something 'going on'; it can refer to future plans.)

The answer is to seek a noun to replace the verb which captures the essence of the form, and there is such a noun (at least for this particular meaning):

> The present progressive refers to something <u>in progress</u>. (Or a plan for the future that is 'in progress'.)

Dependent on the level, it is not certain that the learner will know what 'in progress' means, but it is surely better than the circularity of the previous definition.

Of course, most such rules will be given in the learner's L1, so there will be no problem with the language used, or with circularity. However, another problem then arises: namely, that learners will come to associate some form in their L1 with the L2 target form because it has been used in the rule or explanation.[2] In the absence of rules, learners may make up their own, as is demonstrated in Section 7.5 in respect of article usage.

Swan believes that rules of thumb are in general useful – if they are well designed. Evidence that even inaccurate rules may be seen as useful comes from the study cited in Section 3.3.1 (Berry 2014), where some learners said they preferred demonstrably incorrect rules to nothing. Clearly, more research is required, but surely this should not hold back the search for more accurate formulations.

On another dimension, we should also bear in mind the interaction of the content of the rule with issues of modality and personality, as described in Chapter 5. This can influence the way rules are formulated and how well they are received. As regards the expression of 'personality', there are several options. Taking one rule as an example, the teacher could say:

1. The continuous <u>is not used</u> with verbs such as *want* and *like* which suggest a state.
2. We <u>do not use</u> the continuous with verbs such as *want* and *like* which suggest a state.
3. You <u>do not use</u> the continuous with verbs such as *want* and *like* which suggest a state.

As was pointed out in Section 5.4, option 1 – the impersonal option – contains the most difficult formulation grammatically, i.e. the passive, but it may be what learners expect. The personal options have their own problems. Option 2 may sound very distant, and imply a distinction between L1 speakers or teachers (the experts) and learners. In contrast, learners may find option 3 (the so-called youser-friendly formulation) too direct; they may wonder 'why am I being addressed'?

6.4 Exercises and Activities

Exercises and activities (the latter implying more freedom and less structure) come in many shapes and sizes but they all have the aim of encouraging practice in a selected item. In all grammatically based methods and approaches there is an assumption that learners should produce or select the form in focus, hopefully after they have been exposed to it and understood it (but this is not always the case). Such practice relies heavily on production; comprehension exercises on particular grammatical points are rare. (But see the case studies in Chapters 7–10.)

First of all, we must distinguish different types of grammar exercise and activity. There are the much-criticised automatic or controlled exercises characteristic of audiolingual drills and the practice stage of presentation/practice/performance (PPP) methodology (see Chapter 2), in which one form is to be turned into another without any reference to a situation or context. There is only one possible answer; for instance, a present tense is to be transformed into the past via a prompt. For example:

We go to the cinema every week. (YESTERDAY) *In fact, we went to the cinema yesterday.*

Then there is the more meaningful or free type of exercise in which learners have to think before they answer because there is more than one possible answer; even if they have just been taught a particular form, it may not be appropriate in every item. This type of exercise/ activity is characteristic of communicative/task-based teaching and the production stage of PPP as described in Section 1.3. The creative vs conventional distinction outlined in Chapter 2 is also relevant here.

However, meaningful or creative exercises are not without issues themselves. The point is: meaningful to whom? Just because there is some choice does not mean that the exercise replicates real life in a meaningful way. Widdowson's (1978) distinction between authenticity and genuineness, as discussed in Section 5.6.5, applies here. The language of a text or an activity may well be original (i.e. not contrived), but if taken away from its origin and thrown into the classroom it is in some way incomplete; it is genuine language but not fully authentic. In any case, is it really justifiable to expect classroom activities to mirror 'real life'? Isn't the classroom itself part of real life, with its own 'communicative' value?

To illustrate these points let us examine one particular and very common type of exercise.

6.4.1 Gap-Filling Exercises

Gap-filling exercises are very popular in EFL teaching; they are easy to produce and applicable to some of the most difficult and frequent areas of English grammar, such as the tenses and the articles. The recipe is simple: take a text (presumably authentic rather than scripted) and remove all of the instances of the item being practised. This is not quite as simple as it sounds; for articles, gaps need to be made where there is no article in front of nouns (the so-called zero article). For verb phrases there are often intervening adverbs in the so-called middle position (*They have not yet responded*), so where is the gap to be left?

But beyond these technical issues there are a number of philosophical problems with such exercises, the first one being redundancy. Learners may well reason as follows: I am told that I can complete this exercise by looking at the rest of the text; all the information for comprehension is contained there. But if that is so, why bother filling in the gaps? In other words, gap-filling reinforces the notion that a lot of grammar is redundant.

However, that is not always the case. In many gap situations the inserted item adds to or distinguishes meanings; there may be a choice between two possibilities. In other words, creativity rather than convention (see Section 2.4) is involved. But of course the text does not belong to the learners so how do they know what meaning is intended? As a result, they may be obliged to look for formal rather than semantic criteria in making their choice.

As an example, take exercises which practise the difference between the present perfect and past tense when referring to past events. This is a major problem for many learners (not to mention academics[4]), and practice grammars devote space to contrasting the two, with gapfilling being one obvious exercise format. Usually only one of the two is possible but not always, as the following item shows:

"*Where's Ken?*" "*He ... out. He'll be back in about an hour*" (Murphy: 27)

The answer in the key is *has gone* (or *'s gone*) but *went* is also perfectly feasible. Grammarians need to be constantly on the lookout for unintended alternatives. A similar example of a gapfilling exercise concerning the use of articles is given in Section 7.6.

There are various modifications of a straightforward gapfill. In one a multiple choice is offered for each gap, thereby restricting the learners' problem. In another, reverse gapfill, it is the focused item itself that is given and an associated item that is missing. For example, with noun phrases it is usually the article that is omitted, but it is also possible to omit the noun, thereby emphasising the close link between the two. See Section 7.7.5 for an example of this.

6.4.2 Other Types of Exercise

Before moving on we should perhaps consider other exercise types that may be relevant to grammar; drills/transformation exercises have already been discussed:

- Multiple choice. This is a very difficult format to devise; it is hard to find decent distractors, though this may be easier with verb phrase options. And there is always the argument that by presenting incorrect forms mistakes may be encouraged. Therefore this format is more suited to carefully constructed tests.
- Translation. Despite its unfortunate association with the grammar-translation method (described in Section 1.3) this is still a major activity for learners around the world, particularly those engaged on academic courses at a tertiary level.
- Analysing concordance lines. First proposed by Tim Johns (1991), under the heading of 'data-driven learning', this sees the use of sets of concordance lines as a useful means of

practising particular grammatical (and vocabulary) points. Concordance lines derived from electronic corpora offer an easily obtained concentration of examples of the desired form (compared to, say, contrived texts with multiple examples of the same form). They offer a genuine text, although it cannot be totally authentic, since the original communicative purpose has been lost. The difficulty of language and culture involved makes them only suitable at an advanced or teacher-training level (and even then it may be necessary to edit them). See Berry (1994) for words of caution on their use, and Berry (2015) for an extended exploitation based on key lexico-grammatical items.
- Identifying and perhaps correcting erroneous sentences. This technique has been used for many years in the school-leaving exam in Hong Kong.
- Quizzes. These can be extremely authentic and motivating. Chapter 8 exhibits a quiz on comparative and superlative adjectives. Ur (2009: 41) has a similar activity; including the following question:

Which is the larger country: Russia or China?

Similar questions are posed regarding other factual matters, including superlatives. This can be taken a stage further by inviting learners to make up their own quiz questions, perhaps with a prompt (e.g. 'river' – 'which is the longest river in the world?') The only problem is that quizzes involving other grammatical features are not always so easy to devise.

There is a myriad of further formats for which there is no room for discussion here.

6.5 Error Correction

Here we need to make a distinction between the correction of speech and of writing. Nevertheless, similar pedagogic issues apply to both: does it do any good? does it demotivate learners? What is the point of the activity? Is it designed to encourage fluency or to emphasise accuracy (and eradicate mistakes)? It is well known that too much correction can inhibit learners, can make them anxious when required to produce language. Pedagogic considerations are uppermost when it comes to deciding whether and how to correct.

We saw in Chapter 4 an example (from Tsui 1995: 33) where the judicious use of terminology (with learners who were familiar with it) allowed the successful correction of an error (the incorrect use of a verb form after a modal). This constituted an explicit form of correction, and presumably it was appropriate to the purpose of the lesson, given that it took up a fair amount of classroom time. A more implicit form, known as recasts, can be used in situations where the teacher does not wish to focus on accuracy too obviously. In this the teacher picks up a learner's spoken error and recasts it correctly as if it were a part of natural conversation. For instance, if a learner says 'I go to the cinema last night', the teacher might retort 'Oh, I didn't know you went to the cinema last night. What did you see?' But despite the best attempts of teachers to make recasts sound natural, learners generally realise that they are being corrected, that accuracy is the goal. (And, as with any error, a generalisation may be missed by simply giving the correct form.)

So much for spoken correction. Written correction, increasingly carried out online, allows for more time and consideration, but it can be equally daunting and demotivating for the learner. The same issues as with spoken correction apply: how to give learners appropriate advice without causing harm? Should everything be corrected, with the correct forms inserted in the text? There are several arguments against this (apart from its demotivating effect). Firstly, though the error is obvious, in many cases it is not possible to say what the correct form is; there may be several possibilities. Secondly, there are often multiple, possibly interdependent, errors in the same sentence. Attempts at total correction may result in gobbledegook.

Beyond this, learners may switch off after a quick glance at the text, and not pay any attention to the exact nature of the error, hence missing out on any learning opportunity. By doing all the work for them, the correction discourages any involvement on their part. This has led to arguments for the use of guided correction in order to involve them – for the use of a coding system whereby the location of the actual error is highlighted in some way and a symbol, usually a capital letter, is placed in the margin to identify the grammatical type of error; for example, A for articles, WO for word order, V for verb phrase construction, T for tense, and so on. (Areas other than grammar are catered for by such a system, e.g. spelling.)

Coding systems are not without their problems. Some codes may be beyond the competence of the learner, and the appearance of multiple corrections can again be demotivating. Some errors may be hard to indicate since they affect longer sequences. Coding systems need to be tailor-made for the level and L1 background of the learners; and at times the temptation to correct everything (if possible) should be resisted; certain types of error, e.g. tenses, can be focused on.

6.6 Tests

When the teaching and learning (theoretically) is done, the obvious step is to check it. Language tests (or exams) have many roles. They range from the spot test at the end of a class to check on progress to multinational, multi-skill, high-stakes tests such as IELTS and TOEFL.

There are a number of criteria used in designing and evaluating tests, the most important of which are:

- Reliability: would two markers (or the same marker at different times) arrive at the same score? Essay-style tests are notoriously unreliable.
- Validity: is the test actually testing what it says it aims to test? Many grammar tests lack 'purity' in that they are of necessity prompted by written language, which involves some limited reading comprehension. A typical format requires learners to identify and/or correct an error typical of the L2 learners' background. However, testees may fail to perform because they have not understood a vocabulary item, rather than lacking proficiency in the grammatical item. Since the text is not theirs the error exhibited may be one that they themselves would not make.
- Ease of marking: with millions of people taking some tests annually, how can marking be speeded up? As a general rule, the easier a test is to mark, the harder it is to devise (if done properly) and the less valid it is.

These criteria are often at odds with each other. A test which is easy to mark reliably (e.g. online), such as multiple choice, will usually have to compromise on validity. Thus designing tests of grammar requires great expertise in testing. But this is not the only requirement; a full knowledge of grammar on the part of the setter is also needed. The examples in this section will show that both requirements are not always met.

There are a number of constituencies at whom tests are aimed: L1 speakers, L2 learners and teachers. These are dealt with one by one.

6.6.1 Tests of L1 Speakers

For L1 speakers tests of grammar may be involved as part of their (written) language awareness education (see Section 1.6). As indicated, these concentrate mainly on written language. However, Crystal (2017: 258) cites the following test item in which testees are required to insert a pair of commas into the sentence below 'to clarify the meaning':

My friend who is very fit won the 100-metre race.

Clearly, the answer that the test seeks is

My friend, who is very fit, won the 100-metre race.

However, as Crystal points out, the original sentence, though perhaps unlikely, is perfectly grammatical and meaningful. It is quite possible that there is another friend who is not fit. The test designer appears not to be familiar with the difference between so-called defining relative clauses (as per the original) and non-defining relative clauses, as in the desired correction. It also has a problem with validity, since demonstrating grammatical awareness relies on a knowledge of punctuation.

The issue of a lack of grammatical awareness on the part of the designer is one which crops up time and time again in tests of grammar (and, as we have seen, in the design of exercises, though in that case the stakes are not so high, and there is a teacher present who may be able to mitigate the situation).

6.6.2 Tests of L2 Learners

There is a multiplicity of tests of grammar aimed at L2 leaners, with several different aims. Two of the most obvious aims are to check on proficiency and to check on progress. The former takes (hopefully) a snapshot at a certain point; this includes placement tests and school-leaving exams, not to mention forward-looking exams evaluating a person's potential for university study. The latter requires a comparison of two tests at two different points in time.

As with L1 speakers, in either case the learner's grammatical ability may be tested in conjunction with writing, particularly in essays, where learners have more freedom to express themselves, even though such an activity is not entirely authentic or valid (who otherwise writes essays nowadays?). In addition, aware that they are being tested on their grammatical ability as well as on their written fluency, learners may exploit such freedom to avoid grammatical structures that they know are problematic for them (e.g. complex verb phrases). This is why, in the marking process, credit must be given not only for grammatical accuracy but also for range and complexity of structures.

To avoid such problems, more controlled objective formats may be used. Multiple-choice tests are popular since they are easy to mark, especially by machines; but what they gain in ease and reliability of marking can be compromised by a lack of validity, especially if the distractors are not well chosen.

6.6 Tests

One other aim of testing learner (or indeed teacher) proficiency comes in the field of second language acquisition studies, as described in Section 1.4. Such tests tend to be much more open to scrutiny. We have already seen that there are problems with tests used by SLA researchers: tests that failed the criteria of good test design and proper knowledge of English grammar. These problems do not seem to have been completely resolved in more recent studies. Take this example used in a test of adult learners of Russian and Korean (Ionin et al. 2004):

> (man to security guard) *Can you help me? I am looking for (a/the/–) train; I think it came in 10 minutes ago.*

This is characterised as [-definite, +specific) so presumably the answer is 'a (train)'. But obviously 'the train' is a highly plausible answer if the speaker considers that they and the guard share the same presupposition. As with the problems with gap-filling exercises, this item does not display a full awareness of English grammar.

Research has also been carried out into learners' explicit metalinguistic knowledge (in an attempt to see if it is linked to proficiency). Various types of prompt have been used (see Berry 2014), for example, explaining errors, or giving a sentence or text where subjects have to identify a given term, e.g. 'verb'. However, as outlined above, designers need to pay attention both to issues of good test design and to the grammatical facts.

An example of both kinds of failing can be found in Elder's (2009) 'Metalinguistic Knowledge Test'. In one part of the test subjects are given a text and asked to identify among others 'the definite article'. However, many subjects will be able to give the answer 'the' without needing a text. And others may not be familiar with the term 'definite article', being accustomed to it being simply referred to iconically (see Section 1.4) as 'the'. What subjects are therefore being tested on is their knowledge of metalinguistic terminology, not their explicit knowledge of grammar. In other words, the test's validity is in question. This kind of item, requiring the identification of grammatical forms based on a terminological prompt, is more suited to situations where there is no one-to-one correspondence between term and form, e.g. identifying a relative clause introduced by 'that' when there are other uses of 'that' in the text.

The other part of the same test requires the subjects (teachers) to account for the mistakes in erroneous sentences – not by explaining them verbally, but by selecting from a menu of options. (This is a partly valid technique – the point being to tap into metalinguistic knowledge without interference from a lack of productive ability; however, it is not a task that teachers are ever confronted with.) One item contains the following supposedly erroneous sentence:

> *If Jane had asked me, I would give her some money.*

The 'correct' option, from a selection of four, was (somewhat elliptically phrased):

> When 'if' clause is in the past perfect tense, main clause verb is in the past conditional.

This is clearly suggesting that the correct form was:

> If Jane had asked me, I would <u>have given</u> her some money.

But actually there is nothing wrong with the original sentence, as I pointed out in Berry (2014). It is quite possible that the opportunity for asking occurred in the past, while the contingent event (the giving) occurs in the future. It would seem the designer has bought into the long-discredited three- or four-conditional approach (see Chapter 3 for such misconceptions). The original sentence is actually a mixture of the so-called third and second conditionals and such mixtures are quite common (e.g. *If we <u>had won</u>, we'd <u>be</u> top*). At least in this case the test instrument was open to scrutiny; many SLA researchers think that the grammatical basis of their tests should go unquestioned.

As suggested, there is a pattern emerging here, in that test designers present sentences for correction, without realising that the original may be perfectly grammatical.

There is another, broader, problem here stemming from the concept of 'backwash' in testing, by which the test becomes more important than the teaching that precedes it and adversely influences it – it 'washes back' over it, as with a boat's wake. In terms of grammar, there are certain items which are easier to test and which therefore are more likely to appear in an exam, if there is one. Thus teachers will spend more time on these areas, to the detriment of a full coverage. This is even more detrimental when it comes to the presentation of incorrect grammar rules, as highlighted in Section 3.3. Many times I have been told by teachers that they know the rule is wrong but that they have to teach it because it may be exploited in the exam.

6.6.3 Tests of Teachers

Most language teaching institutions around the world, whether at the level of state education or private school, require a qualification to be acquired by would-be teachers. In some pedagogic ability is paramount; in others it is linguistic (including grammatical) proficiency that counts.

As an example of the latter we may take the Language Proficiency Assessment for Teachers of English as an example (Coniam and Falvey 2018). Though it is an assessment rooted in the needs of contemporary Hong Kong, it has several implications for attempts to test teachers anywhere. The assessment arose out of the specific circumstances of

ELT in Hong Kong at the end of the twentieth century. Throughout the 1980s and 1990s there had been, at the behest of government, a vast expansion of ELT in schools in the territory. However, the demand had not been matched by a supply of trained and qualified English Language teachers. Instead, the demand was filled by recruiting teachers from other subjects across the curriculum – teachers who, though qualified in their own subjects and mostly having studied them in English, were lacking in knowledge about the language and whose proficiency in the language varied. The learners' exposure to their teachers' limited English was widely seen as the cause of their so-called Chinglish.

This is what led, controversially, to the establishment of LPATE: a high-stakes raft of papers that would determine whether the teachers of English (in primary as well as secondary schools) would be allowed to continue as such. It consists of a number of papers covering various areas of language proficiency, including one on writing and grammar. Part Two of this paper on writing and grammar consisted of two sections: the first where candidates were asked to identify and correct errors in a (partly authentic but somewhat-manipulated) learner essay; the second where they were asked to explain such errors (originally the same errors as in the first part; latterly a different set, to avoid teachers being punished twice for the same failing).[5]

It was established that the ability to explain errors consisted of two parts: one, the localisation or classification of the error, which would probably involve terminology (the rubric for the paper advises the use of terminology); and two, a reason for the error, as in this hypothetical example of an explanation (Berry 2014: 30):

The <u>present perfect</u> is wrong as the event has <u>no relevance to present time</u>
LOCATION/CLASSIFICATION   REASON/JUSTIFICATION

This insight led to the abandonment of a (fairly unreliable) system of scales and descriptors (used elsewhere in the exam) for a more reliable and objective marking system.

However, the question of validity still remains. The question is: what is the aim of such items? What exactly is being tested? The distinction raised in Chapter 1 between pedagogic and linguistic teacher skills is relevant here since it might be thought that this is a test of a teacher's ability to explain errors to learners in an appropriate way. However, the extensive list of terms given in a sample paper as part of possible answers includes several of a highly scientific nature (as described in Section 4.2), such as 'subordinating conjunction', 'non-defining relative clause' and 'adverbial phrase'. This makes it clear that this is a test of a teacher's linguistic knowledge rather than of their pedagogic ability.

Items in the test itself are not without design problems. In one an underlined student error 'I remember to feel very frightened' was given to testees, who were given the following frame and asked to fill in the gaps:

> The problem is with the (a) _____ 'to feel'. It should be replaced by 'feeling' because the writer wishes to describe (b) _____ rather than an intended action.

(Gap-filling had been introduced to make the marking more objective, since in the previous open format many different responses had to be evaluated.)

The intended answers were (a) 'infinitive' (= location/classification, as above) and (b) 'a mental state' (or a similar phrase; = reason/ justification, as above). The problem lay with the answer for (a), since it could be given without reference to the actual error; a teacher could look at the prompt and work out that it was an infinitive. Indeed, 'verb' would also need to have been accepted.

6.7 Attitudes to Grammar: Innovative Activities

Everything so far in this chapter has unavoidably been about the cognitive domain: what has been learnt, what has not; what is correct, what is not. But we also need to consider the affective domain: what learners think about grammar and how they react to it. Krashen himself allowed for such a dimension with his 'affective filter', as mentioned in Chapter 1. This was meant to account for the fact that some learners expect an explicit formal focus and would be demotivated if this were not present. But for many others grammar is regarded as a dull topic, involving the memorisation of rules or the imposition of boring exercises. If grammar is to be taught explicitly, learners need to be motivated; so teachers need to 'sell' grammar.

One point has already been made above about the selling of grammar: materials should avoid giving the impression that grammar is full of redundancy. Though redundancy is a fact of grammar, exercises such as gap-filling reinforce this impression. Teachers and materials should show learners the role the grammatical item has in communication; often explanations do not do this. Take this example from one of the texts compared in Chapter 5:

> For example, if you say *The swift has long narrow wings*, you mean that all swifts have long narrow wings.

My reaction to this was: if the two mean the same, what is the point? But of course, they do not mean the same, or have the same function. 'The swift...' allows the writer to give the statement an academic tone. The concepts of creativity and convention (see Section 2.4) can explain this, in that learners have a choice between the two forms according to the impression they wish to make. Even apparently wholly conventional items, such as the indefinite article, can have a role in the determination of meaning, as Section 2.4 showed.

The use of dull, contrived texts and dialogues, where the grammatical item being introduced is repeated ad infinitum, are mostly a thing of the past. Or should be since there are many resources offering a variety of authentic and enjoyable activities – for example, Ur (2009) or Celce-Murcia and Hilles (1988). The classic works by Rinvolucri (1985) and Wright et al. (2006) offer many interesting activities based on the idea of games – an activity that would have been thought heretical not so many years ago.

A well-known example of a game is where learners start off with a lengthy sentence and in turn remove one word at a time while attempting to retain a grammatical sentence – a kind of word 'Jenga'. A point is lost when a removal creates ungrammaticality. (So with a sentence such as *The people are very unhappy about this new tax* 'the', 'very' and 'new' could safely be removed; this can lead to discussion about grammatical principles.) But such games should be chosen with care according to their level and relevance. The same applies to authentic extracts from literature, poems especially; they too need to be well chosen and used with the right groups of learners.

The devising of texts with a particular learning point in mind does not need to be dull and repetitive. Stories and dramas, may have a motivating, entertaining effect. An example, perhaps more appropriate for advanced levels, concerning the use of the ergative as described in Section 6.2 on syllabuses, is given below. A further text is to be found as an activity.

A story: The Broken Window, or how grammar can get you out of trouble

This story originally appeared in Berry (2012: 164–165) as an illustration of the ergative. It was suggested in Section 6.2 that this structure, whereby a normally transitive verb is used intransitively but with the transitive object becoming the intransitive subject, might be a worthy addition to traditional syllabuses at an advanced level.

The broken window, or how grammar can get you out of trouble

> Four boys were playing football in their school playground – where it was not allowed. One of them mis-kicked the ball and it smashed a window in one of the schoolrooms.
> Now they were honest lads and, instead of running away and hiding, they decided to report the broken window to the principal. But first they discussed how to describe the breakage.

The first one, who was a little naïve linguistically, suggested *I'm sorry; we have broken the window*. But the other three said that it was much too obvious; it would get them into lots of trouble.

The second student, who had taken a basic course in English grammar and knew something about the passive, suggested *The window has been broken by us*. 'It focuses more on the thing affected than on those responsible for the action', he said. But the other two said it was still too obvious who was responsible.

The third student, more advanced, knew that the actor could be omitted in the passive. So he suggested *The window has been broken*. The first two nodded their agreement, but the fourth said 'But the principal will still know that someone did it and will ask "Who by?"'

Now this fourth student had read this book and so he knew all about the ergative, and how it could be used to present an action as a happening without any 'actors'. So he suggested *The window has broken*. The other three looked at him in awe, and agreed. So that is what they said when they went to see the principal; and the principal just nodded and thanked them for telling him.

6.8 Conclusion

This chapter has covered areas that might be thought rather unrelated, and which are generally the responsibility of different groups of people: syllabuses, tests, classroom activities. However, what they have in common is that they are all practical applications of grammar. The field is an extensive one; several more didactic devices could have been included, such as timelines. These will have to await another study. Two final points may be stressed here:

1 that it is necessary to get the grammar right throughout all these applications;
2 that it is not enough to get the grammar right; it must be sold to learners.

Activity

Read the following short play (or act it out) and work out what the grammatical point and how to explain it. (See Section 2.8.1 and the Activity at the end of Chapter 2 for an account of grammatical functions.)

A Drama: Call Me a Taxi

Scene: in front of a five-star hotel. It is raining.

GUEST 1 (to concierge):   Excuse me – could you call me a taxi?
CONCIERGE: Are you sure, sir?
GUEST 1:   Of course. Call me a taxi!
CONCIERGE: Alright, sir. You're a taxi!

GUEST 1:   Thank you. (He trots off, manipulating an imaginary steering-wheel and making revving noises before coming to a sudden halt and looking back over his left shoulder.) Where to, guv? (Pause.) Right you are. (He turns back and trots off.)
GUEST 2   (approaching the concierge, having witnessed the whole scene): Would you be so kind as to call me a genius?
CONCIERGE: Are you sure, sir?
GUEST 2:   Absolutely. Go ahead – call me a genius!
CONCIERGE: As you wish, sir. (He steps forward and raises an arm.) Genius! (Someone looking remarkably like Einstein rushes past.) Genius! (A Leonardo look-alike races by. The concierge turns to the guest.) I'm sorry, sir. It's the rain – they won't stop. (© Roger Berry 2020)

Comment

The point of this is to demonstrate two different meanings and uses of the verb 'call': one as a ditransitive verb with two objects (= 'Call a taxi for me'), the other as what is sometimes called a 'link transitive' verb (see also Berry 2018: 115–117), where the meaning is 'Say that I am a taxi'. A rather arcane point grammatically, but one that is relevant at an advanced level when complex verb patterns are introduced.

Notes

1 The second book in the series has the same twenty-two areas, but at a more advanced level. The third book recycles some of these issues while adding more complex structures such as noun clauses.
2 A well-known example of overusing translational equivalents in rule of thumb is the misleading association of imperfective verb forms in Slavonic languages with progressive forms in English. For example, in Croatian the imperfective verb *čekati* – 'to wait' – (as opposed to its perfective counterpart *pričekati*), can be used to express both the simple and progressive forms in English:

> *Čekam* autobus. I *am waiting* for the bus.
> *Čekam* autobus svaki dan. I *wait* for the bus every day.

3 A further question asked why they thought incorrect rules were useful; some said that they were better than nothing - i.e. they had come to expect some form of explicit instruction.
4 Should one say, in introducing a quotation *As X said*, or *As X has said*? A delicate issue involving creativity.
5 I was briefly Chief Examiner for this paper, and made several of the recommendations that led to the changes described.

References

Berry, Roger. 1994. Using concordance printouts for language awareness training. In D. Li, D. Mahoney and J. Richards (eds) *Exploring Second Language Teacher Development*. Hong Kong: City Polytechnic of Hong Kong, 195–207.
Berry, Roger. 2014. Learners' use of and reaction to incorrect rules of thumb. Paper delivered at the 12th Biennial Conference of the Association for Language Awareness, Hamar, Norway.
Berry, Roger. 2015. *From Words to Grammar*. Abingdon: Routledge.
Berry, Roger. 2018. *English Grammar: A Resource Book for Students*. 2nd edn. Abingdon: Routledge.
Celce-Murcia, Marianne and Sharon Hilles. 1988. *Techniques and Resources in Teaching Grammar*. New York: Oxford University Press.
Coniam, David and Peter Falvey (eds). 2018. *High-Stakes Testing: The Impact of the LPATE on English Language Teachers in Hong Kong*. Singapore: Springer.
Crystal, David. 2017. *Making Sense: The Glamorous Story of English Grammar*. London: Profile Books.
Elder, C. 2009. Validating a test of metalinguistic knowledge. In R. Ellis, S. Loewen, C. Elder, R. M. Erlam, J. Phelp and H. Reinders (eds) *Implicit and Explicit Knowledge in Second Language Learning, Testing and Teaching*. Bristol: Multilingual Matters, 113–138.
Ionin, T, H. Ko and K. Wexler. 2004. Article semantics in L2 acquisition: the role of specificity. *Language Acquisition* 12/1: 3–69.
Lee, Jackie and Peter Collins. 2009. English grammar: an investigation of Hong Kong ESL textbooks. *Hong Kong Journal of Applied Linguistics* 11/2: 51–70.
Johns, Tim. 1991. From printout to handout: grammar and vocabulary teaching in the context of data-driven learning. *ELR Journal* 4: 27–45.
Murphy, Raymond. 1994. *English grammar in Use*. 2nd edn. Cambridge: Cambridge University Press.
Rinvolucri, Mario. 1985. *Grammar Games: Cognitive, Affective and Drama Activities for EFL Students*. Cambridge: Cambridge University Press.
Swan, Michael. 1994. Design criteria for pedagogic language rules. In Martin Bygate, Alan Tonkyn and Eddie Williams (eds) *Grammar and the Language Teacher*. Hemel Hempstead: Prentice Hall International: 45–55.
Swan, Michael and Catherine Walter. 2011. *Oxford English Grammar Course Basic*. Volume 1: *Basic*, Volume 2: *Intermediate*, Volume 3: *Advanced*. Oxford: Oxford University Press.
Thomson, A. J. and A. V. Martinet. 1980. *A Practical English Grammar*. London: Oxford University Press.
Tsui, Amy M. B. 1995. *Introducing Classroom Interaction*. London: Penguin.
Ur, Penny. 2009. *Grammar Practice Activities*. 2nd edn. Cambridge: Cambridge University Press.
Widdowson, Henry. 1978. *Teaching Language as Communication*. Oxford: Oxford University Press.
Wright, Andrew, David Betteridge and Michael Buckby. 2006. *Games for Language Learning*. 3rd edn. Cambridge: Cambridge University Press.

7 Case Study 1
The Articles

7.1 Introduction

The following four chapters contain case studies of important areas of English grammar. Each one in its own way is critical of the current state of affairs, suggesting that pedagogic descriptions, and therefore pedagogic practices such as rules of thumb and exercises, are inadequate, and that by applying some of the principles outlined in the first six chapters improvements can be made. The first case study aims to present a critical investigation into current beliefs about, and practices involving, the English articles.

The definite article *the* and the indefinite article *a/an* are two of the most frequent words in English. *The* is by far the most frequent word in English while *a* and *an* together constitute the fifth most frequent word in most frequency counts. Together they make up almost 10 per cent of words in running texts. Moreover, most languages in the world do not possess anything that can be said to be equivalent (see Section 7.4) and therefore most EFL learners will have no point of reference when confronted by them. Mistakes in article usage are often the last sign that someone is not an L1 speaker. Furthermore, unlike most grammatical features they cannot be avoided in even the simplest controlled text; learners will encounter them from day one. Some form of explanation will be essential in any formal approach to teaching. However, the one that is usually given is highly misleading, as will be shown.

7.2 Understanding Articles

The articles, especially the definite article, have presented grammarians, as well as learners and teachers, with something of a headache over the years. In descriptive accounts they are usually discussed in terms of two distinctions to do with the concept of **reference**, i.e. what we are referring to or talking about. The articles do not have any referential meaning themselves, but they help noun phrases to refer to real-world entities. The first of these distinctions is between **specific** and **generic reference**, that is, whether reference is to a particular individual or group, or to all the members of a class denoted by the noun, i.e. generalising.

While by far the most common way of generalising in English is to use a plural noun phrase (<u>Bicycles</u> *can be lethal weapons*), both articles can, given the appropriate circumstances, be used for generic reference:

> <u>A bike</u> *can be a lethal weapon* (picking out one individual as representative of a class).
> <u>The bike</u> *was invented in the nineteenth century* (a formal, academic statement).

However, generic reference with the articles is comparatively rare, and it is specific reference to which most attention has been paid by grammarians. The following discussion concentrates on this.

The second distinction, as the labels given to these forms implies, is between two types of specific reference: **definite** and **indefinite reference**. *The* is said to confer definite reference on noun phrases while *a* and *an* are said to confer indefinite reference. The essence of the difference between the two is discussed in the following two sections.

7.2.1 The Indefinite Article

We can perhaps deal with the indefinite article first since its use is less problematic. Accounts usually identify a number of situations where it is used (apart from the generic use described in the previous section; see Berry 2018: 89):

- in introducing or establishing something in discourse: *Suddenly they heard <u>a gunshot</u>*;
- in referring to something not existing: *I'm looking for <u>a cheap flight</u>*. This use can be distinguished from the previous one because the pronoun used to refer back would be *one* ('Let me know if you find <u>one</u>') as opposed to *it* ('No one else heard <u>it</u>');
- in describing (but not referring to) someone or something: *She's <u>a teacher</u>*. (This use is often not matched in other languages with articles, e.g. in French *Elle est <u>professeur</u>*);
- in rates: *Take these three times <u>a day</u>*. (This use is interesting historically; see Note 2.)

7.2 Understanding Articles

A fifth possibility arises in cases where the indefinite article seems to be combined with other determiners, as in *such a* and *many a*, but these are best treated as single units.

The extent to which these uses are separate may be questioned. (See the discussions of lumpers and splitters in Section 5.2.1.) Indeed, there is one factor that unifies them all, and it is purely formal in nature. It can be expressed as a scientific rule:

> 'If the head of a noun phrase is singular and count, and if there is no other determiner, the indefinite article is obligatory.'

In other words, if you have a noun that is the most important word in a noun phrase and it is singular and countable then you must have at least one determiner; if no other is appropriate then use the indefinite article. In this way it may be seen, as I have termed it, as the 'default determiner' rather than the 'indefinite article'.

While this formulation is not for most learners, containing as it does several partly scientific terms and concepts ('head', 'noun phrase', 'count' and in particular 'determiner') it does cover all the instances of its use.[1] The difficulty comes in interpreting these terms. For example, which nouns are count/countable and which are non-count/uncountable? Many can be both; for example:

> *This puts the issue beyond doubt* (uncountable).
> *I have some doubts about this* (countable).

In this case there is little difference in meaning between the two, as in this further example (for more, see Berry 1993: 9–11):

> *Their marriage seems to be heading for (a) divorce.*

But in other cases there is a clear difference in meaning related to the grammatical difference (Berry 1993: 13–14):

> *...the cost of paper...*
> *...the cost of producing a paper...*
> *He's lost his reason.*
> *He didn't have a single reason to quit.*

It seems that the indefinite article can serve as a lexical marker, distinguishing meanings (cf. the case of *wood*, discussed in Section 2.4).

There are also pairs of nouns which appear to be in a 'symbiotic' relationship, the one countable, the other uncountable, but broadly having the same reference:

> *The room was full of machinery/machines.*

In other words, the difference between 'machinery' and 'machine' seems to be the same as that between the countable and uncountable interpretations of a word like 'divorce'. It sometimes seems that countability is determined by the presence/absence of the indefinite article, rather than reflecting the countability status of nouns.

This countable/uncountable distinction – and therefore the need for the indefinite article or not – can sometimes appear rather mysterious, especially to learners. Take this example:

She has expertise in <u>crisis management</u>.

Why not 'a crisis management' since 'crisis' is a count noun? The answer is that it is not the head; 'management' is, and of course it is non-count.

7.2.2 The Definite Article

Moving on to the definite article, we can at an early stage set aside some more idiomatic uses, such as its use with proper nouns, e.g. *the Thames, The Times* (a list of such cases is given in Berry 1993: 54–65 and Quirk et al. 1985: 288–297), and various uses with adjectives (*the rich/poor*, etc., e.g. *you're trying to defend <u>the indefensible</u>, <u>the sooner the better</u>*). We can also include here a use that Quirk at al. call 'sporadic' but which I prefer to call 'institutional' since it refers to institutions of human society such as forms of entertainment or transport:

Take <u>the train</u> – it's quicker than <u>the bus</u>.

Here we are not talking about specific buses or trains; rather we are comparing forms of transport. In contrast,

Let's go to <u>the theatre</u> tonight.

is potentially ambiguous, as Quirk et al. (1985: 269) point out, referring either to a particular theatre or to the form of entertainment.

This leaves us with a number of situations where the definite article has specific reference with common nouns. The following list is based on Quirk et al. (1985: 265–272), though I have split one usage into two and added one (Berry 2018); Celce-Murcia and Larsen-Freeman (1983: 177) and others give a similar list:

1 Immediate situation, e.g. *Where's <u>the</u> butter?*
2 Larger situation, e.g. *<u>The</u> President is going to make a speech.*

These two 'situational' uses involve knowledge of one's environment, and they are very common in spoken English. For example, if you are in a kitchen, you could expect *the fridge, the floor, the table, the light*, etc. If you are in a particular country, you could expect *the government, the economy, the president*, etc. What is sometimes called 'unique reference', as with *the sun* and *the moon*, is just an extreme extension of this.

3 Direct anaphora, e.g. *I ate a cake and a roll; the roll made me sick.*
4 Co-referential anaphora, e.g. *The first time I rode my bike, the machine fell apart.*
5 Indirect (or associative) anaphora, e.g. *The first time I rode my bike, the bell fell off.*

In these three uses 'anaphora' simply means referring back to something earlier in the text. In (3) it is the same noun, *roll*, in (4) it is the same referent but a different noun is used (*bike/machine*), while in (5) there is something associated with an already mentioned noun, something that could be expected (e.g. on a bike: *the seat, the handlebars, the bell*).

6 Cataphora, e.g. *The girls sitting over there are my cousins.*

Cataphora means referring forward; in this case it is the post-modification, 'sitting over there', which makes the reference of the noun identifiable.

7 'unique' adjectives, e.g. *He's the best person for the job.*

Sometimes pre-modification (that is, what precedes the noun in a noun phrase) can be the reason for definiteness. Superlative and similar adjectives (e.g. *first, next, same, only*), which give an idea of uniqueness, tend to have this effect (e.g. *Do you remember the first time we met?*)

8 the pre-emptive use, as in these examples:

> *The boy with the fair hair lowered himself down the last few feet of rock and began to pick his way towards the lagoon.* (The first line from the novel, *The Lord of the Flies*, by William Golding.)

This last case is a use that is typical of the first line of stories, where to all appearances an indefinite article would be correct since nothing has yet been introduced or established. Why does the writer not say 'A boy with fair hair'? Here the definite article is used to introduce something unknown to the reader. I called it the 'pre-emptive' use (Berry 1991, 2018: 90) because it seeks to create in advance, rather than reflect, a state of affairs; the reader's attention is being drawn to this pack of cigarettes because it is going to be significant. It is somewhat similar to the cataphoric use above; what makes the noun phrase definite is later information, rather than a postmodifying phrase.

Is there something that holds all of these uses together, as with the indefinite article? Previous attempts at establishing a unifying factor for all these specific uses of the definite article (excluding the idiomatic uses described above) were based on the idea that definiteness was equal to something being 'known', that if something was familiar then *the* should be used. This foundered on cases where the referent was either clearly unknown, particularly as in indirect anaphora above, or where the referent was arguably unfamiliar, as with the situational uses.

However, there is something to the idea of familiarity, as grammarians including Hawkins (1978) have pointed out. But in the case of indirect anaphora, it is the relationship between the two referents that is familiar or expected, not the referents themselves. Bikes have bells, as well as wheels, brakes, handlebars, etc.; cruise ships have crews, captains, passengers, decks, restaurants, etc. In both cases once the root idea has been introduced the associated items can be treated as definite without any need for prior mention. As regards situational uses, in a classroom you might expect the teacher, the students, the desks, the board; if you are already in that situation you do not need to introduce the nouns first; you can proceed directly to using *the*.

But it is not only what you as a speaker expect, it is what you expect your hearer to expect; it is the shared assumptions you have. And in both cases the assumptions and expectations may be invalid. There may be a place where bikes are not expected to have bells and so indirect anaphora would not apply, even if you wanted to refer to a bell. And there are certainly cases where classrooms do not have desks. A teacher from outside may ask 'Where are the desks?' and find that their expectations are incorrect. Breakdowns in conversation may also arise when situational assumptions are not met, as in this example where a visitor is asking for directions on a campus:

> A Can you tell me where the canteen is?
> B The canteen? I can tell you where there is a canteen. (Because there is more than one.)

Given all this complexity is there anything in common to all these uses? There is, but it is not formal, as with the indefinite article. It is more pragmatic in nature (see Section 2.9.3) and it was best expressed by John Hawkins in what he termed 'location theory':

> the speaker performs the following acts when using a definite article. He [sic] (a) introduces a referent (or referents) to the hearer; and (b) instructs the hearer to locate the referent in some shared set of

objects ...; and (c) he refers to the totality of objects or mass within this set which satisfy the referring expressions. (Hawkins 1978: 167)

To simplify this somewhat, we might say that, with regard to common nouns which have specific reference, *the* is basically used to help the noun phrase refer to a thing or things that the speaker (or writer) thinks the listener (or reader) can locate or identify uniquely, that is, without confusing it or them with other possible referents. Again, this is not a formulation that can be passed on to learners, but it is a starting point.

7.2.3 Further Information about the Articles

Another factor which may have pedagogical implications is the frequency of these different uses.

Biber et al. (1999: 266) show the frequency of different types of definite noun phrase usage according to different genres. Of course, in definite noun phrases they include other definite cases with other determiners and definite pronouns, but the major exponent of definiteness will be the definite article, so there is some value in their findings. According to them, situational use is by far the most frequent in conversation, while cataphora is the most popular in academic writing. Direct anaphora is first in fiction and joint first with cataphora in news (both genres where story-telling is important). One other statistic, which will be important later on, is worth stating: when a noun is mentioned for the first time in discourse it is more likely to be with the definite than indefinite article.

We can make two final comments which may have pedagogic relevance. The first issue is whether the definite and indefinite articles constitute a coherent system. As respectively the basic markers of definite and indefinite noun phrases, they are actually members of two different sub-classes of words: definite determiners (in the case of *the*, along with *my, you, this, that*, etc.), and indefinite determiners (*a*, along with *some, any, all, many, few*, etc.). The main reason why they are usually grouped together in teaching is a contrastive one: the fact that many languages do not possess equivalents for them (see Section 7.3). So while there may be a pedagogic reason for putting them together, there is no overwhelming linguistic reason for doing so. The concept of metalinguistic relativity is relevant here (see Chapters 3 and 4): we are conditioned to thinking of them as a coherent system because of the terminology (and because books – such as mine (Berry 1993) – and textbook units and exercises, not to mention linguists, group them together).

A further difference between the two articles lies in the types of nouns they combine with: *the* with uncountable nouns as well as with singular and plural countable nouns (*the dog, the dogs, the money*) and *a/an* only with singular countable nouns (*a dog*). This provides more evidence for treating them separately.

7.3 The Contrastive Background

As stated in the introduction, the majority of the world's languages, including Chinese, Japanese, Hindi/Urdu, most African languages and almost all Slavonic languages (Russian, etc.) do not possess articles. In some cases (e.g. Arabic, the Celtic languages) there is one article – always the definite, it seems. But we must be careful in equating exponents from different language systems. Even in cases where two languages may reasonably be said to possess articles (i.e. most European languages), there will be differences. For example, English and French make generalisations with plural or singular uncountable nouns differently:

> *J'adore les pommes* ('I love ~~the~~ apples').
> *Je n'aime pas le vin* ('I don't like ~~the~~ wine').

And German, like French, does not use the indefinite article when denoting a nationality or profession: *Ich bin Student* ('I am a student'). The most famous article mistake in world history was made by President Kennedy with his famous pronouncement 'Ich bin ein Berliner', which should have been 'Ich bin Berliner' since 'ein Berliner' in this case apparently refers to 'a doughnut'. He was translating directly from English, but in German no article is required to talk about one's provenance.

A different kind of discrepancy is found with some other languages, in that while they do mark nouns for definiteness, they do so as a suffix on the noun, e.g. Swedish. Other languages can mark definiteness in noun phrases through adjectival endings (e.g. Croatian: 'dobar čovjek' – a good man vs 'dobri čovjek' – the good man).

While many languages do not possess articles, this does not mean they cannot mark definiteness. Word order, or more precisely, information structure can help to render the difference between definiteness and indefiniteness, in that noun phrases placed at the start of a sentence are likely to be interpreted as 'given', or known, while those placed later will be interpreted as new information, as indefinite, as in this example from Croatian:

> *Upekla me osa* (literally 'stung me wasp') is likely to be interpreted as 'A wasp stung me'

(or 'I was stung by a wasp') whereas

> *Osa me upekla*

is more likely to be translated as 'The wasp stung me'.

This is not a foolproof method for determining definiteness, of course, since sentences may be devoid of new information or composed entirely of it.

7.4 The Historical Background

Originally English did not have articles, like other European languages. They arose as a major structural change was taking place in the nature of English whereby it moved from marking grammatical functions (subject, object etc.) by case endings, which allowed word order to denote information structure, towards the use of word order to denote grammatical functions and the use of articles for information structure. (This was partly motivated by concurrent sound changes that neutralised case endings.) These changes can be understood in terms of the four strategies discussed in Section 2.5: the use of little function words (the articles, prepositions) in place of changing the forms of words or altering the word order.

Both the definite and indefinite articles developed from still-existing determiners – from *that* in the case of *the*, and *one* in the case of *a/an*. The indefinite article shows its origin in certain situations where the choice between it and *one* seems to make little difference, as in *a/one hundred*. This is just another, albeit small, example of how previous systems of grammar leave traces and how a historical perspective can help to understand current anomalies (cf. the subjunctive, Section 2.9.1). Another example is the use of the indefinite article in rates and speeds (where other languages use a preposition), e.g. £90 a night, twenty miles an hour, can also be explained in diachronic terms, since it is a reinterpretation of the preposition *on*.[2]

7.5 Learners and Articles

Learners – at least those from article-less languages – seem to reappraise the articles in terms of the distinction discussed in Chapter 2 between convention and creativity. From the preceding description, it should be clear that articles are very much a creative device, allowing speakers as they do to create different meanings. Yet learners seem to regard them in conventional terms, as something that is determined by formal rules, similar to, for example, the use of third-person *-s*; this can be seen in the formal rules that some make up themselves, as discussed below. This point will play a part in the approach to teaching the articles later on in this case study

Left to their own devices EFL learners appear to undergo a development process whereby they initially underuse articles followed by a later stage where they overuse them, especially the definite article, before perhaps settling back to the correct level of use. The following examples of typical errors, which many teachers will be familiar with, are taken from Swan and Smith (1987):

> *New house is building near cinema that is near us.* (p. 125, Russian speaker)
> *Where is pen I gave you? Please close a door.* (p. 204, Bantu speakers)
> *He was soldier.* (p. 151, Arabic speaker)

However, many if not most learners of English, whether in formal or informal learning situations, do not achieve proficiency with articles; with highly advanced learners article errors may be the only grammatical sign that English is not their L1. Learners may make also up their own rules, based on their own experiences and observation, for example that if a noun is followed by *of* then it should be preceded by *the* (*the driver of a passing car*); this works quite well, but falls down at times (**the friend of mine*) and prevents further progress. (I even had a student once who reported that she used a criterion of 'balance'; she would distribute articles evenly throughout a text!)

Another strategy used is avoidance, for example, using *one* instead of *a*, and demonstratives (*this, that, these, those*) instead of *the*; this can lead to rather odd, though not necessarily incorrect utterances:

> *She is one good friend.*

7.6 The Current Situation

How does current pedagogical practice then attempt to deal with this notoriously difficult area of English grammar? It cannot be ignored, given the frequency and ubiquity of articles and the contrastive situation as described above.

Apart from rather vague suggestions that *the* is used for 'known' things, the main instructional thrust comes in the shape of a rule of thumb:

> 'The first time you mention something use *a*, the second time *the*.'

Most learners, at least those from article-less languages, seem to be aware of this rule in one form or other. In a recent paper investigating grammatical myths comparatively in different parts of the world I found this belief to be widespread among first-year English majors in Poland and Hong Kong (Berry 2015; already discussed in Section 3.3 in respect of the Hong Kong findings). Out of 195 Hong Kong students 136 held this statement to be true; the relevant figure for Poland was 33 out of 44; the percentages for Hong Kong and

7.6 The Current Situation

Poland were similar (70 and 75 per cent respectively). However, in a third country, Hungary, the figure was 8 out of 32. This discrepancy is explained by the fact that Hungarian does have an article system, and therefore the need for such a sweeping statement is absent.

This rule of thumb arises from a laudable attempt to make two of the most difficult words in English amenable to learners. It appears to deal with both of them together in very simple terms. However, it is for the most part wrong, and if applied generally and faithfully, would result in numerous errors. A significant amount of 'unlearning' is needed here, with both learners and teachers. This can be carried out by applying the description above; there are three situations where the rule can be shown to be false.

1 Firstly, and most importantly, as pointed out above, the first time something is mentioned, you do not have to use *a*: in fact, *the* is more common than *a* for 'first mention'. This may sound strange: if, as is the case, *a* is used to introduce something new into a discussion (or a piece of writing), how could *the* be appropriate? The answer is that mentioning something for the first time is not the same as introducing it. There are many things that do not need to be 'introduced' because we and our listeners (or readers) are already familiar with them, because we expect them in a particular situation or can work them out from the context, as in the case of situational and indirect anaphoric uses described above Thus a conversation in a hotel room might go as follows:

   A: *Turn on the TV.*
   B: *Where's the remote control?*

   In both cases *the* is used even though the objects have not been mentioned before; speaker A says *the* as both of them are aware of the TV, while speaker B uses *the*, assuming there is one because of the TV. Applying the rule above, however, a learner would say *turn on a TV; where's a remote control?* – both of which are absurd.

2 Secondly, first mention with *a* does not always 'establish' something (or, as we said above, make it 'specific'):

   Jonny wants a bike but we're not sure a bike is a good idea.

   Here the first mention with *a* does not actually establish any specific bike. So for the second mention we cannot refer back to it using *the*; there is nothing to refer back to, so we continue using *a*.

3   Thirdly, even if we try to refine the rule by saying that 'when something is introduced use *a*; then, since it has been established, use *the*; if it needs no introduction, use *the*', this unfortunately does not work either, because even when something has been established, *the* is still not the most logical choice. Consider this example that I found in a pedagogic grammar:

> *I have found a̱ coin; the̱ coin is worth 50p.*

This seems to be a perfectly formed example of 'second mention', but in fact it is nonsense. If a student wrote this in an essay for me, I would take a red pen to it. Why? Because there are far more obvious choices:

> *I have found a coin. I̱t is worth 50p.*
> *I have found a coin wẖich is worth 50p.*
> (or more concisely, *I have found a coin worth 50p.*)

The point is that repeating the noun with *the* in place of *a* is totally unnecessary here; a pronoun is more appropriate. This is a perfect example of what Henry Widdowson has called 'usage' (and what I call 'grammarspeak'). Usage is the manipulation of language to demonstrate grammatical rules, as opposed to 'use', which is how people use language naturally.

To exemplify 'second mention' accurately and succinctly it is necessary to have two possible referents, as in this example:

> *John bought a̱ TV and a̱ video recorder, but he returned the̱ video recorder.* (Quirk et al. 1985: 267)

Here the pronoun *it* would be wrong, because it would not be clear which of the two possibilities is intended. The unjustified obsession with direct anaphora, out of all the uses mentioned above, is one of the major causes of confusion when teaching the articles. It may have arisen because of a concentration on story-telling in beginners' materials. Narrative is one field where we can reasonably expect to find cases of second mention; in stories people and things have to be introduced using *a* and then referred back to. However, even here the logical and predominant means of referring back is a pronoun, although authors may have recourse to *the* for reasons of elegant variation. Consider this further example from Agatha Christie (*Elephants Can Remember*, Collins Crime Club, 1972):

> *Just then he smelled a̱ do̱g approaching and heard i̱t curiously scuffing. Somehow he sensed that i̱t was not his enemy. But then, as tẖe do̱g came closer...*

7.6 The Current Situation

> This is a common pattern in narrative: something is introduced with *a*, then referred to using a pronoun, and finally, when the introduction is some way off, the noun is repeated with *the*. To repeat *it* throughout might be considered boring.

So, the desire to offer clear advice is understandable, but the formulation is a gross oversimplification, and in most cases inappropriate.

Current practice exercises involve mainly gap-filling, whereby all articles are deleted and replaced with a gap in front of every noun phrase in the text (including places where there was no article; see Section 6.4.1). Unfortunately, many such exercises have not been properly controlled and unforeseen alternatives are possible, reflecting different possible meanings. A recent book which aims to help teachers prepare lessons on grammar starts off the unit on articles with the following gap-fill text:

> *Every day I walk to _____ town centre. There are always lots of _____ people there. I usually buy _____ ice cream, _____ packet of _____ sweets and _____ newspaper. Then I go to _____ beach and sit on _____ bench...* (Scrivener 2010: 46)

Out of the nine gaps in this extract there are at least three which are questionable, i.e. could have more than one possibility. The most egregious is the penultimate one; the intended answer is 'the beach' but it would be quite possible to say 'a beach' if there is more than one and the writer does not want to be precise. Furthermore, as an answer 'the beach' is actually ambiguous; it could be a specific beach that the writer thinks the reader can identify uniquely, or it could be regarded as an 'institutional' feature of seasides, as in 'A day at the beach will do you good' (i.e. no particular beach). Other problematic gaps are the ones before 'bench' (supposedly 'a', but no reason why it could not be 'the bench' if both writer and reader know there is only one in question), and before 'ice cream' (supposedly 'an', but 'ice cream' can be uncountable as well as countable, so no article is a possibility).[3] The activity could be improved by having a plan of the town which would constrain the possibilities. (See such an idea in Berry 1993, 84–85.)

Ur (2010: 158–159) has an exercise which involves turning headlines into complete sentences, which involves adding articles as well as other elements (e.g. 'Bus in accident' becomes 'A bus was involved in an accident'). Although highly authentic as a linguistic exercise, it is very difficult for any but the most advanced leaners to complete, and suffers from the same problem as other inserting exercises: it emphasises the redundancy of articles (see Section 6.7).

There is a whole range of alternative exercise types which stress the value of articles that can be found in Berry (1991 and 1993). Some are described below.

7.7 What to Do

First of all, we must believe that articles are important. There are many cases where communication breakdown is possible if they are used incorrectly. The completely opposite meaning may be derived; for example, 'It is uninteresting play' might be heard as 'It is an interesting play'.

7.7.1 Overall Strategy

It is impossible to ignore *a/an* and *the* in any kind of teaching approach where there is a grammatical focus. As mentioned above, both words are very frequent in English. Given this, it should be worth devoting some time to them. However, there is no simple formula that caters for both words, as the description outlined above should have made clear. They are not in a formal one-to-one relationship; the choice between them – and between them and nothing – depends on meaning.

Of the two articles, more classroom time should be devoted to *the* since it is far more common and harder to learn. Indeed, because of its frequency, it may be worth starting with the definite article. It is easier to construct texts which contain it alone. Of the different uses cited above, less emphasis should be given to second mention (or direct anaphora) – unless narrative is the focus. Instead I would recommend concentrating on immediate situation (the TV example above) and indirect anaphora (the remote control example). Both are easy to exemplify and give a better insight into the nature of the definite article. Though it is common in writing, cataphora can be left till a later stage since it involves potentially complex noun phrases and is most common in academic writing

7.7.2 Introducing the Definite Article

Immediate situation – especially if it is chosen as the first use of *the* to be taught – can be practised by utilising the context in which teachers and learners find themselves, i.e. the classroom. The teacher can exemplify it through reference to common features there:

> *Turn on <u>the light</u> please.*
> *Clean <u>the board</u> please.*
> *Where is <u>the _____</u>?*
> *Who is <u>the class representative</u>?*

7.7 What to Do

Pictures of common scenes can also be used to establish the appropriate context, for example a picture of a kitchen with familiar objects in different colours:

The fridge is white.
The cupboard is green.

But whatever the choice of situation, it is necessary to be culturally sensitive.

7.7.3 Rules

If rules are needed – and this is not indisputable, nor should it be the first step – the following might be offered.

Starting with the indefinite article, a useful rule of thumb would go as follows:

> Use *a* and *an* in front of singular countable nouns when they are the head (i.e. the main word) of a noun phrase, and when there is no reason for using another determiner like *some, this, the, my*, etc.

This rule, however, involves quite a lot of concepts and terminology and so is not for beginners, unless they are linguistically sophisticated and the explanation is given in the L1. It treats the indefinite article as the 'default' article or determiner, as stated above.

As we saw above, there is no similar simple rule for using the definite article. Trainee teachers may be told that it is used by the speaker (or writer) to instruct the hearer (or reader) to distinguish something uniquely from all other possible referents, but it should be made clear that this is not a rule for learners. Other, more inductive procedures, such as exercises, should form the major part of practice.

If a generalisation for both articles is required then Table 7.1 might be offered.

Of course, this is a simplification and does not apply to all situations; in particular, what is meant by 'known' needs to be refined,

Table 7.1 The difference between the *and* a *with singular count nouns.*

	Known to speaker	Known to hearer	'Rule'	Example
1	+	+	use *the*	Can I have the car?
2	+	–	use *a*	I bought a new car today.
3	–	–	use *a*	I need a new car.

(After Allsop 1983: 35; see also Celce-Murcia and Larsen-Freeman 1983: 177.)

along the lines of familiarity and expectations as discussed above. But it is a useful starting point. It simplifies the concepts of specificness and definiteness; the former becomes 'known to speaker' and the latter 'known to hearer as well'.

7.7.4 Terms

As regards terminology to be used in the classroom, there is a choice between 'the definite/indefinite article' and the words themselves: '*a*' and '*the*'. A teacher might say 'use the definite article here, not the indefinite', or 'use *the*, not *a*'. The latter approach is clearly simpler, so long as learners can make out the schwa sound in both words, but it does not cater for *an* ('a' has two forms: 'a' and 'an'?). The former approach would be suitable for more advanced learners. But the decision will depend largely on the classroom culture that is already established in the learning community.

One concept and related term that can be dispensed with in teaching is 'zero article'. Its acceptance may simplify theoretical accounts (in that all common nouns can be said to have one article or other), but it is beyond the grasp, or indeed need, of all but the most sophisticated students.

7.7.5 Exercises

One conclusion that follows from the observation that the choice between articles is a question of meaning, i.e. creativity, is that gap-filling exercises, where learners insert the articles into a text from which they have been removed, are of dubious validity, as was seen in Section 7.6. The learners are told that they can work out the answers based on the meaning in the text, but they may reason that if the meaning is already there, what is the point of inserting extra words? Such exercises emphasise the unimportance of articles, not to mention causing confusion when there are alternatives based on meaning, as in the Scrivener example shown above. The problem is, essentially, that it is wrong to ask learners to take the part of an anonymous writer or speaker, about whom they know nothing, addressing readers or listeners, about whom they equally know nothing, in circumstances which they can only imagine. They have to guess what these interlocutors know about, expect of or share with each other. Where possible learners should be expressing their own meanings.

If the articles are to be learned teachers need to emphasise their value in communication. In my 1993 book I exemplified a number of alternative types of exercise design based on this aim. They are largely based on the insight that the definite article needs to be practised in its role as a feature of noun phrases, as the element which creates reference.

7.7 What to Do

The first type may be termed 'reverse gap-fill' exercises. In this it is the articles that are present and it is the nouns that are to be inserted. For example:

Exercise 1 *Insert an appropriate noun in the gap.*

(a) *There's something wrong with my radio. The _____ isn't clear.*

(b) *There's something wrong with my car. I can't unlock the _____.*

etc. (There may be more than one answer.)

This concentrates on indirect anaphora, as discussed above, where the is used for the first time because of the relationship to something else already mentioned.

The second type again stresses the link between article and noun, but in this case both noun and article are missing, showing how the two go together to create a particular meaning. In this case indirect anaphora in the context of a narration is the focus.

Exercise 2 *Complete this text with words appropriate to the situation.*

The hall was quite small so when all (1) _____ were taken the remaining people had to stand at (2) _____. After a few minutes (3) _____ entered and (4) _____ began.

Suggested answers: (1) the seats/places; (2) the back; (3) the speaker/lecturer; (4) the talk/lecture. There are other possibilities.

Comprehension of articles is as important as production, if not more so. The following exercise asks learners to differentiate between the implications of the two articles.

Exercise 3 *What is the difference between using 'a' or 'the' in the following sentence? Link them to the two meanings below.*

Yesterday a man was murdered in his flat. Police investigating the crime have discovered a/the gun.

(a) *They are not sure if it was used in the crime.*

(b) *They are sure that it was used in the crime.*

This can also be used for awareness-raising, where the value of article is stressed with learners who perhaps already have some intuitions about articles.

Here is another exercise which emphasises the communicative value of articles and how their use depends on the assumptions that speakers make about their hearers:

Case Study 1: The Articles

Exercise 4 Link the questions on the left to the person you would ask them of on the right.

    (a) *Have you seen the cat?*   (i) *A stranger*
    (b) *Have you seen our cat?*   (ii) *A member of your household*
    (c) *Have you seen a cat?*   (iii) *Your usual postman*

The following activity practises immediate situation.

Exercise 5 Find a sentence on the left which matches a situation on the right.

    (a) *I'd like to speak to the manager.*   (i) *At the scene of a car accident.*
    (b) *Did you remember the tickets?*   (ii) *At the entrance to a sporting event.*
    (c) *Maybe the driver had a heart-attack.* (iii) *In a hotel.*

The next exercise practises cataphora in the context of what is called 'nominalisation': turning a verb into a noun followed by an *of* phrase denoting the subject of the action. This involves the addition of definite articles along with the noun. It is for more advanced learners

Exercise 6 Reword the short sentences in brackets as noun phrase to complete the longer sentences.

    (a) *(The stars arrived.) Crowds watched _____ (...<u>the</u> arrival of the stars.)*
    (b) *(The shop opened.) _____ was followed by a party. (The opening of the shop...)*
    (c) *(A file has disappeared.) The manager was concerned by _____ (...the disappearance of a file.)*
    etc.

These exercises only exhibit a small range of the more creative formats that exploit the true creative nature of definite article usage.

Stepping back somewhat, it can be argued that that there is a stage before both comprehension and production, namely awareness. Learners often give up on articles at an early stage, sensing that they are too difficult and (mistakenly) of little value. This may be compounded by formal factors: both are short and use (usually) the unstressed shwa vowel. The indefinite article in spoken English is particularly hard to spot, especially its *a* variant. As a result learners may not notice their presence, even when they are asked to repeat sentences containing them. This can be remedied by resuscitating a practice I criticised above: gap-filling, so long as it is a text that they have encountered before. If such an exercise is given regularly as a test (but unexpectedly), learners may be encouraged to notice the presence of articles. In devising such a homemade activity, teachers should remember to place gaps in front of all noun phrases, not just those where *a* and *the* have been deleted. This approach can be taken a stage further by deleting entire selected noun phrases, as suggested above in Exercise 2. These are admittedly rather automatic exercises but they will help when the articles are being sold to learners as creative not conventional devices.

One other broader feature of definiteness could also be exploited. It involves the relationship between *the* and other words in English. Namely, the question word *which* enquires about definite things (as noted above in the canteen example), while *what* asks about indefinite things, for example:

> *Which* road shall we take? (implying that the listener has some knowledge of the options).
> *What* road shall we take? (no such implication).

In other words, if someone uses *the* incorrectly, it may prompt a question using *which*, as the above example about the canteen showed. If someone says 'Give me the keys' and the listener is unsure which, they may ask 'Which keys?' Teachers may use this in class as a corrective feedback technique whenever the use of *the* is not justified.

7.8 Conclusion

There is no need to link the two articles, except perhaps as a comparative exercise after both have been explicitly introduced separately. The linguistic justification for so doing is weak. The use of the indefinite article is formally conditioned, whereas in contrast the definite article represents a classic case of the interplay between creativity and convention (Section 2.4). Its use is dependent on the circumstances in which participants in the act of communication find themselves, on the knowledge that speakers have and think their listeners have, or on the message speakers wish to convey. It is thus subject to creativity, unlike the indefinite article. However, the picture that emerges from the classroom is one of convention; that using the definite article can be determined by a set of formal rules, whether inculcated by teachers or materials, or arrived at by learners themselves.

This linking of the two articles and the attempt to turn creativity into convention leads inexorably to the current situation whereby a rather uncommon usage of the definite article, direct anaphora, is chosen as the key one, and is linked to the indefinite article by a highly misleading rule of thumb. And because of a lack of transmission, or communication between linguists and practitioners, the situation remains unchanged.

This admittedly rather technical but accurate observation taken from the *Longman Grammar of Spoken and Written English* should be taken to heart by all teachers:

> Despite the perception that definite noun phrases are usually used for anaphoric reference [referring back, or second mention], they are more commonly used for other purposes. At the same time, anaphoric reference is marked by pronouns and a range of other devices. (Biber et al. 1999: 266)

(Note that on the first line of this quote we could easily replace *the* with *a* according to the meaning we wish to convey: 'Despite a perception that...'.)

The solution to the issue of misleading conceptions about the article is not an easy matter. Some practical suggestions were made above, the most important of which are summarised here:

1 Focus learners' attention on the articles.
2 Practise comprehension as well as production.
3 Consider treating the two articles separately.
4 For the indefinite article focus on the countable/uncountable distinction.
5 Consider starting with and focusing on the definite article. It is much more common and harder to learn.
6 Introduce the definite article through its situational and/or indirect anaphoric uses;
7 Only focus on direct anaphora in the case of story-telling. Even then the second mention 'rule' should be introduced with caveats.
8 Treat article-only gap-fill exercises with caution, checking for alternatives. Use alternative meaning-dependent formats where possible.

These will all help to bring about progress. But it may be a long time before we see a sea change.

Activity

1 Find a textbook with a gap-fill exercise for learners. Check whether there are any possible alternative answers.
2 Create your own gap-fill exercise. Take a text, preferably a simple one, and replace all the articles with gaps. Don't forget to add gaps in front of noun phrases where there is no article. Then examine it

critically (or give it to a colleague) to check if there are any alternatives to the original.

Notes

1 This use explains another mystery, but a phonetic one: why *on*, unlike *from* and other prepositions, did not develop a weak form using schwa (/ən/). In fact it did, but since this was homophonous with the indefinite article it was reinterpreted as such. (The rule that all count nouns should have some form of determiner may have aided this reinterpretation.)
2 In terms of Swan's criteria for evaluating rules of thumb in Section 6.2, we would rate it highly for truth and demarcation, but not for clarity and simplicity.
3 To be fair to Scrivener (2010), the subsequent account does reflect some advance in the understanding of articles. Alongside a cautious mention of the second mention 'rule', it also refers to indirect anaphora and first mention with *the*.

References

Allsop, Jake. 1983. *Cassells Students' English Grammar*. Eastbourne: Cassells.
Berry, Roger. 1991. Rearticulating the articles. *ELT Journal* 45/3: 252–257. This contains ideas for teaching the articles.
Berry, Roger. 1993. *Collins Cobuild English Guides 3: Articles*. HarperCollins: London. See especially chapter 4, 'Specific uses of the definite article'.
Berry, Roger. 2015. Grammar myths. *Language Awareness* 24/1: 15–37.
Berry, Roger. 2018. *English Grammar: A Resource Book for Students*. 2nd edn. Abingdon: Routledge.
Biber, Douglas, Stig Johannsson, Geoffrey Leech, Susan Conrad and Edward Finegan. 1999. *Longman Grammar of Spoken and Written English*. Harlow: Longman, 260–269.
Celce-Murcia, Marianne and Diane Larsen-Freeman. 1983. *The Grammar Book*. Rowley, MA: Newbury House
Hawkins, John. 1978. *Definiteness and Indefiniteness*. London: Croom Helm.
Quirk, Randolph, Sidney Greenbaum, Geoffrey Leech and Jan Svartvik. 1985. *A Comprehensive Grammar of the English Language*. Harlow: Longman, 265–287.
Scrivener, Jim. 2010. *Teaching English Grammar*. London: Macmillan Education.
Swan, Michael and Bernard Smith. 1987. *Learner English*. Cambridge: Cambridge University Press.
Ur, Penny. 2010. *Grammar Practice Activities*. 2nd edn. Cambridge. Cambridge University Press.

8 Case Study 2
The Comparison of Adjectives

8.1 Introduction

This, the second case study, confronts an issue that is very different from the one which concerned the articles in the previous study. There the main issue was that a phenomenon that was essentially creative was turned by pedagogical practice into something conventional (see Section 2.4); semantic/pragmatic considerations were transferred into formal ones. Here we are faced with an issue that is principally conventional (though creative matters are also involved) to do with how words are formed. There is a choice but it is not a creative one; it is between competing forms and does not lead to different meanings being expressed. However, there is a similarity in that a rule (or rules) of thumb is placed under a spotlight, but this time it is a corpus study that provides the evidence. In this way the chapter serves as an example of pedagogic grammar as process (Section 2.7), whereby a descriptive study feeds into the pedagogic filter and produces an output in the shape of a revised rule.

All teachers and other practitioners, as well as most learners, will be familiar with the grammatical phenomenon known as the 'comparison of adjectives', whereby certain adjectives may be modified to produce three different forms:

- the base: *big*;
- the comparative: *bigger*;
- the superlative: *biggest*.

Not all adjectives can have comparison, e.g. *electric*. The idea of comparison is related to the concept of 'gradability', whereby adjectives can be modified by an intensifying adverb (e.g. <u>*very* *big*</u>; see Chapter 3 for more on different types of adverbs), but the two are not the same. Some adjectives are subject to one phenomenon but not the other (e.g. *glad* can be 'graded' (*very glad*) but not 'compared' (*gladder*, *more glad*). It should be noted that comparison also affects adverbs, e.g. *He arrived <u>later</u>. She sang <u>more gracefully</u>.*

8.2 The Background

While there are a number of prescriptive issues to do with the meanings of comparison,[1] the phenomenon is mostly of interest to grammarians because there are two systems of comparison in operation, and to some extent they may be said to be in competition, namely:

- So-called 'inflectional comparison' (or 'analytic comparison'), as exemplified above, where the comparative and superlative are formed by respectively adding in writing *-er* and *-est*.[2] (There are also certain spelling rules involved, such as adding only *-r* and *-st* after a final *-e*, and the doubling of final consonants, but these are not peculiar to comparison and need not concern us here.)
- So-called 'phrasal comparison' (or 'periphrastic comparison'), where the comparative and superlative are formed by respectively prefacing the adjective with *more* or *most*: *more beautiful, most successful*.

It has long been recognised that these two systems 'overlap' in their application to adjectives, that there is no totally hard and fast rule for deciding under which circumstances the one or the other is used. However, it is accepted that there is a tendency to use inflectional comparison with shorter adjectives and phrasal comparison with longer adjectives, while certain adjectives may have both forms of comparison: *common, handsome, pleasant, remote, polite*, are just some examples.

What do the authoritative grammars say? Quirk et al. (1985: 461–462) offer the following findings (amongst others):

> 'The choice between inflectional and periphrastic comparison is largely determined by the length of the adjective.'

> 'Monosyllabic adjectives form their comparison by inflection...' (*real, right* and *wrong* are cited as exceptions). 'However, most other monosyllabic adjectives can take either inflectional or periphrastic comparison.'

> 'Many disyllabic adjectives can also take inflections, though they have the alternative of the periphrastic forms... Disyllabic adjectives that can most readily take inflected forms are those ending in an unstressed vowel, /l/ or /ə/.' They cite the following endings: *-y* (*early*), *-ow* (*mellow*), *-le* (*able*), *-er* (*clever*), and *-ure* (*mature*).

> 'Trisyllabic or longer adjectives can only take periphrastic forms' (but they note the exception of adjectives with the *un-* prefix, e.g. *unhappier*).

In other words, Quirk et al. present a rather complex and confusing picture of comparison, particularly regarding two-syllable adjectives. This would be very hard to distil into a brief but helpful account for teachers and learners. In particular there is extensive hedging (see Section 5.3) to avoid being wrong, using words such as *largely* and *can*.

Biber et al. (1999: 522) present the following findings:

> 'Gradable adjectives of one syllable usually take the inflectional suffix, except for a few forms such as *right, wrong* and *real*. Longer adjectives usually take phrasal comparison.'

They cite corpus evidence for phrasal comparison for the following monosyllabic adjectives (where the inflectional forms would have been expected): *fair, full, fierce, proud* and *rude*. An explanation offered for such uses is that phrasal comparison 'makes the comparison more prominent'; it is easier to give stress to the idea of a comparison if it is contained in a separate word: 'more fair', rather than 'fairer'.

As for disyllabic adjectives, they note that a whole range of adjectives ending in *-y* 'are usually inflected', while those ending in *-ly* 'are more variable'. They list the same other types of ending as Quirk et al. that engender inflectional comparison. They also observe that inflectional comparison is possible with three-syllable adjectives ending in *-y* (*almightiest*).

Overall these studies in major descriptive grammars point out the problems in the analysis of adjectival comparison. However, apart from the odd insight, they do not offer a systematic solution, still less a platform for useful pedagogic advice. The use of 'largely' in Quirk et al. and 'usually' in Biber et al. indicates the lack of certainty in their accounts (cf. 'hedging' as discussed in Section 5.3) and the absence of a general rule.

We should also note the potential ambiguity of the phrasal forms, both comparative and superlative, since *more* and *most* both function as determiners ('more people', 'most people') as well as in the adverbial role that they have in comparison. For example, with *more*:

> *This should get us more regular coverage...*

Does this mean 'more coverage' which is regular, or coverage which is 'more regular'?

And with *most*:

> *Most common cells in the brain help us anticipate rewards.*

Here the proximity of *most* to an adjective should not deceive us: it refers to 'common cells' as a determiner. There is also the rather formal use of *most* as an adverb to modify adjectives with the meaning 'very' (i.e. no comparison is being made):

> *That was most interesting.*

8.3 The Meanings of Comparison

While the choice of form is the central feature of this case study, we should not ignore other important elements of comparison, in particular the meanings of the three forms, or rather the relationships between them. It is sometimes erroneously assumed that, because of the way the three forms are ordered, they represent three increasing degrees of that particular quality or attribute. Thus the comparative is said to be 'more' than the base, and the superlative 'more' than the comparative. For example, the adjective *strong* might be characterised as having three degrees of 'strength': *strong, stronger* and *strongest*. However, this is not the case; it has long been recognised that something or someone can be identified as 'stronger' or 'strongest' without necessarily being 'strong', for example:

> He may be <u>stronger</u> than his brother, but I wouldn't say he's particularly <u>strong</u>.

8.4 Other Comparative Structures

A discussion of adjective comparison does not end with the debate about the competing forms or their meanings. There are also structural elements, for example the use of *than* after the comparative (*bigger than...*), as in the above example, to specify the item being compared, not to mention the existence of negative comparison with *less* and *least* (i.e. using exclusively phrasal comparison). Then there is the use of intensification and reduplication with comparative adjectives: <u>much</u> *bigger*; <u>bigger and</u> *bigger*. And we should not forget the use of the definite article with superlative adjectives and nouns (<u>the biggest</u> *fool*) to reflect the 'unique' nature of what is being referred to; see use 7) under the definite article in Section 7.2.2.

Other structures can express 'comparison', for example '(not) as big as...' etc. The use of the term 'comparison' to refer to the above phenomenon involving the choice of adjective form is somewhat 'unfair' to other structures which also have the function of comparing. The question here is: is the concept of comparison a formal one, referring to the above-discussed grammatical choice, or is it a semantic concept wherein any structure that reflects comparison is included?

8.5 The Comparative and Historical Background

Comparison, that is comparing different degrees of the same quality, such as age, height, size (*older, taller, bigger*), or selecting some referents as standouts as regards that quality (*oldest, tallest, biggest*), is a universal feature of languages. But the methods of modifying adjectives to convey these ideas are varied. Some languages have adjectival suffixes, as with English, e.g. German, Farsi. Others have phrasal comparison but the modifying word comes after the adjective (e.g. Vietnamese). French has phrasal comparison preceding the adjective, but the distinction between the comparative and superlative is carried only by the presence or absence of the definite article (*plus intelligent/le plus intelligent*). But no other languages, it would seem, have two competing systems the way English does; hence the desire (ultimately fruitless) to separate the two systems completely by means of an absolute, exception-free rule.

Adjectives in English originally relied entirely on inflections for comparison (in the same way that nouns and verbs used suffixes to indicate factors such as grammatical function and person respectively); this can still be seen in the forms used in current Germanic languages. The introduction of phrasal comparison can be associated with the importation into English of French structures (via translation, i.e. *more* for *plus*, *of* for *de*), similar to the process which led to the competing forms of the genitive in English, as described in Section 2.9.1. And as with the two systems for the genitive, no clear distinction has emerged between the inflectional and phrasal forms of comparison, despite the best efforts, and much to the disappointment, of pedagogic grammarians.

8.6 Learners and Comparison

Regarding learners' familiarity with the 'rules' for the formation of comparison, the issue was the subject of one of the items in the grammatical myths research reported in Chapter 3 (Berry 2015). Although this 'belief' did not reach the stringent threshold for inclusion there as a 'myth' about English grammar, the figures are still worth mentioning. Here are the statement and results:

> 'The comparative of adjectives is formed by adding '-er' to one syllable words and 'more' to words of two or more syllables.' (*TRUE 42, FALSE 80, DON'T KNOW 7, PARTLY TRUE 66*)

Clearly, there is a fair amount of uncertainty among the participants, first-year English majors in Hong Kong; similar figures were obtained for a comparable group of Polish and Hungarian students in an earlier study (Berry 1994). But in spite of there being a significant proportion who held it to be true without exception (more than one-fifth), a majority were aware of the fact that the 'rule' is far from watertight, that the situation concerning the formation of comparative adjectives is not clear-cut.

Learners around the world have difficulty with comparison, partly because of the contrastive issues identified above, but particularly because of the two competing systems. Some problems with formation that I have come across are:

- the application of both forms of comparison: e.g. *<u>more</u> cleverer*, *<u>most</u> cleverest* (Swan and Smith (1987: 179) report this as a typical problem for speakers of Indian languages);
- mistakes with irregular forms, e.g. *goodest*;
- confusion of an irregular comparative or superlative with a base form: e.g. *worser* or *bestest*. (A colleague was once told by a student, much to her amusement, that she was his 'bestest teacher' – a super-superlative?)

Overall, I have found a tendency for learners to prefer phrasal comparison, perhaps because it is semantically transparent, in that both ideas have a separate word. However, this observation must be tempered by several factors, such as the influence of the equivalent structure in their L1. But one factor that is common to all learners of English is the decision they have to make about which form of comparison to use with which adjectives.

8.7 Researching Comparison

Corpus analysis is very suitable for investigating this issue, as outlined in Chapter 3. Indeed, the scientific grammars referred to be above rely on corpora to some extent (more so in the case of Biber et al. 1999). And yet they reach the same basic unconvincing conclusions, dilutions of which are found in most pedagogic grammars.

In a research article, Martin Hilpert (2008) examined the British National Corpus for the occurrence of phrasal and inflectional comparatives.[3] He found, much against expectations, as many as 245 adjectives which had both phrasal and inflectional forms. This finding alone should counsel against any attempt to formulate a simplistic rule for the choice between the two systems. And while many adjectives did largely follow expectations (e.g. *free*, which had 270 occurrences of *freer*, but only 21 of *more free*; or *shallow*, which had 125 occurrences of *shallower*, but only 6 of *more shallow*), many did not. It is a moot point as to whether forms such as *more free* should be characterised as 'errors'; believers in the above rule may wish to do so. But this may be a convenient way of avoiding a complex truth.

Overall there were a number of anomalous results:

1 One-syllable adjectives which preferred phrasal to inflectional comparison, for example:
   DEAD: 19 cases of *more dead* vs 4 cases of *deader*;[4]
   REAL: 105 *more real* vs 4 *realer*.

174   *Case Study 2: The Comparison of Adjectives*

Readers are invited to consider via their own intuitions the acceptability of *deader* and *realer*, and why they should be so rare compared to *freer*. A possible explanation is offered below.

2 One two-syllable adjective ending in -*y* which greatly preferred phrasal comparison, namely:

LIKELY: 3,724 *more likely* (!) vs 17 *likelier*

as opposed to those which preferred inflectional comparison, e.g.:

EASY: 28 *more easy* vs 4,031 *easier*;
HAPPY: 10 *more happy* vs 1,007 *happier*;
HEALTHY: 26 *more healthy* vs 500 *healthier*;
WEALTHY: 15 *more wealthy* vs 148 *wealthier*.

Following the descriptions in this section, and the patterning of similar adjectives, one would expect *likelier* to be more common than *more likely*. An explanation for this is offered later in this section.

3 Discrepancies between the findings for two-syllable adjectives ending in -*er*, e.g.:

CLEVER: 21 *more clever* vs 101 *cleverer*;
TENDER: 15 *more tender* vs 4 *tenderer*.

These would appear to make it difficult to draw any conclusion regarding -*er*-ending adjectives.

4 similar discrepancies for adjectives ending in -*le*, e.g.:

SIMPLE: 60 *more simple* vs 1,115 *simpler*;
SUBTLE: 339 *more subtle* vs 114 *subtler*.

Again, this would appear to make a generalisation about such adjectives difficult. Readers are again invited to assess how their intuitions correspond to the findings. The activity at the end of this chapter tests intuitions about several such forms.

5 The existence of inflectional comparison with *three*-syllable adjectives ending in -*y* (even though the phrasal comparison is more common), e.g.:

UNHAPPY: 18 *more unhappy* vs 15 *unhappier*.

Why one of the three-syllable adjective breaks the ban on inflectional comparison, while the others do not, needs to be investigated.

6 The preference for phrasal comparison in the cases of two-syllable adjectives noted in Section 8.2, where both systems are said to be acceptable, e.g.:

PLEASANT: 90 *more pleasant* vs 50 *pleasanter*;
COMMON: 594 *more common* vs 73 *commoner* (which leads to the delightful explanation that '*more common* is *more common* than *commoner*' as well as that '*more likely* is *more likely* than *likelier*').

Hilpert offered several explanations for these unexpected findings and discrepancies:

- Pronunciation. The preference for the inflectional option in *simpler*, as opposed to the phrasal choice in the case of *more subtle*, may have something to do with the juxtaposition of consonant sounds: /pl/ is easier to pronounce in English than /tl/ in the middle of a word. One can suppose that a preference in speech may transfer to writing in the largely written corpus.
- Morphology. For example, the possibility of *unhappier* (though slightly rarer than *more unhappy*) is predicated on its relationship to *happier*.
- Structure. In the preference for *more likely*, cited above, a factor may be that the adjective is usually followed by a complement beginning with *that* or *to*, i.e.:
    It is more likely that… (cf. It is likelier that…)
    They are more likely to… (cf. They are likelier to…)
  Why this should be so is another question, but the structure does seem to be involved; the inflectional alternatives seem less felicitous.
- Frequency. Above all, there seems to be the influence of frequency at work. Whenever an adjective is rare in its comparative form, phrasal comparison seems to dominate, or at least rival, the inflectional option. We have already seen the cases of *dead* (19 inflectional out of a total of 23) and *tender* (15 out of 21), which are both rare, comparatively speaking, and which go against the grain of their category. To this we can add the case of *yellow*. While other adjectives ending in *-ow*, for example *shallow*, as discussed above, and *narrow* (14 *more narrow* vs 550 *narrower*) have a huge predominance of inflectional comparison, *yellow* bucks the trend: 8 *more yellow* vs 9 *yellower*.

I suggested that planning may also be a factor: the decision to use a comparative may precede the choice of adjective, resulting in the phrasal rather than the inflectional option (Berry 2018: 155). Reduplication may be another factor promoting the use of phrasal comparison: *more and more polite* sounds more natural (and is more economical) than *politer and politer* (notwithstanding Lewis Caroll's deliberately rule-breaking 'curiouser and curiouser' in *Alice in Wonderland*).

But overall it seems frequency is a factor that may have pedagogical implications. It may well be that L1 speakers, far from having a rule based on the length of the word, with exceptions, are relying on what they have heard before. And in cases of doubt the phrasal option seems to be the default. One might ask if there is still a general trend away from the inflectional towards the analytic in English morphology, as evidenced by this preference, and as noted in other areas of grammar. It would be too soon to answer this, however. Many of the above findings are hardly absolute.

8.8 In the Classroom

As far as describing the meanings of comparison is concerned, a major problem seems to be circularity (see Section 6.3): using the form being described in its own definition. Note how this description from Wikipedia (entry for 'Comparison', accessed 19 September 2018) involves circularity for the superlative but avoids it for the comparative:

> The comparative expresses a comparison between two (or more) entities or groups of entities in quality, quantity, or degree; the **superlative** is the form of an adverb or adjective that is the greatest degree of a given descriptor. [my underlining]

Another issue is whether the two forms need to be introduced together. The general approach taken in this book has been to challenge the juxtaposition of related forms, to avoid basing the introduction of one on an earlier form (e.g. of *any* on *some*), where the relationship may have been misunderstood. Scrivener (2010), for example, has two separate units (albeit short), one for the comparative and one for the superlative.

8.8.1 Rules

A major component of pedagogic practice, if not the main one, will be the rule that is presented to learners for the choice between phrasal and inflectional comparison. The precise formulation of the rule (and the terminology used) will depend, of course, on the maturity and level of sophistication of the learners. At the simplest level it might consist of saying that inflectional comparison is for shorter adjectives and phrasal for longer, as does Scrivener (2010), though he doesn't use the terms 'inflectional' and 'phrasal'. This, of course, is far from the picture painted above, but is perhaps acceptable as a first step.

At a slightly more advanced level, learners may encounter the rule of thumb that was presented in the myths research cited above:

> 'use *-er* and *-est* with one-syllable adjectives, *more* and *most* with two- and three-syllable adjectives'.

Of course, if applied this rule would lead to numerous 'errors', such as *more happy* instead of *happier*. But 'errors' is the wrong word. L1 speakers would not blink if a learner said

> *I have never been more happy.*

However, teachers may apply the 'rule' strictly and so condemn such a usage. Their justification might be stronger if a learner said 'more large', but in this case the suggestion in point 2 below may come into play.

A more advanced version of the rule would go like this:

> 'use *-er* and *-est* with one-syllable adjectives, *more* and *most* with two-syllable adjectives (except those ending *-y*, *-ow*, *-le* and *-er*) and three-syllable adjectives'.

A further elaboration might specify the possible exceptions, such as *common*. And so on. But one wonders if this increasing complexity is actually helping learners. If we turn to the conclusions of the research described above we might find more helpful advice. The following suggestions could be given in place of the prescriptive rules cited above based on the length of the adjective:

1. You can use *-er* and *-est*, or *more* and *most*, to form the comparative and superlative forms of adjectives.
2. If you have heard or seen a comparative form, whether inflectional or phrasal, use it.
3. If not, use phrasal comparison; you will rarely be criticised.

At a later level the trend for adjectives ending in *-er*, *-y*, *-le* and *-ow* to take inflectional comparison can be mentioned, but this should not be presented as a hard and fast rule. As we saw in the study, both kinds of comparison occur with such adjectives.

The third suggestion above is the crucial one. This results from the insight that the (lack of) frequency of occurrence of an adjective is a major influencing factor in the use of phrasal comparison, far more than the length of the word. Thus the forms that learners encounter are likely to be the phrasal versions of more frequent words.

This formulation is admittedly not watertight, but it is simple for learners to use. It de-emphasises an obsession with so-called correctness, which leads to the learning of rules, followed by extensions of the rules and then of exceptions to these rules. Learners may hesitate in their production because they are unsure about which form to use.

In this way the learning load is lessened and as a result more time can be devoted to learning when and how to use comparatives and superlatives. The choice between phrasal and inflectional forms is after all a relatively trivial matter in comparison with other grammatical phenomena; the wrong choice will rarely, if ever, lead to a breakdown in communication.

However, we have to accept that the pedagogic rules for comparison are well entrenched and it will certainly take a long time before they could be dethroned. But surely there is no reason for propagating misleading information, especially if there is a simpler, more economical and truthful explanation.

8.8.2 Exercises

If it is thought necessary, the choice between the two forms of comparison can be practised by simply presenting the two options in a context, for instance:

This is the _____ way to peel an orange. (most easy/easiest; most quick/quickest)

However, this type of mechanical exercise has been criticised elsewhere (see Section 6.4.2) for its inauthenticity and reliance purely on the memorisation of rules. While L1 speaker intuitions might clearly indicate 'easiest' or 'quickest' as the 'correct' answers, the 'wrong' choice would hardly be crucial. And if 'likelier' vs 'more likely' were to be offered as choices, then correctness would not be an issue, unless some inaccurate rule were applied. As we saw above, many adjectives take both forms of comparison.

Meanwhile, the practice of other aspects of comparison would be more rewarding for learners. For instance, a more appropriate (but also unrealistic) exercise would involve choosing between the three forms, for example, where learners fill in a gap from a choice of the three forms of comparison, perhaps with the help of some form of visual hint:

John is _____ in his class. (tall/taller/the tallest)

This can be turned into a more realistic and classroom-related activity whereby the learners in a class can be used as a prop; the teacher asks certain students to stand up and the rest of the class is asked to make comparisons regarding their relative height. However, the number of attributes that can be compared in this way without making invidious comparisons is very limited.

More authentic, challenging activities to practise adjective comparison – but not the choice between phrasal and inflectional comparison – are not hard to come by. One such activity can be built around a geography quiz (see also Section 6.4.2). Learners have access to a map of the world and corresponding statistics (on paper or online) and are first of all asked questions about it, for example:

>What's the largest country in the world?
>What's the highest mountain in the world?
>What's the largest country in South America?
>What's the most populous country in the world?
>What's the longest river in Africa?
>Which country is larger, France or Italy?
>Which river is longer, the Danube or the Rhine?
>etc.

Then, at a suitable point, the learners become the questioners (in group work if so desired). A written alternative or follow-up would be to reformulate the questions as statements, with the adjective missing, thus:

>Russia is the _____ country in the world.
>France is _____ than Italy.

At a slightly more advanced level the associated words can also be omitted:

>Russia is _____ country in the world.
>France is _____Italy.

8.8.3 Terminology

Another issue that could bear scrutiny is that of the terms involved (as per Chapter 4). The superordinate term 'comparison of adjectives' attempts to be transparent through the idea of comparing. But it is somewhat misleading; it is not different adjectives that are being compared,[5] or indeed different degrees of the same adjective in the case of the superlative (see Note 1).

But to the extent that any superordinate term is required, we are probably stuck with it; a better term is improbable. The only alternative would be to devise an opaque (see Chapter 4), form-based term, such as the 'modification of adjectives'.

The same is true of the terms 'comparative' and 'superlative', precisely because of the issue of the two types of comparison described above. They are useful, not so much because of their transparent nature helps learners with the concept, but because they offer a level of generalisation in the classroom. A teacher might say, using an eponymous term:

>'Use an -er adjective here.'

In a particular case this would be fine, but to make it clear that the advice also applies to phrasal comparison it would be more helpful to say

> 'Use a comparative adjective here.'

But of course there will be times when teachers wish to distinguish the two types of comparison, where it might be more economical to use eponymous options (see Chapter 5) and say

> 'This adjective usually has *more* rather than *-er*' (pronouncing *-er* as two letters).

The terms 'phrasal comparison' and 'inflectional comparison', as used above, should be avoided except at an advanced level. Similarly, the term 'base', for the basic form of the adjective, can be dispensed with in any but the most advanced account. (There are also competing terms: *absolute*, etc.)

8.9 Conclusion

The aim of this case study has not been to critique teaching practices in general but rather to arrive at a reformulation of the rule for deciding between phrasal and inflectional comparison. Hilpert's study is a classic example of how corpus analysis can aid our understanding of linguistic and pedagogic issues. It presents results that can be easily understood by teachers and can be easily adapted into material for learners. If it does not bring closure on this issue, then so be it; at least we are better informed and able to construct better explanations. Of course it is not the final word on the comparison of adjectives. Another study twenty years hence may give different results and provide evidence of another trend.

The formation of comparative and superlative adjectives is a much-debated area in scientific and pedagogic circles. But should this affect learners? The concept of comparison is not alien to them, unlike many of the important issues in English grammar, because it exists in their own languages. So, apart from a few irregular forms (see Note 2), it is really down to a fairly unimportant choice between two competing forms, over which there is much variance among L1 speakers. While an 'inappropriate' choice may lead to eyebrows being occasionally raised, it will rarely cause problems.

Thus, the comparison of adjectives – or more precisely the debate about phrasal and inflectional comparison – is rather over-rated as an issue for learners of English. Indeed, it could be entirely omitted from syllabuses. In its place other related areas can be focused on, such as how to make comparisons with *than*. But if it is included, then at least a more realistic rule can be applied.

Activity

Try out your intuitions on the following two-syllable adjectives which were also included in Hilpert's study: *sorry, worthy, lively, slender, humble, polite, remote, handsome.*

(a) Which form of comparison do you prefer in each case? Are there any forms that you would reject?
(b) Compare your intuitions with the figures from the study below. Do they match?
(c) Compare your intuitions and the figures from the study with those from the adjectives in the comparable groupings above (i.e. those ending in *-y*, in *-er*, in *-le*, and others).
(d) Does this throw any more light on the findings above or on the traditional rules?

Comment

Table 8.1 gives the figures from Hilpert with my comments.

Table 8.1 Results from Hilpert

Adjective	Frequency of phrasal comparative	Frequency of inflectional comparative	Comment
sorry	12	18	A mixed picture; *worthy* seems to buck the trend for inflectional comparison with adjectives ending in *-y*.
worthy	38	17	
lively	19	46	
slender	15	44	Similar to *clever* but not to *tender* (because of frequency?) in preferring inflectional comparison.
humble	25	77	Similar to *simple* but not to *subtle* in preferring inflectional comparison (because of ease of pronunciation?).
polite	23	7	All three in this group follow the trend identified above, preferring phrasal comparison, and in similar proportions – by two or three times.
remote	179	87	
handsome	24	10	

Generally speaking, these further figures confirm the main point made above: that the comparison of adjectives does not follow strict rules and that there are various factors affecting the choice between phrasal and inflectional comparison.

Notes

1 We can dispense with the prescriptive notion that the superlative should not be used when comparing two things, that, for example

   He is the <u>youngest</u> of the two

   is wrong, that it should be

   He is the <u>younger</u> of the two.

   Huddleston and Pullum (2002: 532) decry another prescriptive notion, that adjectives such as *unique, correct* etc., which denote an absolute quality, should not allow comparison, that to say something is 'more unique' than something else is tautologous. This of course ignores the way people use language for rhetorical purposes, as is the case with 'more dead' in the survey above.

2 These endings are among the few inflectional morphemes remaining in English (alongside the plural and genitive for nouns and the participle and past-tense forms for verbs), which exhibit the strategy 'change the shape of words' outlined in Section 2.5.2.

   Another grammatical oddity relating to inflectional comparison is the existence of irregular forms: *good/better/best, bad/worse/worst*, as well as adjectives which have alternatives to the regular forms (which have acquired different meanings to some extent): *far/further/furthest, old/elder/eldest*.

3 Hilpert did not investigate superlatives, which might have thrown further interesting light on the phenomenon of comparison.

4 Some purists object to the use of (any form of) comparison with adjectives such as *right, wrong* and *dead*. The argument is that one is either dead or not; there cannot be different degrees of 'deadness'. This argument fails on two counts: firstly, the creative use of comparison, e.g.

   You couldn't be <u>more right</u>.
   I have never seen a body that looked <u>more dead</u>.

   Secondly, there may be metaphorical meanings of the adjective for which comparison is entirely feasible:

   A: *I'm feeling totally dead.*
   B: *Yeah, well, but I'm more dead than you.*

5 There is, of course, a way of comparing two adjectives, to say that one is more applicable than another, and it also uses *more . . . than*, for example:

   I would say they were <u>more sleepy than</u> exhausted.

   This is not the same 'comparison' as discussed in this chapter. You cannot say '. . .sleepier than exhausted'.

References

Berry, Roger. 1994. 'Blackpool would be a nice place unless there were so many tourists': some misconceptions about English grammar. *Studia Anglica Posnaniensis* XXVIII: 101–112.

Berry, Roger. 2015. Grammar myths. *Language Awareness* 24/1: 15–37.

Berry, Roger. 2018. *English Grammar: A Resource Book for Students*. 2nd edn. Abingdon: Routledge.

Biber, Douglas, Stig Johannsson, Geoffrey Leech, Susan Conrad and Edward Finegan. 1999. *Longman Grammar of Spoken and Written English*. Harlow: Longman, 260–269.

Hilpert, Martin. 2008. The English comparative: language structure and language use. *English Language and Linguistics* 12/3: 395–417.

Huddleston, Rodney and Geoffrey K. Pullum. 2002. *The Cambridge Grammar of the English Language*. Cambridge: Cambridge University Press.

Quirk, Randolph, Sidney Greenbaum, Geoffrey Leech and Jan Svartvik. 1985. *A Comprehensive Grammar of the English Language*. Harlow: Longman, 265–287.

Scrivener, Jim. 2010. *Teaching English Grammar*. London: Macmillan Education.

Swan, Michael and Bernard Smith. 1987. *Learner English*. Cambridge: Cambridge University Press.

9 Case Study 3

The Personal Pronouns

9.1 Introduction

This case study turns the spotlight on an area of English grammar that some may see as sacrosanct: the personal pronouns. It seeks to establish new ways of looking at them which may lead to a re-evaluation of the way they are organised and accounted for, with implications for teaching.

How could such a basic area of English grammar be controversial and in need of re-examination? Surely the personal pronouns in English correspond precisely to pure communicational and grammatical principles that are matched in other languages. Unfortunately, they do not and are not. Although most accounts, both scientific and pedagogic, present a similar, well-established picture, the evidence is that this is a very fluid area, both historically and synchronically. One issue that needs a re-examination is the way existing pronouns are used. Another is that the membership need to be reconsidered. Below I will propose the acceptance of one, possibly two new forms, as well as new additional roles for two of the traditional pronouns.

What follows takes a critical look at the state of play, along the lines of the critical approach outlined in Chapter 3. The evidence I will present is not entirely new or unknown, but again we see the issue of poor transmission, whereby facts that have long been known have failed to reach the pedagogic arena (see Section 3.7).

9.2 The Background (1)

Several writers have pointed out how personal pronouns in English are not restricted to their traditional uses but may be also used for rhetorical and even ideological or political purposes (e.g. Fairclough 1989; Pennycook 1994; Flowerdew 1997). There are numerous situations where speakers have a choice of pronouns, according to the impression they wish to give, rather than their selection being determined by objective circumstances (i.e. it is creative rather than conventional). For example, in a study of chairmen's statements in company annual reports (Berry 1997), I noted that some chairmen chose to project their own individual authority by using *I*, while others (the majority) preferred a corporate identity through the use of *we*, as in these examples:

> We believe there is a great deal of growth potential ...
> I am pleased to report another year's record results ... (Berry 1997: 13)

The choice may not only be between competing personal pronouns; it may be between a pronoun and an impersonal construction, such as the passive in English. Tarone et al. (e.g. 1998) observed how in scientific articles writers tended to use the passive for standard, accepted moves, while using *we* for more unique, innovative decisions. In another area, one that is central to the purpose of this book, writers of grammatical description have a choice between being purely impersonal, via the use of the passive and other constructions, or personal via a pronoun, typically *we* (potentially ambiguous, between an inclusive or exclusive interpretation) or *you* (involving the reader). This issue was discussed more fully in Chapter 5.

To fully understand the problems posed by personal pronouns we need to re-examine critically the dominant model accounting for their use.

9.3 The Personal Pronoun Paradigm

Descriptions of the English personal pronouns are dominated by a tabular depiction of what is commonly called the 'personal pronoun paradigm' (PPP). Table 9.1 shows one particular variant of this paradigm.

Table 9.1 The traditional personal pronoun paradigm, with axes for person and number.

	Singular	Plural
1st person	*I, me, my, mine*	*we, us, our, ours*
2nd person	*you, you, your, yours*	
3rd person	masculine: *he, him, his, his* feminine: *she, her, her, hers* neuter: *it, it, its, its*	*they, them, their, theirs*

In Table 9.1 each box contains four forms: the subjective case, the objective case, the 'possessive' determiner (and so strictly speaking, the paradigm is not just about pronouns) and the 'possessive' pronoun. (See Section 9.9.3 for a discussion of the accuracy of 'possessive' as a term.) This is the paradigm at its most comprehensive as found in scientific grammars with slight variations (for instance, the axes may be exchanged, or the reflexive pronouns may be added). Simpler versions, with just the subjective and objective case forms, may be found in more pedagogically oriented grammars.

I have suggested that the whole PPP can be called into question, not only because of its content, but also because the whole concept of a paradigmatic model is inappropriate for this complicated, multi-layered area of grammar (Berry 2013, Berry 2018: 83–85). In the first place there are too many dimensions to capture in this way – not just those identified above. For example, Wales (1996: 45), stresses the importance – and absence from descriptions – of generic uses (see Section 9.5). Then there are numerous inconsistencies, for example the fact that number is neutralised for the second person, that *we* is not really the plural of *I*, and so on. Here is a more detailed analysis of these categories.

9.3.1 Person

In standard accounts English has three 'persons', labelled 'first', 'second' and 'third'. In these accounts the first person (*I*, *we*, etc.) refers to the speaker or writer in the act of communication. We can point out here that these pronouns are not the only way of referring to the first person; there are other formal and euphemistic ways according to the situation, such as 'the present writer', 'yours truly', or the royal 'we'.[1]

The second person refers to the other participant(s) in the act of communication: the hearer(s) or reader(s); see below for more on the pronoun, *you*, used to realise this. The third person is somewhat different, in that it refers to something or someone outside the act of communication; unlike the first and second persons, whose reference is 'deictic' (i.e. pointing, in that it depends on the situation; see Section 10.4.2), the referent is said to be identifiable from the text. This view, that *it* and *they* (etc.) refer back to and take the place of noun phrases (i.e. are 'pro-nouns') is somewhat misguided; in particular *it* often has no reference and fulfils grammatical roles, as in these examples:

> <u>It</u>'s going to rain. (*It* is a dummy subject, fulfilling the needs of sentence structure.)
> <u>It</u>'s the bugs I can't stand. (A 'cleft' sentence.)

I would appreciate it if you could bring forward my appointment. (A case of 'extraposition'; *it* is a dummy object, warning of the lengthy object to come.)

Even when it has reference *it* is by definition not a 'personal' pronoun since it does not refer to people, but we can perhaps ignore this quibble. Thus on several levels we can question whether *it* really belongs in the PPP.

9.3.2 *Number*

'Number' basically refers to the obligatory choice in English between singular and plural (for nouns as well as pronouns). In some languages there are other options, including 'dual' to specify two of something; in others (e.g. Mandarin and Cantonese) the choice is not obligatory for nouns.

While the first and third persons distinguish singular and plural, in standard English there is no distinction for number for the second person; *you* serves as both singular and plural. However, there are various non-standard forms which take up the role of plural, restricting *you* to singular reference: *yiz* in Irish English, *youse* in Liverpudlian (spellings may vary), and the iconic *y'all* in southern American English. There is one more form which, deceptively, since it is written as two words, is slowly acquiring the status of a personal pronoun, namely *you guys*. (Phonetically it behaves as one word, with a single stress on the first syllable; however, writing it as one word 'youguys' does seem rather unattractive.) It would seem to be restricted to informal, spoken contexts, and lacks some related forms (**It's you guys' turn* or **It's your guys turn*), but it is very common and has clearly spread extensively into British English from its source in American English. One objection, that *guys* is clearly masculine in reference, does not hold here; *you guys* can not only refer to mixed groups but also to groups of women. There were 15,409 examples of the string *you guys* in the 2017 Corpus of Contemporary American English[2] (COCA). Here are two examples from it:

Now, you guys have to finish the job...
That's where you guys come in.

(Both are potentially ambiguous in writing; *guys* could be functioning as a plural head noun, with *you* as a determiner, but then in speech the stress would be on *guys*.)

In this way the number distinction for the second person is being restored, with *you* as the singular option (whereas before it was the plural form and *thou* the singular).

The other major issue with number is the role of *we*. Although supposedly the plural of *I*, it is clearly very rare, almost impossible, to have more than one 'first persons', especially in speech. Two exceptions to this would be the classic situation in films where two twins are speaking in unison, or where several people append their name to a document as 'we, the undersigned'. For the most part, the plurality of *we* derives from combining the first person with the second or third person. In some cases *we* refers to both hearer and speaker:

What are we doing tonight?

In others it is third-person reference that accompanies the first, and the hearer is expressly excluded:

We're staying in tonight. What about you?

This is the well-known distinction between 'inclusive' and 'exclusive' *we*, according to whether the hearer is included or excluded. In some languages it is lexicalised. In English the clearly inclusive *let's* is the only situation where the distinction is reflected in usage. There are, of course, situations where the reference of *we* is not just inclusive or exclusive, in particular the politician's all-embracing *we* (i.e. all three persons). Politicians also exploit the referential ambiguity of *we* to be deliberately vague or to shift without drawing attention from one interpretation to another (Wales 1996: 62; Flowerdew 1996: 578).

Other deviations from this notion of *we* as referring to the first-person plural include the classic royal *we* (*We are not amused*), not to mention the authorial use in academic writing whereby single authors represent themselves as more than one in order to gain authority (a genre convention that is probably well past its sell-by date nowadays). Then there is the patronising *we* of doctors and nurses when speaking to patients, e.g. *How are we doing?*, which technically excludes the first person (the speaker), while trying to suggest – inappropriately, some would say – a joint enterprise. Whether these are genuine cases, or a scriptwriter's invention, they all chip away at the characterisation of *we* as the plural of *I*.

9.3.3 Gender

Gender only applies to the third-person singular in English, as a way of narrowing down reference (which is clearly not needed for the first and second persons). The singular makes a three-way distinction between masculine *he* etc., feminine *she* etc. and neuter, or inanimate *it* etc., whereas the plural makes no such distinction. This leaves the issue of how to refer in the singular to a referent that is animate/human but whose sex is unknown; this issue does not arise in the plural. The factors surrounding this problem are discussed in Section 9.4.

9.3.4 Case

Case is one of the few areas where English uses the strategy of changing the form of a word for a grammatical purpose (Section 2.5.2). This only applies to the first- and third-person pronouns in English (excluding *it*). The second person is neutralised for case, as it is for number; in standard English, *you* serves as subjective as well as objective form. Note the terms 'subjective' and 'objective' here. In common parlance these forms are referred to as 'subject' (*I, he, she, we, they*) and 'object' pronouns. This is not quite accurate at least in scientific terminology, because, although they do parallel the subject/object distinction found with noun phrases in grammatical structure (see Section 2.5), the objective form also serves the grammatical function 'complement' (or 'predicative') in that form of analysis:

> *Who's that? – It's me.*

This has become a prescriptive issue for some native speakers (see the discussion in Section 2.6.2), who claim that the subjective should be used after the verb *be*:

> *Who's that? – It is I.*

Both forms can be heard, but the former is far more frequent and is of greater antiquity while the latter is restricted to very formal contexts and can sound pompous. It appears to have been introduced through analogy with Latin grammar, where the nominative case would be used for both subject and complement. But English grammar, as we have seen in Chapter 2, differs from Latin grammar. However, to be fair, the issue is less clear-cut when the complement pronoun is itself the antecedent of the subject in a following relative clause:

> *It is they/them who are responsible.*

The reader is invited to compare the two possibilities. But in cases where linking verbs other than 'be' are followed by a complement/predicative, to use the subjective would sound bizarre:

> **That's when I became what I am today – when I became I.*

Bauer (1998) conclusively demolishes this myth; and yet it still persists.

9.3.5 Related Forms

There are two other sets of forms that are sometimes included in the paradigm (as in Table 9.1): the so-called possessive determiners (*my* etc.) and possessive pronouns (*mine* etc.). A third set, the reflexive pronouns (*myself* etc.), may also be included in the paradigm since they parallel the other forms. We should note here that the reflexive pronouns also have an emphatic use, as

> *Myself*, I feel it's overdone (emphatic) in addition to
> I hurt *myself* (reflexive).

A further issue with the paradigm for the third-person-singular neuter box is the questionable status of *its* as a possessive pronoun. It seems strange to say 'The bone is its' (referring to a dog). However, valid examples can be found, as with these two from COCA:

> ... *perhaps it was more used to her shape than she was to its.*
> *Mars moved on its orbit, Earth moved on its.*

It is hard to say how frequent it is, however; most citations of *its* that I found in COCA when not used as a possessive determiner were in fact mistakes.

9.3.6 Summary

From the discussion above we should appreciate that there is nothing 'absolute' about the PPP; it is an artifice of linguistic description. A look at the multitude of ways in which different languages handle pronominal reference discussed in Section 9.6.1 will strengthen this conviction. This is just another case of metalinguistic relativity (Chapters 3 and 4) whereby a linguistic device – a paradigm in this case – has become so dominant that it prevents us from looking beyond, to a rather messy reality. The point is, if we were to start entirely afresh, with the knowledge we have now, we might end up with a very different picture.

The rest of this case study concentrates on two areas of concern of personal pronoun usage which fall outside the narrow confines of the PPP and which as a result receive little attention in teaching:

– the use of *they* as a singular pronoun,
– the use of *you* as a generic pronoun.

9.4 *They* as Singular Pronoun

For several decades there has been an awareness that certain pronominal usage is sexist, in particular the use of masculine third-person-singular forms to refer back to people whose sex is unknown or not determined, as in this example:

> *A member who has his membership revoked may not reapply for two years.*

Such a usage jars on the ears of most people nowadays. Unlike other changes in English identified in Section 3.2, this is distinctly a conscious change resulting from socio-political pressure. However, certain alternatives to the use of *he* in this situation, such as using *it* etc. or the invented form *s/he*, have not found favour; the former is too strongly identified with its non-human status (except possibly with little children), while the latter is impossible to pronounce and lacks the related forms; a further possibility, 'his or her' is laborious. Writers are advised to avoid this issue by pluralising the noun phrase wherever possible so that *they* etc. can be used to refer back, i.e.:

Member<u>s</u> who have <u>their</u> membership revoked...

But there are cases where this is not possible (see below), and even where it is, English already has an answer to the problem: to use *they* to refer back to <u>singular</u> antecedents. This use has already drawn the notice of scientific grammarians; Huddleston and Pullum (2002: 493) give it their approval, as does Wales (1996: 125–133).

While in the past this use may have been somewhat restricted in its range, nowadays it would appear to extend even to respectable written English. It is particularly common referring back to indefinite pronouns such as *everyone* and *anyone* which, though singular grammatically, are plural semantically:

If <u>anybody</u> had been there to observe the gentle-looking elderly lady who stood meditatively on the loggia outside her bungalow, <u>they</u> would have thought she had nothing more on her mind than deliberation on how to arrange her time that day. (From Agatha Christie's *A Caribbean Mystery*, HarperCollins, 1993, p. 126)

<u>Someone</u> would need to vouch that he was with <u>them</u> at the time of the murder... (Robert Harris, *Dictator*, Hutchinson, 2015, p. 87)

However, indefinite singular noun phrases are also possible as antecedents:

<u>Any fool</u> knows that 'they' can be singular, don't <u>they</u>?

If <u>a parent</u> wishes to remove a child from school early then <u>they</u> should apply to the Principal in writing...

...one of our volunteers lost their life... (Spoken on Episode 8 of *Designated Survivor*, viewed on Netflix, 4 October 2018)

He looked like <u>a child</u> who had had <u>their</u> favourite toy taken away... (BBC Sport Website, 28 November 2016)

In the last example *its* could also have served as a way of avoiding *their*; but as mentioned above there is a reluctance to use the impersonal *it* or *its* for children. Equally, pluralisation would not be appropriate; even in the second example above to use the plural ('If parents...') could imply a group rather than individual action.

Indeed, a further development seems to be taking place. Huddleston and Pullum (2002: 494) note that cases where the antecedent is referential (i.e. referring to a specific or known individual) are rare. But this no longer seems to be the case, as these six recent examples from my own experience, the first four spoken, the last two written, demonstrate; in all six cases the antecedent is a definite noun phrase (underlined):

> The next Prime Minister and their cabinet... (Former British PM David Cameron in Parliament, 29 June 2016)
> When that person walked into the police station there was no child with them. (On ITV programme The Investigator, 14 July 2016)
> This employee is another senior member of staff. They told us ... (BBC Watchdog programme, 23 May 2018)
> This person has no signs of ... deficiency in their diet. (On Channel 5, 6 October 2018)
> The drone operator is still at large and police said it was possible they were an environmental activist. (BBC News Website, 21 December 2018)
> ... this was the first time the head of a major international organisation had been forced from their position. (From The Silk Roads: A New History of the World by Peter Frankopan, Bloomsbury, 2015, p. 502)

As described above, the employment of gender-neutral *they, them* or *their* in these examples allows the speaker or writer to avoid specifying the sex of the person involved. (In fact, in the fourth and last cases the antecedent was actually male, as the context made clear, and so *his* would have been uncontroversial.) All this suggests the acceptance of *they* as a singular pronoun.

9.4.1 A New Reflexive Pronoun?

This acceptance of *they, them, their* and *theirs* as valid gender-neutral third-person forms leads to an interesting question regarding the use of the related reflexive pronoun: in cases where *they* is singular in reference, can it be appropriate to say *themselves* as the reflexive form? Would not *themself* be preferable, a logical consequence of using *they* with singular antecedents? The reader is invited to judge the acceptability of the two forms:

> Just because a person has low self-esteem, it doesn't mean that they will self-harm themself/themselves.
> Give someone enough rope and they'll hang themself.

9.4 They as Singular Pronoun

All the objections that applied to alternatives for *they* (*he*, *he and she*, *s/he*) that were discussed in Section 9.4 also apply here.

How common is it? There were 113 examples of 'themself' in the COCA corpus compared to 114,011 examples of 'themselves' (including emphatic forms). In most cases there is an antecedent indefinite pronoun such as *anyone* or *someone*, as was the case with singular *they*.

> He stipulated in his will that <u>anyone</u> able to prove <u>themself</u> to be his widow or child would be entitled to fifty dollars.

But there may be a noun phrase in the antecedent:

> <u>That witness</u> has placed <u>themself</u> on the scene of a murder...

This also applies to its emphatic use:

> Does that mean then you want stem cells from <u>the patient themself</u>?

In all these cases here the advantage of using *themself* lies in the gender neutrality. But there are even cases with obviously plural reference:

> ... students were asked to assess the fit between <u>themself</u> and macro social work practice...
> ... sometimes <u>boys</u> have to learn those things for <u>themself</u>.

Presumably in both cases *themselves* would have sufficed.

One can ask if this is evidence of a growing trend towards the use of *themself*. There are certainly enough examples of it to be found in corpora, enough to rule out a claim of error. However, the results from COCA would, surprisingly, seem to argue against this. Taking five-year periods as our yardstick we can see from Table 9.2 that the frequency of *themself* has apparently decreased over the last twenty-five or so years.

Table 9.2 Frequency of themself *over twenty-five years*

Period	Frequency
1993–1997	33
1998–2002	22
2003–2007	16
2008–2012	15
2013–2017	13

In 2013–2017 the occurrence of *themself* was only 40 per cent of what it had been twenty years before. Now this is no hard proof that its use is actually declining; the sample is small and it can be influenced, as with any corpus, by variations in the sources selected. If there is a decline it may be because this use has been stigmatised – at least in writing. The Microsoft spellchecker constantly changes my citations of it to *themselves*, so it may have had a somewhat sinister role to play. But it seems that we are not yet at the stage where it can be advocated as a fully fledged form in descriptions of English. Nevertheless, teachers should be aware of it in case their learners come across it.

9.5 Generic *You*

There is another major structural issue with the PPP, one that is perhaps more problematic than the others alluded to so far. It concerns the reference of the personal pronouns. The PPP assumes that reference is specific (that is, to identifiable individuals: *I* the speaker, *you* the hearer), but in fact much of the time reference is generic, referring to all people, not just the speaker, hearer or third party. (For more on the distinction between specific and generic, see case study 1 on articles in Chapter 7.) Take the following examples (cited in Berry 2013: 239):

> One must be careful with firearms (formal).
> We now live in a global village (all-inclusive, as used by politicians, claiming solidarity with the speaker).

In both cases the pronouns could be replaced with 'people' without significantly affecting the reference (though perhaps losing some of the creative nuances). Wales (1996: 45) argues that overall the generic uses of personal pronouns warrant more attention in descriptions of English since they are 'exceedingly common in speech'. It would seem that they constitute a further dimension for the PPP to handle.

Nowhere is this generic dimension more pronounced than with *you*, as in these examples:

> It's awful when you can't remember someone's name.
> You add the eggs to the butter, not the other way round. (Quoted in Siewierska 2004: 11)

Is *you* referring to the hearer here? Not specifically. The sentence is making a generalisation, and *you* refers to people in general; i.e. it is generic. Siewierska (2004: 212) summarises this use as follows: the addressee is directly invited to imagine himself [sic] in the situation or event expressed by the speaker and thus share the world-view being presented or entertained.

This neatly captures various situations in which generic *you* is found, for example where it includes the speaker:

> *It wasn't a bad life. You got up at seven* ... (Quirk et al. 1985: 354)

or where reference cannot possibly include the reader since the event is in the past:

> *Indeed, until September 1942 you were more likely to die if you were a British civilian* ... (Quoted in Berry 2009: 31)

Amongst others, Quirk et al. (1985: 354) characterise generic *you* as 'typically an informal equivalent of *one*'.[3] Though a popular belief, this is somewhat contradicted by evidence that generic *you* occurs in formal, written circumstances, and that the two can co-occur:

> *I don't feel that one can ever be a therapist to somebody that you are closely involved with emotionally.* (Cited in Wales 1996: 81)
> *The best you can do is to use the little voice one has.* (Stephen Fry in an interview on BBC TV, 8 November 2018)

How frequent is generic you as a proportion of *you* overall? In a 2009 study I examined 100 concordance lines taken randomly from the *Collins Cobuild Wordbanks Online Corpus*. Using substitution with *one* as a test and interpreting for generalisation, I found thirty-three (i.e. one-third) to be generic. This finding should be treated with great caution of course, given the size of sample and the make-up of the corpus. Nevertheless, it would seem that generic *you* is indeed a significant phenomenon in modern English. *You* itself is generally a very common word (not mentioning *your* and *yours*); Kennedy (1998: 98) ranked it as the fourteenth most frequent word type in English according to the Birmingham Corpus (a forerunner of Cobuild's Bank of English), so it seems sensible that its generic use should receive the attention of grammarians. (See the activity at the end of this chapter for more evidence of this.)

One final point may be made about generic *you*. Since the addressee is involved, speakers must take care not to make offensive statements (unless they intend to). For example, when the metalanguage of definitions was being devised for the Cobuild Dictionaries, the authors realised that they could not extend their preferred 'youser-friendly' (see Section 5.4) *you* to all entries for verbs ('When you X something, you...'), for this would have resulted in definitions such as 'When you murder someone...'. Their solution was to impersonalise through the use of infinitives ('To murder someone...').

9.6 The Background (2)

9.6.1 Contrastive Evidence

The traditional personal pronoun paradigm, which is assumed to hold for all languages, with minor variations, is in fact multilaterally inconsistent. Siewierska (2004), in a study of person from languages around the world, cites numerous different arrangements. For instance, some languages have different pronouns for inclusive and exclusive *we*, e.g. northern Mandarin Chinese. While each language may be said to have something resembling a paradigm, it may be very different from that for English, and different factors may be involved.

Some such differences from English will be familiar to readers, especially those concerning major European languages. Thus French distinguishes third-person gender for both singular and plural, but at the same time only distinguishes number in the written form: *il* and *ils* ('he' and 'they' masculine) are not distinguished in speech in most cases, as are *elle* and *elles* ('she' and 'they' feminine). There is also the matter of grammatical gender, in that these pronouns will be used to refer back to nouns according to their established grammatical status as masculine or feminine, regardless of their natural gender (as is the case in English). An iconic example is the German noun 'Mädchen' ('girls'), which is neuter in gender.

Then there are the so-called honorific second-person pronouns in many European languages, whereby the singular, so-called T forms (*tu* in French, etc.) are restricted to use in informal, familiar relationships, while the originally plural V pronouns (*vous* etc.) are used as markers of respect, even with singular addressees, reflecting the distance between speaker and hearer. These are a great difficulty for English L1 speakers. However, this area is notably fluid, as with other aspects of personal pronoun usage; for example, the honorific 'usted' in Spanish is now considered old-fashioned.

A further issue is that of the so-called pro-drop languages, such as Italian and the Slavonic languages, where person is usually marked by verb endings, making the use of pronouns for subject use unnecessary, for example, Italian *vengo* ('I come'). In fact, pro-dropping, rather than being a hard-and-fast rule, as some linguists would wish, is often not observed. Conversely, supposedly non-pro-drop languages, e.g. Chinese and even English, may 'lose' their pronouns given the right circumstances; in English this usually occurs in informal language, e.g. *Saw you last week*.

From all these examples we can see the difficulty in trying to map one language's pronouns onto another's.

As regards generic *you*, English is far from being the only language that uses the second-person pronoun in this way. According to Siewierska (2004: 212), it is widespread throughout European languages, but in this case it is the singular, the informal T version, rather than the plural which is utilised, in some cases because the plural is used honorifically (see above). However, according to her, in none of the many languages which use a second-person-singular pronoun to refer generically is its use as common as in English, though it may be increasing under the influence of English. Meanwhile, for those languages which do not use second-person pronouns in this way, it does not mean they are incapable of referring generically with pronouns; other personal pronouns may be used, especially the third-person plural (Siewierska 2004: 211).

9.6.2 Historical Evidence

Over the centuries there have been many changes in personal pronouns in English, which further emphasises the fragility of the PPP. As we saw, English originally distinguished singular and plural in the second person: *thou* (etc.) for singular and *you* (etc.), itself an introduction from Norse, for plural. By the time of Shakespeare, the distinction was not only based on number but on the relationship between speaker and hearer; *you* for plural and for formal situations, as a marker of respect, even for singular, while *thou* was restricted to intimate, singular use, similar to the distinction developed in other European languages, as noted. However, the distinction in at least standard English disappeared with the 'demise' of *thou* in current parlance.

Regarding the use of *they* for singular reference, prescriptive grammarians (and teachers) may argue that it is a recent anomaly. However, this use has in fact been around in English for a long time. Huddleston and Pullum (2002: 493) point out that the use of *they* (and its related forms *them*, *their* and *theirs*) with singular antecedents goes back to middle English. The *Oxford English Dictionary* gives its first mention as 1577. Wales (1996: 126) also stresses its longevity:

> Singular *they* has, in fact, been well established in informal usage for centuries...

although she notes a certain reluctance on the part of earlier descriptive grammarians, in particular Quirk et al. (1985), to give it their approval.

9.7 Learners and Personal Pronouns

As we saw above, far from being a case of one-to-one mapping of personal pronouns in one language onto the corresponding ones in English, the contrastive situation is much more complex; there are many mismatches. However, learners seem to make an assumption of direct equivalence, as evidenced by the errors they make in English, for example these from Swan and Smith (1987):

Omission of subject pronouns:

* * I bought the book before left the shop. (Chinese learner, p. 232)
* * Was raining. (Spanish/Catalan speaker, p. 85)

Confusion of case:

* * I am like she. (Chinese learner, p. 232)

Confusion of gender:

* * I've a brother and she's working in a factory. (Chinese learner, p. 231)
* * This cooker doesn't work as well as she used to. (French learner, p. 52)

Use of the objective instead of reflexive:

* * I hurt me with a hammer. (French learner, p. 53)

My 2009 article on generic *you* was predicated on a court case in Hong Kong in which a litigant's testimony (in Cantonese) was translated by an interpreter into English (for the benefit of the non-Cantonese-speaking judge) as 'You could say that', which was interpreted by the court as having generic reference, i.e. agreeing with the defence counsel's point. However, what the litigant meant was 'You' (the counsel) 'could say that' (but not me), i.e. reference was specific.

But even English L1 speakers can get confused by the reference of *you*, as in this example from Wales (1996: 79), where clarification is needed:

A: Friends can be two-faced.
B: What do you mean?
A: The way they talk about you.
B: Me?
A: No, me!

As regards the awareness of the PPP among learners, in an informal survey, I found that two-thirds of first-year English majors at my Hong Kong university were familiar with the PPP (Berry 2013: 234). This was a familiarity they had presumably acquired during their years of secondary education. I suspect a similar situation would pertain elsewhere.

9.8 The Current Pedagogic Situation

9.8.1 Coverage in Materials

Outside of scientific grammars mention of the use of *they* as singular in any EFL materials is rare. Wales (1996: 133) comments acerbically on this omission:

> Because of grammarians' general conservatism the prevalence of indeterminate *they* [she stresses its gender-free nature rather than its use as singular] foreign students are likely to be unaware of its existence, until they encounter native-speakers or 'real' common-core spoken and written usage.

A notable exception is in the pedagogically-oriented *Collins Cobuild English Grammar* (2011: 37), which gives the following account:

> You can also use *they* in subject position, or *them* in object position, to refer to an individual when you do not know, or do not want to specify, whether the individual is male or female

though the subsequent discussion only refers to indefinite pronouns or noun phrases as antecedents.

The picture is worse with *themself* and *you guys*. There is no mention of the former and mention of the latter is rare. Biber et al. (1999: 330) give an example of it as a way of making *you* more specific, rather than recognising it as a pronoun per se; and the *Collins Cobuild English Grammar* (2011: 30) lists it and exemplifies it only as one of several ways of making *you* plural (alongside, for example *you two*).

9.8.2 Coverage of Generic 'You'

The situation with generic *you* is somewhat different. In Berry (2009) I surveyed a sample of various types of grammatical comment across the scientific/pedagogic spectrum. At one end, the three most authoritative scientific grammars (Quirk et al. 1985, Huddleston and Pullum 2002 and Biber et al. 1999) all mention generic *you* but the descriptions are brief, and in two cases are derived from that for *one*. At the other end of the spectrum, in EFL classroom coursebooks and grammar practice books, no mention was found. In between there were varying findings.

Of the five pedagogic grammars surveyed, all mention this use. There is a fairly lengthy discussion of it in Carter and McCarthy (2006: 286), and the *Collins Cobuild English Grammar* (2011: 36) includes it in a separate table for generic pronominal reference (alongside *one*, *we* and *they*) followed by a description and exemplification. As regards alphabetically ordered reference grammars, Swan (1995) mentions it twice: on page 432 along with other personal pronouns and on page 393, where it is compared to *one*:[4]

> 16) <u>One</u>/<u>You</u> can't learn a language in six weeks.

Chalker (1990), however, gives not just a generic but also a self-referring use, while Leech et al. (2001:612) refer to it as a 'general' use.

In introductory coursebooks for students of English (important because such students often go on to become teachers), of the six books surveyed three give the personal pronoun paradigm but do not mention generic uses at all. One, Wardaugh (2003), gives a brief mention of generic uses (including *you*), while Downing and Locke (1992: 413–414) mention generic *we* but not *you*. Huddleston and Pullum (2005:103) discuss it under the label of a 'non-deictic use'; i.e. as non-specific. Four grammar courses for teachers were examined: Yule (1998), Parrott (2000), Master (1996) and Celce-Murcia and Larsen-Freeman (1999). Not one of them mentioned generic *you*. This may be due to the fact that they are reflecting classroom practice, but of course this may result in a vicious circle.

If anything is done to explain generic *you*, it is as an informal version of *one*. As shown above, this is misleading: generic *you* itself can be rather formal, and can be found in the same circumstances as *one*. More importantly, generic *you* is far more common than generic *one*, and so if anything the relationship should be reversed; generic *one* should be regarded as the markedly formal version of generic *you*.

9.9 What to Do?

9.9.1 Strategy

As regards a general approach to the personal pronouns, it would seem advisable – given the extensive differences between them in English and other languages – to tailor (where possible, i.e. not in multilingual classes) any formal instruction to the needs of learners according to their L1 background. So, for example, in EFL classes for French L1 speakers, there would be a focus on the third-person-singular pronouns, in order to train them to use third-person-singular pronouns according to natural gender rather than the grammatical gender that they are accustomed to in French. A further task for teachers (amongst others) would be to dispel any perceived equivalence between French *on* and English *one*; the latter is, as we saw, a rare formal generic pronoun, while the latter has become a very common replacement for *nous*.

But what about the specific areas discussed above? Namely, the use of *they* as a singular pronoun and of *you* for generic reference, not to mention the existence of *you guys* and *themself* as new members of the paradigm? Are these areas sufficiently frequent or enough of a problem for learners to warrant their introduction into the classroom, in the shape of a syllabus and associated teaching materials (assuming there is a grammatical focus)? I would argue that this is the case for both generic *you* and singular *they* – perhaps at a relatively advanced level. While it may be possible to control texts at beginner and intermediate level (in which case materials writers need to take care not to introduce them unwittingly), they are frequent and appear in all sorts of authentic texts, formal and otherwise, not to mention the lack of equivalence in learners' L1s.

As for *you guys* and *themself*, perhaps the time has not yet come for them to be accorded a place in any formal course. The latter, while a logical extension of singular *they*, is still rare and controversial. The former, though frequent in colloquial speech, is not an indispensable alternative to *you* for beginners, nor does it stand out as a novel phenomenon. At a more advanced level learners may well acquire it naturally when they come to adopt more informal language into their repertoire.

9.9.2 Activities

A typical exercise for generic *you* might be to take some sample sentences and ask learners to say who is being talked about. In a recent article I quoted a delightful example from Pete McCarthy's *McCarthy's Bar* (Hodder & Stoughton, 2000, p. 368, quoted in Berry 2009) in which two drunken tourists are leaving a hotel and the manager calls after them:

You *can tell* you're *not Irish.*

This can be exploited by the teacher asking: 'Who does *you* refer to here? Is it the same people in both cases? A similar exercise can be used with a gap for the pronoun, asking learners to fill it in to make a generalisation, as with this example cited above:

It's awful when ____ can't remember someone's name.

Similar activities can be devised for singular *they*. But the main thrust here must be on the level of teacher awareness in the first place (Section 1.6): awareness of all the aspects of the personal pronouns discussed. Teachers need to be conscious of them above all in case the issues are raised by their learners. If a learner comes across a case of *they* referring back to a singular pronoun or noun phrase, should the teacher have to resort to saying it is a mistake? Surely not.

9.9.3 Terminology

There are a number of interesting issues pertaining to the terminology used in describing the personal pronouns; this warrants a separate section for this case study based on the discussion and criteria described in Chapter 4.

Firstly, we can question the accuracy of 'possessive' as a term to refer to both the so-called possessive determiners (*my* etc.) and possessive pronouns (*mine* etc.). As with many transparent terms, while some instances of both forms clearly refer to possession (*It's my book, It's mine*), many do not: *It's your loss, their defeat was totally unexpected*. This is similar to the inflected form of nouns (e.g. dog's), which is also somewhat misleadingly labelled 'possessive'. However, a better term is not easy to recommend, and the two labels are widely accepted (cf. the concept of 'familiarity' in Section 4.6).

Secondly, we might mention the point that the possessive determiners are sometimes erroneously called 'adjectives', which they clearly are not. The place in noun-phrase structure that they occupy is the same as other determiners: they appear in front of adjectives (*my red pen*) and cannot appear after other determiners (**the my pen*). This is one terminological change that should be vigorously pursued in the pedagogic arena.

Thirdly, a comment is in order on the use of the three terms 'number', 'person' and 'case'. These words are in common usage as countable nouns with different meanings (*a large number, a brave person, an important legal case*). However, in their terminological use, both are used as uncountable nouns and thereby achieve the quality of distinctiveness discussed in Section 4.2 (e.g. *in English person has three categories, while number has two*), although we can talk about 'the three persons'. In spite of this, all three terms are little used in teaching and should be considered as belonging to the scientific end of the terminological spectrum (apart from the one-off 'third-person -s').

9.10 Conclusion

The personal pronoun paradigm is a classic case of metalinguistic relativity (Chapter 3). A model that we have inherited limits our grammatical worldview and hides the rather messy reality; even scientific grammarians are complicit in this. The other major problem identified in Section 3.7 – poor transmission – is not so relevant here, unlike in the other case studies, since the problem is not so much with facts that are known which do not reach the pedagogic arena as it is with facts that are ignored in the first place.

The reason why a paradigm such as that depicted in the model is unsuitable is that personal pronouns are subject to socio-pragmatic forces rather than purely formal ones. This is somewhat similar to another area that is problematic for grammatical description, namely the modal auxiliaries. Personal pronouns, as has been shown, are chosen according to interpersonal factors, such as the power relationship between interlocutors, or the impression that a speaker/writer wishes to convey, rather than relying on objective factors (i.e. it is highly creative).

So are we stuck with the PPP? Surely some adjustment is possible. The problem is that there are too many dimensions involved. Even the current model at its simplest, catering for number, person and case, has too many dimensions to account for in two axes. At the very least we would need to insert *they* as a fourth option alongside *he*, *she* and *it*, as in Table 9.3.

This shows person, number and case only; the possessive determiner and possessive pronoun forms have been omitted from Table 9.1 at the start of this chapter. The non-generic pronominal uses of *one* (see Note 3) are also not included, nor is the informal *you guys*. As for the generic dimension, involving, above all, *you*, but also other pronouns, it is difficult to see how it could be included; a separate treatment would be required. As was pointed out above, the *Collins Cobuild English Grammar* (2011: 36) does just this in the shape of another table. Overall, the paradigm seems hard, if not impossible, to sustain if it has to include all dimensions.

However, the personal pronouns are a valid sub-class of English grammar (even though the membership is not entirely agreed upon), and so some account of their uses is necessary (if only in reference grammars). One alternative to the PPP, or as a back-up to it, is to list the individual pronouns and then specify their uses (as in e.g. Carter

Table 9.3 A revised version of the personal pronoun paradigm

	Singular		Plural
1st person	*I, me*		*we, us*
2nd person		*you, you*	
3rd person	masculine: *he, him* feminine: *she, her* neuter: *it, it* non-gender-specific: *they, them*		*they, them*

and McCarthy 2006: 377–380) and, correspondingly perhaps, to introduce them slowly over the course of a syllabus.

Certain lessons can be derived from this case study. It is another good example (along with the case study in Chapter 8 on adjective comparison) of how corpus analysis can help with a re-evaluation of particular areas of English grammar (though the evidence in that case study was purely based on a corpus). The chapter is also an example of areas of English which have escaped pedagogic attention, not because pedagogy has created its own alternative reality (as with the case studies in Chapters 7 and 10), but because pedagogy has received little help from scientific accounts because of its dependence on the PPP.

A Postscript

A further boost to the use of singular *they* may come from the issue of how to refer to transgender people. An article in *The Times* (13 October 2019) reports that BBC employees have been instructed to use *they* in such cases rather than *he* or *she*. Such linguistic 'engineering' may meet some resistance, but it does solve the same problem that has caused the popularity of singular *they* in the first place. One can wonder whether the next step will be for all the BBC's staff to be referred to using *they* to avoid identifying transgender staff. From there it is still a very long road to a situation where *they* replaces the singular third-person pronouns. But equally unpredicted things have happened to personal pronoun use in the past, and this does demonstrate how such a seemingly untouchable area as personal pronouns can be subject to change motivated by cultural and societal pressures, rather than being an unchanging monolith, as represented by the PPP.

Activity

(a) Look at this example from COCA. Does it strike you as odd? What alternatives to 'themselves' might there be, and what would the argument for each be?

> [She] said she also wants to 'elect the candidate that can carry themselves as commander in chief of our country'.

(b) Work out whether the following concordance lines (from COCA) containing *you* (underlined) are generic or specific in their reference; the simplest method is to try replacing *you* with *one*, though the two are not necessarily equal.

1 I must be perfectly frank with you. Although you appeal for no commitment, I would be remiss to ask you …

2 So some kids are born to play baseball and you just know it. You can see it.
3 We sort out the best of the bunch and help you choose the one that's right for you ...
4 'You do beautiful work. You're a real artist', Francis said.
5 Fifty years ago you could put all the big boys in one room, lock the door and say ...
6 Chris Black, same question to you about the vice president's campaign.
7 I guess I dozed off. That's what happens when you get old.
8 And I respect you, but wait a minute, I think I love you more.
9 When you listen, you hear distant echoes of current music.
10 This makes it too – very, very difficult when you – when you have two foreign policies for one country.
11 ... what did you do to make Mandy blush?
12 And you know, Nancy, the number is going up.
13 'My friend is twenty-three', Kenel said. 'You can see it already. The disease is eating his eyes ...'
14 I hope he's wrong on it, to be frank with you.
15 Take a look again because you never quite know.
16 When it starts to happen, you'll see a domino effect where everything starts shifting...
17 ... where you can't keep tabs on every individual, you have to rely on intelligence and you have to rely on good law enforcement.
18 The wizard shook his head. 'I fear that you must learn a lesson.'
19 ... don't dwell on the things over which you have no control.
20 I am sorry that I have made you sad, Khang told me again.

Comment

(a) The oddness in this example resides in the pairing of the singular antecedent 'candidate' with the anaphoric plural 'themselves'. Obviously, the speaker did not want to refer back using 'himself' (or 'herself'), implying that the only possible candidate was male (or female). So would 'themself' have been acceptable? What about the lengthy 'himself or herself'?

(b) These lines have been chosen rather randomly but they are not meant to be representative of the proportion of generic *you*; if anything, they are slanted slightly towards it. Nevertheless, they show that it is a significant factor in the use of *you*. Lines 1, 3, 4, 6, 8, 11, 12, 14, 16, 18 and 20 are specific; the speaker/writer is addressing a particular audience of one or more. Lines 2, 5, 7, 9, 10, 13, 15 and 17 are generic. Line 19 is an interesting case, in that it could be either – a piece of advice to a particular person or a general statement. This indicates that the dividing line between the two types of reference is not always clear. Note how the generic use is – as one would expect – associated with the present tense.

Notes

1 One more technique of self-reference is to use the third person, as in these examples from the TV series *Poirot*, viewed on ITV3 24 October 2018:

> *Poirot, he is not your love.*
> *You ask Poirot to be gentle.*

when it is Poirot himself (David Suchet) who is actually speaking. This brings this comment from Simon Callow: '*Poirot, why do you insist on referring to yourself in the third person? It is intensely irritating.*' This is just another example of how the selection, or avoidance, of a pronoun may be controversial.)

2 The Corpus of Contemporary American English currently consists of 560 million words from several genres equally: spoken, fiction, popular magazines, newspapers and academic texts. There are 20 million words from each year 1990–2017.

3 This is, of course, only one type of pronominal *one*. There are two other, relatively common, non-formal uses (Berry 2018: 83); the first is where it refers back to a non-specific noun phrase (rather than *it*, which would make the reference definite):

> *We need a new television.* – *Where are we going to find the money for one?*

The second is where it replaces a head noun only, rather than a noun phrase:

> *Which tie would you like?* – *I'll take the blue one.*

The former at least should be added to the PPP, but this is not the place for that battle.

4 The 4th edition of this work has basically the same text (Swan 2016: point 181).

References

Bauer, Laurie. 1998. You shouldn't say 'It is me' because 'me' is accusative. In Laurie Bauer and Peter Trudgill (eds) *Language Myths*. London: Penguin, 132–138.

Berry, Roger. 1997 'We' as marker of power in business and academic communication. *Unesco Alsed-LSP Newsletter* 20/1: 4–15.

Berry, Roger. 2009. 'You could say that': the generic second-person pronoun in modern English. *English Today* 25/3: 29–34.

Berry, Roger. 2013. Metalinguistic relativity and the personal pronoun paradigm. In K. Droździal-Szelest and M. Pawlak (eds) *Psycholinguistic and*

Sociolinguistic Perspectives on Second Language Learning and Teaching: Studies in Honour of Waldemar Marton. Berlin: Springer Verlag, 233–244.
Berry, Roger. 2018. *English Grammar: A Resource Book for Students*. Abingdon: Routledge.
Biber, Douglas, Stig Johannson, Geoffrey Leech, Susan Conrad and Edward Finegan. 1999. *Longman Grammar of Spoken and Written English*. Harlow: Pearson Education.
Carter, Ronald and Michael McCarthy. 2006. *Cambridge Grammar of English*. Cambridge: Cambridge University Press.
Celce-Murcia, M. and D. Larsen-Freeman. 1999. *The Grammar Book*. Rowley, MA: Newbury House.
Chalker, Sylvia. 1990. *English Grammar Word by Word*. Walton-on-Thames: Nelson.
Collins Cobuild English Grammar. 2011. 3rd edn. Glasgow: HarperCollins.
Downing, Angela and Philip Locke. 1992. *A University Course in English Grammar*. Hemel Hempstead: Prentice Hall International.
Fairclough, Norman. 1989. *Language and Power*. Harlow: Longman.
Flowerdew, John. 1996. Discourse and social change in contemporary Hong Kong. *Language in Society* 25: 557–586.
Flowerdew, John. 1997. The discourse of colonial withdrawal: a case study in the creation of mythic discourse. *Discourse and Society* 8/4: 453–477.
Huddleston, Rodney and Geoffrey K. Pullum. 2002. *The Cambridge Grammar of the English Language*. Cambridge: Cambridge University Press.
Huddleston, Rodney and Geoffrey K. Pullum. 2005. *A Students' Introduction to English Grammar*. Cambridge: Cambridge University Press.
Kennedy, Graeme. 1998. *An Introduction to Corpus Linguistics*. London: Longman.
Leech, Geoffrey, Susan Conrad, Benita Cruickshank and Roz Ivanic. 2001. *An A–Z of English Grammar and Usage*. 2nd edn. Harlow: Pearson Education.
Master, Peter. 1996. *Systems of English Grammar*. Englewood Cliffs, NJ: Prentice Hall Regents.
Oxford English Dictionary. http://dictionary.oed.com
Parrott, Martin. 2000. *Grammar for English Language Teachers*. Cambridge: Cambridge University Press.
Pennycook, Alistair. 1994. The politics of pronouns. *ELT Journal* 48: 173–178.
Quirk, Randolph, Sidney Greenbaum, Geoffrey Leech and Jan Svartvik. 1985. *A Comprehensive Grammar of the English Language*. Harlow: Longman.
Siewierska, Anna. 2004. *Person*. Cambridge: Cambridge University Press.
Swan, Michael. 1995. *Practical English Usage*. 2nd edn. Oxford: Oxford University Press.
Swan, Michael. 2016. *Practical English Usage*. 4th edn. Oxford: Oxford University Press.

Swan, Michael and Bernard Smith (eds). 1987. *Learner English*. Cambridge: Cambridge University Press.
Tarone, E., S. Gillette, S. Dwyer and V. Icke. 1998. On the use of the active and passive voice in astrophysics journal articles: with extensions to other languages and other fields. *English for Specific Purposes* 17: 113–132.
Wales, Katie. 1996. *Personal Pronouns in Present-Day English*. Cambridge: Cambridge University Press.
Wardaugh, Ronald. 2003. *Understanding English Grammar*. Oxford: Blackwell.
Yule, George. 1998. *Explaining English Grammar*. Oxford: Oxford University Press.

10 Case Study 4
Reported Speech

10.1 Introduction

This concluding case study looks at an area which has been described by some writers as a pedagogic fiction. The chapter therefore looks at a number of issues concerning the status of reported speech and asks whether it is justifiable to include it in grammatical syllabuses.

In Chapter 3, one of the statements in the research into grammar myths in Berry (2015) was as follows:

> 'In reported/indirect speech, the past tense should be changed to the past perfect tense if the introductory verb is in the past tense.'

This was counted as a serious problem since three-quarters of the participants (147 out of 196) thought it was correct (and only 21 thought it false). To cast doubt on its veracity, we can take one example from Thompson (1994: 109):

> An opposition group <u>said</u> it <u>carried</u> out the attack.

Presumably the original sentence was 'We <u>carried</u> out the attack', i.e. the tense has not changed. But the introductory verb, that is, the verb in the reporting clause, is 'said', a past tense, so the rule should apply; the reported clause should be 'we <u>had carried</u> out the attack', which is also a possibility. In fact, it has long been known that this particular 'change' rarely takes place: an original past tense usually remains a past tense when reported. There is a rather simple reason for this, though it is not one discussed in pedagogic circles; it will be presented in Section 10.6. But first we need to look at the wider picture, of which this misconception forms only a small part

10.2 Backshift

This rule is just one of a series, under the heading of 'backshift', designed to help learners report what other people have said, in other words to turn direct speech into indirect (or reported) speech. I have seen school textbooks and teacher handbooks which have a whole unit or page dedicated to this and other so-called backshift rules (for a recent example, see Scrivener 2010: 255; though he does mention exceptions). The text usually goes something like this:

> In reported speech (if the reporting verb is in the past) change
>
> (a) the present tense into the past tense
> (b) the present perfect into the past perfect
> (c) the past into the past perfect
> (d) the present continuous into the past continuous
> (e) the present perfect continuous into the past perfect continuous
> (f) the past continuous into the past perfect continuous.

not to mention a similar tranche of rules regarding modals.[1] They are called 'backshift' rules because in each case the time of the event is apparently shifted one step backwards by the introduction of a 'reporter'. They are usually accompanied by injunctions to change adverbs of time and place (*here* to *there* and *now* to *then*) as well as personal pronouns. Learners are meant to memorise these rules and apply them in exercises (as well as in authentic speech). Apart from failing to capture the generalisation across the verb forms, since all involve changing some form of the present to the corresponding form of the past, apart from (c) and (f), which are rarely applied, such rote learning is a very laborious process and a great waste of time.

One more example, from Thompson (1994: 108), will suffice for the moment to cast doubt on the reliability of these rules:

> *Yeltsin, for his part, said he is willing to try.*

Again the reporting verb is 'said' and so it should not be possible to retain the original verb form 'is' in the reported clause; it should be 'was willing to try'. But the sentence is perfectly acceptable and meaningful.

The point behind the above examples is that these statements are not rules but options; they are not automatically applied. The same is true of the other 'backshift' rules listed above; it is quite possible that the original tense will be retained. The question here is: why does the tense change and why not? As before it is creativity, not convention (as the backshift rules would imply), that is at work. The exact mechanism for this creativity is explained in Section 10.6.

10.3 The Status of Reported Speech (1)

First, however, we must deal with a larger problem. Namely, such rules refer to a classroom invention; in real life when we report what

10.3 The Status of Reported Speech (1)

someone has said we usually do not base it on the exact words used but on how the meaning that we remember applies to the current situation (i.e. it is just like other tense usage in English). If the exact form of words is important – and if we remember it – we tend to use direct speech. If not, then we may express the meaning in our own terms, retaining the original tense if desired.

A further problem with indirect speech (or 'reported speech', as it sometimes called) is that authentic examples of it are very hard to investigate and exemplify. If we want to report something that somebody told us to a third party it is usually because the third person was not present at the original moment of speaking – if they were, the original statement would not need reporting. Therefore, some time has usually elapsed between the time of speaking and the time of reporting; the two utterances are not linked. Such instances are not easily recoverable, e.g. by corpus analysis.

Of course, there are cases where the tense in the reported clause has 'changed', for example:

We asked how she was feeling.

A reported question such as this would presumably be derived from an original question such as:

How are you feeling? Rather than *How were you feeling?*

But there is no need for a special rule to tell learners to use the past tense for reporting it; the state indicated by the verb 'feel' occurred in the past, so it is natural to use the past tense. No 'change' as such has taken place. And if we think it is not a past occurrence, then we are quite free to use the present:

We asked how she is feeling.

Indeed, there are cases where both tenses are possible, even referring to the same time, depending on the attitude of the speaker; these are explained later in this section. There may even be cases of variation in the same text, with one tense different and another not, for example:

> *A Foreign Ministry spokesman said government policy is not to sell arms to sensitive areas. But he said his country needed the income to convert arms factories to non-military production.* (Thompson 1994: 108–109)

which is presumably from 'Government policy is ... but my country needs...'. Clearly the situation is much less simplistic than backshift rules would have us believe.

Where accounts do allow for backshifting not to take place it is usually explained in terms of the recency or continued validity of the original statement, but this is not a complete explanation; if anything it would be better to focus on the limited cases where backshift does appear to take place. And, as will be seen in Section 10.6, there is a general explanation for these.

10.4 The Background

10.4.1 Origin

Reported speech, along with its rules for backshifting and other changes, has become part of the 'canon' of English grammar, like other myths discussed in Chapter 3; it seems to be an essential part of any syllabus, as per Section 6.7. How it came to be so is not quite clear. It may be something to do with the identification of slight differences in tense usage in this area between English and other European languages, where there is a tendency to maintain the original tense in the reported clause (and where the distinction between reported and direct speech is not so obvious). There may be a slight relevance here for certain learners in helping them to avoid making mistakes in English, though not of a serious manner. However, it is not helpful to extend the practice of backshifting worldwide, e.g. to learners whose L1s do not possess the grammatical category 'tense' in the first place, for whom the problem is no different than that they face with tense and word order in general.

Another factor in the creation of the myth – again similar to other myths – is the mistaken belief that such difficulties, which ultimately reside in meaning choices available to the speaker or writer (i.e. are creative), can be reduced to automatic rules of grammar, based on a range of objectively verifiable criteria, such as the distance in time or the continued validity of the statement (i.e. are conventional).

Once established in this largely Eurocentric 'canon' of grammar, other mechanisms reinforce the myth, such as classroom exercises and backwash from testing. The terminology used, especially 'indirect/direct' speech, also encourages a false connection between what actually are two rather distinct phenomena (see Section 10.6); henceforth the term 'reported speech' will be used. Then there is the matter of other factors which have been spuriously added to the area, which the next section addresses.

10.4.2 Deixis

Reported speech is part of a much broader phenomenon in language, namely that what we say has to take account of when and where we say it and who we say it to. Put another way, words like *here* and *you* mean different things according to the context, as this imaginary mobile phone conversation indicates:

A: *Where are you?*
B: *I'm here.*
A: *(looking around and not seeing B) No you're not – I'm here. And by the way, you're not 'I' – I'm 'I'; you're 'you'.*

This concept is called 'deixis' (see e.g. Huddlestone and Pullum 2002: 1023). The less controversial changes involved in reported speech mentioned above, such as *here* to *there* and *now* to *then*, as well as changes in personal pronouns, are all part of this. Deixis is a universal feature of languages and learners will be familiar with it (intuitively) from their first language. If they are in a situation where they are concerned with the meaning of what they are saying, rather than the form, they will have no need to be instructed in it. They will know, for example, that if someone says to them

I'<u>ll</u> meet <u>you</u> <u>here</u> <u>tomorrow</u> at nine

and they later report it to a third party, the words they choose vary according to the circumstances. The rules for backshift would impose the following text:

She said <u>she</u> <u>would</u> meet <u>me</u> <u>there</u> <u>the next day</u> at nine

whereby *I* has become *she, will – would, you – me, here – there, tomorrow – the next day*. But these last two changes would only occur in real life if they are in a different place on a different day. If they are in the same place on the same day then the end of the sentence would remain the same: ... *here tomorrow*. In a meaningful situation learners would know which to choose, as with the pronouns. As to the possible change from *will* to *would*, see below. It is only in artificial, meaningless exercises, where form takes precedence, that rules for deictic changes are to be applied automatically. And yet textbooks still contain a list of such changes, in addition to backshifting, to be made when converting direct speech into reported speech.

10.5 The Status of Reported Speech (2)

All this leads us to question the idea of reported speech as a special grammatical category, as suggested above. Some writers take great exception to it; Dave Willis for one argued that the rules for backshift in reported speech are a pedagogic fiction:

> There is nothing difficult about tense in reported speech. The logic that it follows is the same as for the rest of the language. In spite of this, many coursebooks insist on regarding reported statement as a structure of some kind which has a system of rules to itself. (Willis 1994: 61–62)

In fact, I have suggested that there is 'everything difficult' about reported speech because tense choice in English is a tricky matter in any context, especially for learners whose L1 does not have the category of tense (Berry 2004: 40). So any rule of thumb which offers a way of making decisions will be seized upon.

Michael Swan is only slightly less critical (but more cautious) than Willis:

> Despite the monstrous apparatus of rules about backshift, deictic changes that appear in many pedagogic grammars and coursebooks, nearly all English indirect speech utterances are constructed in accordance with the general rules that determine the form of most other English sentences. (Swan 1994: 53)

10.5.1 The Relationship between Direct and Reported Speech

There is another problem, as Parrott (2000) points out, in that teaching materials generally present learners with an open choice between direct and reported speech. However,

> In fact the two are rarely interchangeable – in reality we almost never use reported speech to convey exactly what someone has said. If we are interested in what was said exactly we generally use direct speech.
> (Parrott 2000: 216)

In other words, as noted, when we use reported speech it is because we want to give the meaning.

However, the fact remains that sometimes the tense of the verb in reported speech is not the same as in the original (as far as this can be ascertained; for a good, if advanced, account of this, see Huddlestone and Pullum 2002: 152). There are indeed cases where the choice of tense is not what would be expected by learners – Swan's words 'nearly all' above suggest this. And there is a reason for this, but it is not the automatic one proposed by backshift rules.

The issue with reported speech here is of a different order from the problems identified above. In a sense it is an ethical problem, and it may be expressed thus: how do I present what someone said to me to a third party? Do I present it as though it comes from me, as though I agree with it entirely? What if I don't? How do I express my (lack of) commitment to the ideas of the first speaker? One solution is to mark the statement explicitly as someone else's. Direct speech does just this – if we can remember the exact words. A word such as *apparently* also invests a statement with someone else's authority while attempting to absolve the reporter of responsibility. But reported speech is unclear on this: who is saying what (in the sense of being committed to it)? Interpreters face a similar dilemma: how do they translate something that might be distasteful, e.g. a swear word, to their listener? The old adage 'Don't shoot me, I'm only the messenger' comes to mind.

10.6 An Explanation: Distancing

So why do we sometimes choose a different tense in reported speech (as far as can be ascertained) to that in the original, even when there is no need in terms of the timing of the event?

It has long been known that there are a number of situations where the past tense can be used to indicate the idea of distance, or remoteness, in general, not only distance in time (Lewis 1986: 69–73; Yule 1998: 274); it can suggest tentativeness or politeness on the part of the speaker, for example:

What name was it?

which might be said by a hotel receptionist to a guest checking in. Or

Excuse me Professor, I wanted to ask you a question.

by a student approaching her lecturer at the end of a class. Here, despite the past tense (can the lecturer respond 'Oh you did, did you, but you don't any longer?' and walk away?), the time of the 'wanting' is now and the past tense indicates a social distance between the speaker and hearer.

Similarly, in the second conditional (see Section 3.3) the use of the past tense indicates another kind of distance, a factual one: unlikelihood, not 'pastness':

If you asked him about a particular coin, he would be able to tell you . . .

The time reference here is future.

The point with backshifting – when it occurs – is that it distances the reporter from the truth value of what they are reporting. Keeping the same tense validates it. Thus in

(I am coming.) He said he is coming.

the reporter shows the same commitment as the original speaker, while if they said 'was coming' commitment would be lacking. Compare these two sentences:

He said he's coming, so that means he is.
?He said he was coming, so that means he is.

The second is improbable because the lack of commitment in 'was coming' contradicts the express commitment in what follows.

10.6.1 Backshift from Past Tense to Past Perfect

This distancing phenomenon explains why one particular form of backshifting, the one in the myth at the start of this chapter, namely from past tense to past perfect, is rare (compared to, say, the shift from present perfect to past perfect). Since the past tense already has the idea of distance, changing it to the past perfect adds nothing, except possibly to imply a change of state (which may not be the desired message.) Thus to turn

> *I believed him.*

into

> *He said he had believed him.*

allows for the possibility that he no longer believes him, whereas

> *He said he believed him.*

does not. And at the same time, the retention of the past allows distancing.

We can now see that direct speech and reported speech are in fact two very different phenomena. When we report someone's words exactly we are not committing ourselves to the statement; we are simply giving the text without investing ourselves in it, like a witness in a court case. When we use reported speech, we have a choice; it is therefore misleading to suggest that the two are alternatives, that one can simply take a quote and turn it into indirect speech.

A similar conclusion, though approached from a different angle, is reached in Semino and Short (2004).

Thus the issue is not so much that these tense changes are not obligatory, as the rules for backshift would have us believe (Lewis 1986: 71); rather, it is inappropriate in the first place to associate direct speech and reported speech so closely, and to talk of changing one into the other.

10.7 Reporting in the Classroom

10.7.1 The Current Situation

Notwithstanding the above, the concepts of direct and indirect speech, along with the backshift rules, are still alive and well in many classrooms, as the research and other evidence presented above indicates. A typical traditional lesson might consist of the presentation of the above rules, followed by practice at transforming direct speech into reported speech. At the very basic level this might consist simply of individual sentences which can be transformed with little understanding of what is going on. (Transformation exercises and drills are discussed briefly in Section 6.4.) At a more imaginative level, situations are created where the production of reported speech is slightly more natural.

A scenario sometimes used is that of a deaf old lady who, unable to hear what is being said to her, constantly asks her companion to report what a third party has said ('What did she say?'). Unfortunately, apart from being potentially offensive, there is a logical problem with this; the immediacy of the response takes away any need for change, above all a change from direct to reported speech, not to mention a change in tense:

> A (visitor): *How are you?*
> B (deaf old lady to her companion): *What did she say?*
> C (companion): *She said 'How are you?'*

or *She asked how you are*, but probably not *She asked how you were*, which could imply a change of state.

Many exercises that I have seen, such as those in Yule (1998: 272–297) and in Scrivener (2010: 256–259), get over the immediacy problem by introducing a period of time between the original and the report. However, they tend to rely on the presence or memorising of the exact words of the original spoken text, thereby reinforcing the link between direct and reported speech. As was pointed out above, the problem with this is that if we know the original words there is no need to use reported speech; in other words, such exercises lack authenticity.

10.7.2 A Revised Strategy

What is really needed here is a new approach to this area. And what is perhaps the first step would be to call it 'reporting', as in the title of Thompson's (1994) book. Thence we can move on to the mechanics of the new strategy.

As was suggested in Section 10.5.1, direct speech and reported speech are really different phenomena and therefore they should be kept apart in teaching as much as possible. Learners can by all means be given practice in how to represent spoken words verbatim in writing, or in reporting the gist of what someone has said – after all, reporting is one of the major communicative functions of language – but not because of the tense and other deictic 'changes' that may take place. The optional case of backshifting for distance in reported speech explained in Section 10.6 might form a small part of a syllabus for advanced learners, but it should not be given much attention in basic teaching materials. It is a waste of time, time that could profitably be devoted to other aspects of reporting; some of these are listed in Section 10.7.4.

10.7.3 Rules and Terms

If an explanation (rather than a rule) is needed to account for the occasional case of backshifting for distance in the reported clause (perhaps because learners have come across an unexpected tense), then it might go something like this:

> Sometimes when you report something you've heard to another person (and you can't remember the actual words), you can change the tense of the verb from present to past to distance yourself from the
> original statement.

A note on terminology is relevant here. 'Reported speech' and 'indirect speech' are both commonly used to describe this phenomenon. I have generally used 'reported speech' here because, it seems to me, it gives a clearer idea of what is going on – speech that is being 'reported'. It also emphasises the difference between it and direct speech. However, all teachers and some learners will need to be familiar with both. Confusingly, some grammars use 'reported speech' as a cover term for both direct and indirect speech.

10.7.4 Alternative Areas of Reporting to Focus On

If we decide to dispense altogether with backshift rules, this does not mean that we should ignore reporting entirely. There are a number of aspects of direct and reported speech that are worthy of a formal focus and on which time can usefully be spent (see Thompson 1994). For example:

1 Different verbs are used in direct and reported speech; some can only be used in reported speech:

> *'You were rude', I criticised him.
> I criticised him for being rude.

The first of these is wrong; *criticise* is not used for direct speech. The same is true of the verb *speak* itself:

> *I spoke 'Let's go now' (a common error).

Learners need information about which verbs in English they can use in direct speech so that they do not make such errors.

2 Learners also need practice in the types of construction that are used with reporting verbs, such as that for *criticise* above, or the difference between *say* and *tell*:

*I said him to go.
I told him to go.

3 Word order in reported *questions* using a '*wh-*' word is another important feature of reported speech. Thus not

*I asked him <u>where is he</u> going.

but instead

I asked him <u>where he is</u> going.

Learners often get this 'wrong'. But this is perhaps one area where a non-standard norm is emerging in English as a Lingua Franca (see Section 3.5); and it must be admitted that communication is unlikely to be affected.

4 Reported thought is similar to reported speech in that it is subject to the same distancing effect of using the past tense:

I thought he <u>was</u> coming tonight.

5 Returning to direct speech, in writing there are some conventions worth noting, for instance, the positioning of the reporting clause, which may come after its quote:

'Sit down!' <u>the judge said</u>.

And when this occurs there is optional inversion of verb and subject:

'Sit down!' <u>said the judge</u>.

6 Punctuation is also important in direct speech, namely the fact that the reporting clause and the quotation belong to the same sentence. A common error is to separate them with a full stop and start a new sentence:

*'Come here.' <u>She</u> said.

The quote in fact functions as the object of 'said'.

7 In speech intonation is important when reporting directly: the reporting clause tends to be said with low, flat intonation.

8 A related matter is the use of nouns to introduce a report:

They put out a <u>statement</u> that ...
He made a <u>comment</u> that ...

9 There is also the issue of informal structures that are used to introduce a statement as direct speech (see e.g. Yule 1998: 283–287), for example, the verb *go*:
And then he <u>goes</u> 'What's wrong with you?'

More prominent and controversial than this is the so-called quotative *like* (see Section 3.2, where it was identified as a bane of purists):

And I'm like: 'where are you going with this story?'

Though some commentators criticise this usage there is no doubt that it is becoming established, at least in informal speech, so learners will need at least a receptive knowledge of it. Interestingly, it is not only speech that is represented in this way; thought (see point 4 above) can also be so represented. In fact, the construction can be easily understood as an abbreviation of the following structure:

I am saying/thinking something like: . . .

Thus there are many other points of grammar that learners need to be made aware of and perhaps given practice in. In fact, reporting is, quite an extensive topic – all the more reason not to waste valuable time teaching obscure rules.

10.7.5 Suggestions for Activities

Two useful initial steps may be:

1 Rather than ask learners to turn direct speech into reported speech, do the reverse, by giving them the reported version and asking them what they think the original statement was.
2 If a focus on backshifting is required, treat the unshifted forms as the default, and focus on cases where backshifting has taken place, asking why it has occurred, rather than seeking explanations, such as recency and continued validity, for why it has not.

Beyond this we need activities that are authentic, where learners might use reported speech naturally. To achieve authenticity the direct speech should not be to hand; then the task becomes to remember and report the meaning. A useful way of doing this is to ask learners what was said to them earlier in the class (Ur 2009: 81). (Such statements need to be prepared in advance, and it helps if they are in the form of promises that would encourage learners to remember them.) But it is best that they do not remember the exact words, so that there is no possibility of using direct speech. For example, the teacher might ask:

'Can you tell me what my first sentence at the start of the class was?'

(Today we are going to visit the park.)

the (attentive) learners might respond – if the lesson hasn't yet reached that point – with

You <u>said</u> we <u>are going</u> to go to the park.

Note the potential change of verb, since they may not remember 'visit' from the original.

If they say

You <u>said</u> we <u>were going</u> to go to the park.

it could be because the lesson and the visit is over, or if they are protesting that the teacher didn't carry out their promise. (Indeed, 'promised' might be used as the reporting verb.) A third possibility is that the lesson is not over but the learners have no confidence in the teacher's promise. In all three cases there is distancing involved: of time, or fact, or belief.

Beyond this, there are numerous ways of practising reporting – in the wider sense – other than by the presentation and drilling of unhelpful rules for backshifting. The precise choice of activity will very much depend on which areas (such as those in Section 10.7.2) are selected for focus.

Here, for example, is an exercise which practises the choice of the most suitable reporting verb in reported speech – an area rarely covered in courses – as well as the grammatical constructions that accompany them:

Exercise 1. Complete the sentences below, using the most suitable reporting verb from the list below. Imagine that that the original sentence is something like 'You forgot to close the window'.

1 She _____ *him of forgetting to close the window.*
2 She _____ *him for forgetting to close the window.*
3 She _____ *that he forgot to close the window.*

claim, tell, accuse, criticise

The first two sentences above remind us that with certain reporting verbs there is no need for a tense at all, so backshifting is not even an issue.

At a slightly more advanced level, this can also be reversed by leaving in the verb, as in the next exercise.

Exercise 2. Complete the following sentences based on the same original sentence 'You forgot to close the window'; there may be more than one possibility.

1 *He apologised* _____.
2 *He admitted* _____.
3 *He denied* _____.

These, of course, are only suitable (or needed) at an advanced level. At a basic level, learners can content themselves with the basic and most frequent reporting verbs: *say*, *tell* and *ask*.

To practise the conventions of expressing direct speech – especially those relevant to writing, such as points (5) and (6) above – a dialogue containing just the words spoken can be given to learners (even in audio form, if they are capable of understanding it word for word) to represent in writing:

A: When will you be home tonight?
B: When I've finished talking to my boss in the States.

Learners can be asked to recreate this in direct speech adding a reporting clause and using appropriate verbs (*ask*, *reply/say*), pronouns (*he, she?*) and word order, e.g.:

A: 'When will you be home tonight?' he asked.
B: 'When I've finished talking to my boss in the States', she replied/said.

More exercises on various aspects of reporting can be found in Thompson (1994: 188–202).

10.8 Conclusion

As was concluded above, backshift rules have little validity, and the meaningless transformation exercises from direct to reported speech applying them that are common in coursebooks are not helpful because

(a) in real life we do not have the original statement in front of us; if we do then we will probably not use reported speech;
(b) usually when we are reporting someone's speech we convey the meaning;
(c) we have the option to retain the original tense when we report speech; this is dependent on our commitment, on how distant we feel.

Agatha Christie was not an English grammarian but she was very perceptive about reported speech. In one of her stories (*A Caribbean Mystery*, HarperCollins, 1993, first published in 1964), a dying man's last words are remembered, mystifyingly, as 'heap of fish'. What he actually said was 'pilocarpine' (a clue to the name of the poison used in his murder); however, this was heard as 'pile o' carp', hence its 'translation' into the remembered phrase above. Her detective sleuth, Miss Marple, solves the mystery of course, and sums up the (lack of) relationship between direct and reported speech very insightfully:

> It is never easy to repeat a conversation and be entirely accurate in what the other party to it has said. One is always inclined to jump at what you think they *meant*. Then, afterwards, you put actual words into their mouths. (*A Caribbean Mystery*, HarperCollins, 1993: 154, first published in 1964)

Or, as Swan and Walker say (somewhat apologetically, after a discussion of backshifting):

> Exercises in books like this are useful for practising the grammar of indirect speech, but they are necessarily rather artificial. In real life, when we report what people say, we re-express their meaning, but we don't necessarily keep very close to the original words.
> (Swan and Walker 2011: 223)

In other words, there is no need to inflict rules for deictic changes and backshifting on ordinary learners. As I once said, these rules

> offer learners and teachers a haven of security in a sea of uncertain usage (Berry 2004: 40).

They suggest that by following a strict algorithm learners can arrive at the correct verb form. But it is an illusion. Life is not like that; we do not have perfect memory of things people said to us, so when it comes to reporting we focus on the meaning. Therefore, backshift rules should not be foregrounded, not only because they are misleading but because direct and reported speech should not be linked so strongly in pedagogy. If they are an unavoidable part of the syllabus then the emphasis should be changed: not why backshift does not occur but why it creatively does. Then it can be regarded as the meaning resource that it really is.

Activity

Look at these three short extracts from *The Times* of 23 November 2019 and consider:

1 the overall approach to the use of direct and reported speech and how this may be influenced by the genre (news reporting);
2 what the original tense of the reported text might have been (relevant verbs have been underlined), and what the reason might have been for changing/retaining;
3 other factors involved in the reporting of speech as outlined above.

(A) *It said that no evidence <u>had been found</u> of similar behavior towards other employees.*
(B) *Experts have said that some midwives and maternity units <u>give</u> women an 'inappropriate push'...*
(C) *An NHS plan to cover doctors' extra pension bills to stave off a winter crisis <u>violates</u> civil service rules against tax avoidance, the government has acknowledged.*

Comment

1 These extracts are typical of newspaper reporting (but not necessarily representative overall). Newspapers often depend for their articles on what people (politicians, doctors etc.) have said, and they are usually reporting what was said some time before, without wishing to give the same commitment to the proposition as the original speakers. It is common to start a contribution with reported speech and then give a direct statement, but this need not be a full clause; the short quotation at the end of B is typical.
2 The original texts must have been 'has been found' in A, 'give' in B and in C 'violates'. Only in A has a tense change occurred, probably because of a desire not to commit to the statement. In B it is clearly necessary to indicate the continued relevance of the 'giving'. In C the retention of the present tense is significant because the past could have been used ('violated'). (The use of the present perfect in the reporting clause may have played a role, as it may have in B.)
3 A and B contain the default structure (reporting clause first) with reporting verb ('said'). C has two interesting features: the reporting clause comes last, and a different reporting verb ('acknowledged') is used.

Note

1 This is the only situation where modals (*can*, etc.) can be claimed to have 'past' tense forms (*could*, etc.), since the backshifting that *may* occur parallels that for present and past tenses of main verbs. Changing an original *can* to *could* achieves the same distancing effect, for example:

('*I <u>can</u> come.*') *She said she <u>could</u> come* (but *can* would also be possible).

But this is hardly an argument for calling *could* a past tense, since it is referring to future time. See a discussion of this myth in Section 3.3.

References

Berry, Roger. 2004. Understanding tense and aspect in English: the roles of creativity and convention. *The Hong Kong Linguist* 23/24: 37–46.
Berry, Roger. 2015. Grammar myths. *Language Awareness* 24/1: 15–37.
Huddlestone, R. and G. Pullum. 2002. *The Cambridge Grammar of the English Language*. Cambridge: Cambridge University Press.
Lewis, Michael. 1986. *The English Verb*. Hove: Language Teaching Publications.
Parrott, Martin. 2000. *Grammar for English Language Teachers*. Cambridge: Cambridge University Press.
Scrivener, Jim. 2010. *Teaching English Grammar*. London: Macmillan Education.
Semino, E. and M. Short. 2004. *Corpus Stylistics: Speech, Writing and Thought Presentation in a Corpus of English Writing*. London: Routledge.
Swan, Michael. 1994. Design criteria for pedagogic language rules. In Martin Bygate, Alan Tonkyn and Eddie Williams (eds) *Grammar and the Language Teacher*. New York: Prentice Hall.
Swan, Michael and Catherine Walker. 2011. *Oxford English Grammar Course: Advanced*. Oxford: Oxford University Press.
Thompson, Geoff. 1994. *Reporting. Collins Cobuild English Guides 5*. London: HarperCollins.
Ur, Penny. 2009. *Grammar Practice Activities*. Cambridge: Cambridge University Press.
Willis, Dave. 1994. A lexical approach. In Martin Bygate, Alan Tonkyn and Eddie Williams (eds) *Grammar and the Language Teacher*. New York: Prentice Hall, 56–66
Yule, George. 1998. *Explaining English Grammar*. Oxford: Oxford University Press.

Conclusion

In this book I have tried to look at grammar, as it affects the teaching of English as a Foreign and Second Language, from every possible angle, from all kinds of grammatical description, both scientific and pedagogic, from syllabus and material design, from teaching and testing. My aim overall has been to bring all these various enterprises together, to 'join up the dots', as I said in the Introduction – a task which has not been attempted before – and to show how they all relate to one another. All the fields that are involved in 'doing English grammar' – including some which would not normally be included – have been covered, though in some cases it has only been possible to give partial coverage – the fields are so extensive.

C.1 Summing Up

The first aim was to establish the place and relevance of grammar in language education (Chapter 1), given the right circumstances, though many readers will not have needed convincing. This was followed in Chapter 2 by a discussion of the nature of grammar and a definition of it, to narrow down the target area. The definition is worth repeating:

> Grammar is the system of rules that enables users of a language to relate linguistic form to meaning.

The chapter then demonstrated how different languages 'do' grammar, before discussing different approaches to it and what fields may contribute legitimately to pedagogic accounts. In Chapter 3 I showed that grammar is not a monolith, that it is a moving, expanding target and our accounts of it need to be constantly updated. In particular, much of the information that reaches learners needs to be improved.

Chapter 4 presented an in-depth study of one of the great 'stumbling blocks' of grammar: terminology. Its nature of and use in language

C.1 Summing Up

teaching were examined, with a stress on its limited and appropriate use. Chapter 5 complemented this by looking at the style(s) of grammatical discourse in the belief that it is itself worthy of investigation – a novel approach, as it is usually taken for granted. Factors such as modality, personality and exemplification were considered in depth. Chapter 6 looked at the various aspects of grammar already discussed as they are operationalised in syllabuses, teaching materials and tests.

These first six chapters considered grammar and grammar teaching from a general standpoint; most of what was said there could be applied to the teaching of other languages. In contrast the case studies (Chapters 7–10) concentrated specifically on four important areas of English grammar, applying the principles elucidated in the first six chapters – namely, what the grammatical 'truth' is and how to bring this to learners. Some of it was original, while some has been known for a long time but not sufficiently exploited.

The key concepts that I have tried to promote to help our understanding of grammar include:

- the interplay between convention and creativity in accounting for the relationship between grammatical form and meaning;
- the distinction between pedagogic and scientific grammar and the associated terminology;
- a view of pedagogic grammar as process, not just as a product that is passed on to learners;
- the potential relevance of contrastive and historical viewpoints to pedagogic accounts;
- the concept of metalinguistic relativity: the possibility that we have been constrained into a distorted view of grammar reality by past developments;
- the concept of poor transmission, as per the vertical concept – that there is insufficient communication between the various communities;
- a classification of terminology in various dimensions, among which the distinction between transparent, opaque and iconic terms is most useful;
- the importance of the choices that grammarians make when writing about grammar; grammar is not just about hard facts, it is about how grammarians, even scientific ones, present their pronouncements to their audience;
- the importance of getting grammar right; regardless of how valid it is to simplify the facts for learners, this should not happen with teachers and other professionals.

C.2 Problems and Solutions

Several problems with grammar have been identified in this book:

- It is sometimes still taught as an end in itself, rather than as a means to communication; the link between grammatical form and grammatical meaning is not made.
- Related to this, there is still an assumption that there is only one way to involve grammar in language teaching, i.e. explicitly and deductively.
- Too much incorrect information about grammar is given to learners in the shape of rules of thumb; while it can be argued that this does not do permanent harm, it is of concern when teachers actually believe in these myths themselves.
- Much grammatical material, in exercises and tests, is poorly designed, for example by not checking for alternatives in answers.
- Boring, unrealistic, automatic drills which do not engage learners are still in evidence.
- Areas such as contrastive and historical studies, which have an occasional role to play in description, are ignored, particularly the former when publishers promote 'universal' courses, regardless of the specific grammatical needs of leaners from different L1 backgrounds.
- Scientific insights into English grammar are occasionally passed directly on to learners; similarly, insights into language acquisition bypass the pedagogical grammar filter and are applied directly.
- Very often too much terminology is used in teaching, terminology that has not been chosen well; while talking about language is important, it must be tailored to learner needs.
- A 'canon' of grammatical structures on which a syllabus should be based has been established which is hard to deviate from; the same old areas seem to be dealt with by each succeeding generation of pedagogic grammarians.

These problems have at least been addressed, if not solved. However, much progress has been and is being made:

- There is a more relaxed, less dogmatic, attitude to 'methods'; in the past grammar was either 'in' completely or 'out' completely (at least in theory); now its presence can be adjusted according to need.

C.2 Problems and Solutions

- The limited, subsidiary role of SLA studies has been recognised, though many interesting findings continue to emerge from this field.
- Corpus studies have become more and more popular, not only because their findings are accessible to teachers (though often not accessed), but also because teachers may access corpora themselves (or even construct them themselves).
- Empty grammatical concepts such as the 'future tense' are being dispensed with.
- Improvements have been made in syllabus design; for example, units on *going to* as well as *will* for future are now common.
- More imaginative, 'authentic' activities are available.
- There have been improvements in terminology – e.g. the slow replacement of 'continuous' by 'progressive'.
- New areas and concepts such as rheme and theme are slowly making their way into pedagogic consciousness.
- Alternative models of grammar are winning recognition; we are no longer restricted to standard British-American English.

To this two major solutions can be added:

- Longer training courses are needed, built around a more extensive and accurate description of English grammar.
- More communication is needed between the various communities that are involved in the teaching of English grammar; the insights of scientific grammarians need to be adapted for a non-scientific audience. (Pedagogically oriented journals and websites can play a greater role in this.) But the connection should work both ways: research should be prompted by pedagogy.

It is hoped that this book, by raising awareness, will contribute to further progress.

Appendices

Appendix 1 (from Chapter 3): Results from Berry (2014)

Questionnaire on pedagogic rules
Please supply the following information:

Year____ Curriculum (3-yr or 4-yr)____ Major programme _____

On this course we have already encountered two pedagogic rules which are sometimes presented to learners of English and which have been shown to be wrong:

- A) The 'rule' about using *some* in positive sentences and *any* in negatives and questions.
- B) The 'rule' about using *a* the first time you mention something and *the* the second time.

This questionnaire aims to find out what effect these statements might have had on you.

44 participants. Results are in bold below

1) First of all, did you know about these rules when you were learning English before university?

    A: YES **21** / NO **23**   B: YES **30** / NO **14**   (Please circle one in each case.)

If your answer to both is NO, you need not continue with questionnaire. If your answer to one is NO, please only answer questions about the other below.

Nine students had 'no' for both and were excluded at this stage.

2) If you knew about these rules, did you ever consciously apply them in your speaking or writing?

    A: YES **13** / NO **8**   B: YES **17** / NO **13**   (Please circle one in each case.)
    No answer 14   **No answer 5**

If your answer to both is NO, please go on to questions 5 and 6. If your answer to one is NO, please only answer the question about the other below.

230

Twelve students had no answer to Q3.

3) In situations where you applied the rule consciously, did you ever find out you were wrong? (E.g. you were corrected by a teacher.)

A: YES 3 / NO 10   B: YES 6 / NO 12   (Please circle one in each case.)
No answer 10   No answer 5

4) If your answer to either part of Question 3 was YES, what was your reaction to finding out you were wrong? (Please describe.) **See separate sheet.**
5) Even though you now know that these rules are wrong, do you feel that they helped you in some way with these difficult areas of English?

A: YES 10 / NO 10

6) If your answer to Question 5 was YES, how did they help? **See separate sheet.**

Answers to questions 4 and 6

4) If your answer to either part of Question 3 was YES, what was your reaction to finding out you were wrong? (Please describe.) BRACKETS REFER TO THE RULE REFERRED TO.
    1. *I was corrected by my teacher and I tried to be more conscious about it. (B)*
    10. *I felt shocked as my teacher told me that the two rules must be correct.*
    14. *confused.*
    29. *Angry because I studied and I'm still wrong.*
6) If your answer to Question 5 was YES, how did they help?
    1. *In my opinion, these rules can help primary learners to learn English easier.*
    4. *It's help me to improve my English and make it more formal.*
    5. *When we write some English papers and are not sure about whether use 'a' or 'the', we could use these rules even though these rules are wrong.*
    6. *Whenever I ask a question, consciously I'd remind myself to use 'any' instead of 'some'. And when I failed to do so, I would feel like 'there was something wrong with what I just said!' But it could help me overcome situations when I used Chinglish.*
    7. *Using rules is easier to write in English.*
    15. *At least my grammar will be better.*
    29. *Decide with less time.*
    37. *Help me write and speak English smoothly because there's a rule for them.*

Appendix 2 (from Chapter 5): Texts Used in METALANG 1

Collins Cobuild English Grammar. 1990. London: Collins.
A Communicative Grammar of English by Geoffrey Leech and Jan Svartvik. 1994. Harlow: Longman.
A Comprehensive Grammar of the English Language by Randolph Quirk, Sidney Greenbaum, Geoffrey Leech and Jan Svartvik. 1985. Harlow: Longman.
English Grammar in Use by Raymond Murphy. 1994. Cambridge: Cambridge University Press.
English Grammar Word by Word by Sylvia Chalker. 1990. Walton-on-Thames: Nelson.
The Heinemann English Grammar by Digby Beaumont and Colin Granger. 1989. Oxford: Heinemann.
The Oxford English Grammar by Sidney Greenbaum. 1996. Oxford: Oxford University Press.
A Practical English Grammar by A. J. Thomson and A. V. Martinet. 1986. Oxford: Oxford University Press.
Practical English Usage by Michael Swan. 1995. Oxford: Oxford University Press.
A Students' Grammar of the English Language by Sidney Greenbaum and Randolph Quirk. 1990. Harlow: Longman.
Systems in English Grammar by Peter Master. 1996. Englewood Cliffs, NJ: Prentice Hall Regents.

Appendix 3 (from Chapter 5): Results from Berry (2009a)

Table A.1 The frequency of the seven items in METALANG I compared to Cobuild Direct (All frequencies are per one million words)

Item	METALANG I		Cobuild Direct corpora		Ratio range between Cobuild Direct and METALANG
	Total	Frequency per million words	Highest frequency	Lowest frequency	
CAN	769	8,992.0	3,494.7	1,157.1	7.77/2.57:1
MAY	234	2,736.2	1,484.5	341.4	8.02/1.84:1
USUALLY	173	2,022.9	227.9	46.0	43.97/8.87:1
NORMALLY	98	1,145.9	157.2	31.0	39.96/7.29:1
GENERALLY	47	549.6	102.9	14.1	38.98/5.34:1
OFTEN	183	2,139.9	542.2	146.6	14.60/3.95:1
SOMETIMES	171	1,999.5	310.4	55.6	35.96/6.44:1

Index

Lexical items are in italics

academic writing 104, 107
access 46
acceptability 99–101, 121
accuracy 9
accuracy (of terminology) 83, 202
adverbial 36
adverbs 28
affective filter 75
American influence 45–46
analogy 46
analytical grammar 26
analytical comparison 169
anaphora 151, 153, 158, 165
antecedent 189, 192
any 48
apostrophe *-s* 89
approaches: see methods
articles 25
aspect 26, 31
at all 61
attach 46
attitudes to grammar 142
audiolingual method 8
authentic examples 113
authenticity 117–118
auxiliaries 35, 56
awareness approach 9

back 20
backwash 140
backshift 49, 209
bare infinitive 24
base (form of adjectives) 168
besides 113–114
Brandreth, Gyles 27

call 143–144
can 50, 96, 103
canon of grammatical items 128, 212
canonical word order 23
cardinal numbers 71
case 155, 189, 202

cataphora 151
circularity 62, 131, 176
clarity (of rules of thumb) 130
clause 24, 35
cleft sentence 186
closed (word) classes 35
coding system 136
cognitive grammar 22
comment: see topic and comment
communicative language teaching 9
communicative value (in syllabuses) 127
comparative (form of adjectives) 25, 88, Chapter 8
comparison (of adjectives) 25, 62, Chapter 8
competence 33
complement or predicative 36, 41, 189
computer mouse 46
conceptual parsimony (of rules of thumb) 130
concordance lines 134
conditional (sentences) 5, 29, 31, 51, 63–66
confusing terms 76
conjunctions 29
construction grammar 22
contact clauses 101
continuous aspect 31, 45
continuous tenses 50
contractions 46
contrastiveness (in syllabuses) 126
contrived examples 113
convention and creativity 21, 59, 133, 142, 155, 162, 168, 185, 203, 210
conversion (of uncountable nouns to countable) 96
could 50
countable 21, 71
counting expressions 57
count (noun) 20, 71
count status 57, 149
corpus studies 39
correctness 4, 99
creativity: see convention and creativity
Croatian 154

234

data-driven learning 134
demonstratives 25
deductive 6
default determiner 149
defective verbs 56
definite article 49, 119, 139, Chapter 7
definite reference 148
definition (of grammar) 18
degree adverb 47
deictic 186
deixis 212
demarcation (of rules of thumb) 130
depth and refinement 93, 120
derivation 24
descriptive grammar 27, 30
determiners 35
direct anaphora: see anaphora
direct method 8
direct object 35, 41
direct speech 209, 214–215
disappear 41
distancing 215
distinctiveness (of terminology) 70–71, 202
ditransitive (verbs) 41, 46, 57, 145
double hedging 110
drills 132
Dryden, John 27
dummy subject 186
dynamic verbs 45

ease of marking (of tests) 137
-ed participle 88–89
emphatic (use of pronouns) 190, 193
empiricist (approaches to language) 33
English as a Lingua Franca 56–59
epistemic hedging 104
eponymous terms 72
ergative 129, 143
error correction 135
exclusive *we* 188, 196
exemplification 112–119, 121
experiential 7
explicit 6
explicit knowledge 11
extraposition 187

familiarity (of terminology) 84
feminine (gender) 188
few 98
fewer 27
fluency 9

formal instruction 10, 11
formality 98, 121
formal linguistics 34
form and function 39
fossilisation 9
French 154, 196
frequency (in syllabuses) 126
function: see form and function
functional linguistics 34
future tense 31, 52

Game of Thrones 27
games 143
gap-filling (exercises) 133, 162–163, 164–165
gender 188, 200
generic reference 148
generic *you* 129, 194, 197
genitive 35, 37, 44, 89
genre analysis 39
gradability (of adjectives) 168
grammar-translation method 7
grammatical functions 34, 35, 155
grammaticality 4, 5

head (noun) 23
hedging 104, 121
honorific second-person pronouns 196
hopefully 28
Humphrys, John 28

iconic terms 72
idiosyncrasy (in syllabuses) 127
if 63–66, 94–95
impact 46
imperative 39
impersonal constructions 108
implicit 6
implicit knowledge 11
inclusive *we* 188, 196
indefinite article 21, 49, 73, 147–150
indefinite pronouns 191
indefinite reference 148
indirect object 35, 41
indirect speech: see reported speech
inductive 6
inflecting language 26
inflections 24
inflectional comparison 25, 169
inflectional genitive 37
informal forms 46

236   Index

informality 46, 98–99
-ing participle 88
innit 58
institutional use 130
integrative motivation for terminology 74
intensifier 47, 168
interface position 11
interpersonal hedging 104
interrogative 25
interrogative sentences 48
intransitive 41
intuitions 27
inversion 36, 219
irregular verbs 59
isolating language 26
iterative 94
its 190

Language Proficiency Assessment for Teachers of English (LPATE) 14, 140
Latin 28
learnability (of terminology) 82
less 99
linking adverb 47
linking verb 41
link-transitive verb 145
little 98
location theory 152

mandative subjunctive 37, 44
masculine (gender) 188
may 103
METALANG 102, 123
metalanguage 69
metalinguistic knowledge 74, 139
metalinguistic relativity 61, 85, 190, 202
Metalinguistic Terminology Survey 79, 82
methods and approaches 6–10
modal adverbs 48
modal auxiliaries 101
modality 26, 101, 121
modals 35, 44, 56
models (of English) 58
modifier 23
more 170
morphology 3, 18
most 170
MTS: see Metalinguistic Terminology Survey
much 98

multifunctionality 35
multiple choice (exercises) 134
multiple choice (tests) 138
myths 48, 172

natural approach (the -) 8
natural approaches 7
negative sentences 48
neuter (gender) 188
nominal clause 36
nominalisation 24, 164
non-count noun 20
non-past (tense) 52
no one 61
noun phrase 21, 24
number 71, 187–188, 202

object 25, 35, 41
objective case 186, 189
object predicative 41
of 24
of genitives 25
one 195, 206
opaque terms 72
operational grammar 26
oral/situational/structural method 8
ordinal numbers 71

parts of speech 34, 61
passive 25, 29, 108, 110, 185
past perfect 216
past (tense) 31, 216
past participle 88
pattern grammar 33, 59
pedagogic grammar 30–33
pedagogic grammar as process 31–33
pedagogic grammar filter 32–33, 62
pedagogic grammarian's dilemma 104
pedagogic terminology 70
perfect (aspect) 31
perfect progressive 94
performance 33
periphrastic comparison 169
person 186–187, 202
personal constructions 107
personality 107, 121
personal pronoun paradigm 185, 196, 197, 198, 200
personal pronouns: Chapter 9
phrasal comparison 25, 169

phrasal genitive 37
phrasal verbs 38
plural 25, 35
polysemy of terms 77
poor transmission 62–63
possessive 89
possessive determiner 186, 189, 202
possessive pronoun 186, 189, 202
PPP: see personal pronoun paradigm
pragmatics 39
precision (of terminology) 70–71
predicate 72
predicative: see complement
pre-emptive use of the definite article 55, 151
prepositional object 35
preposition 22, 29, 85
prepositional verbs 29
prescriptive grammar 27–29, 43, 189
present (tense) 31
present simple 89, 96–98
present perfect 95
primary grammar 26–27
proactive 6
pro-drop languages 196
productivity (of terminology) 83
proform 47
progressive (aspect) 31, 45
progressive verb forms 128, 131
proper noun 150

question tags: see tag questions
quizzes 135
quotative *like* 44

rationalist (approaches to language) 33
reactive 6
recasts 136
recursion 34
redundancy 142, 159
Rees-Mogg, Jacob 28
reflexive pronouns 186
reflexivity 72
relative clauses 101
relevance (of rules of thumb) 130
reliability (of tests) 137
reported speech 49, 88, Chapter 9
reported thought 219
reporting 217–218

right 58
royal *we* 188
rules of thumb 5, 27, 48, 52, 129, 156, 168

saxon genitive 25
say 105
scientific grammar 30–31
scientific terminology 70
secondary grammar 26–27
second language acquisition 10
SEGT: see Standard English Grammatical Terminology
semi-modal verb forms 55
simple present 89
simple (verb) forms 31
simplicity (in syllabuses) 126
simplicity (of rules of thumb) 130
singular *they* 128–129
situational uses 151, 153
specific reference 148
split infinitives 4, 28, 100
splitters and lumpers 93
so 47
some 48
staff 58
Standard English Grammatical Terminology (SEGT) 85
stative verbs 45
story-telling 158
studial 7
subject 25, 35
subjective case 186, 189
subject predicative 41
subject relative pronoun 100
subjunctive 37, 88
subordinate clause 97
subordinating conjunction 47
sub-technical language and vocabulary 70, 111–112, 121
superlative (form of adjectives) 25, 168
suprasegmental features 24
syllabuses 125
synonymy of terms 76–77
syntax 3, 18
systematicity (in syllabuses) 126
sytematicity (of terminology) 83

tag questions 58, 89
task-based language teaching 9
teacher language awareness 13

tense 26, 31, 210
terminology 202, Chapter 4
tests 137
themself 192, 201
theoretical validity (of terminology) 83
they (as singular gender-neutral pronoun) 190–192
third person singular *-s* 25, 36, 73
'time equals tense' fallacy 53
to 24
to infinitive 24, 73
topic 25
traditional grammar 34
transitive 41
translation 134
transparent terms 72
truth (of rules of thumb) 129

unique reference 151
universal grammar 12
universal tags 58
use 105
used to 72
utility (in syllabuses) 126

utility (of terminology) 83–84

validity (of tests) 137
verb (as grammatical function) 35
verb (as word class) 35

want 50
we 95–96, 188
which 165
who 27, 46
whom 27
wh- questions 25
will 52, 72
wood 20
word classes 34–35
word order 23, 155, 219
World Englishes 56–59

yes/no questions 25
you guys 187, 201
youser-friendly (metalanguage) 108, 193

zero article 162

CPSIA information can be obtained
at www.ICGtesting.com
Printed in the USA
LVHW081742140321
681517LV00005B/56